Laban/Bartenieff Movement Studies

Contemporary Applications

Colleen Wahl, MFA, CLMA

HUMAN KINETICS

Library of Congress Cataloging-in-Publication Data

Names: Wahl, Colleen, 1984- author.
Title: Laban/Bartenieff movement studies : contemporary applications /
  Colleen Wahl.
Description: Champaign, IL : Human Kinetics, 2019. | Includes bibliographical
  references and index.
Identifiers: LCCN 2018023831 (print) | LCCN 2018040279 (ebook) | ISBN
  9781492562566 (e-book) | ISBN 9781492562559 (print)
Subjects: LCSH: Movement notation. | Labanotation. | Bartenieff Fundamentals
  (Service mark)
Classification: LCC GV1587 (ebook) | LCC GV1587 .C85 2019 (print) | DDC
  792.8--dc23
LC record available at https://lccn.loc.gov/2018023831

ISBN: 978-1-4925-6255-9 (print)

The web addresses cited in this text were current as of September 2018, unless otherwise noted.

Acquisitions Editor: Bethany J. Bentley
Managing Editors: Carly S. O'Connor and Amanda S. Ewing
Indexer: Andrea J. Hepner
Permissions Manager: Dalene Reeder
Graphic Designer: Denise Lowry
Copyediting and Layout: Westchester Publishing Services
Cover Designer: Keri Evans
Cover Design Associate: Susan Rothermel Allen
Photo Production Manager: Jason Allen
Senior Art Manager: Kelly Hendren
Illustrations: © Human Kinetics, unless otherwise noted; illustrations featured on part and chapter openers and in sidebars are © Sydney P. Celio.
Printer: Seaway Printing

Printed in the United States of America   10   9   8   7   6   5   4   3

The paper in this book is certified under a sustainable forestry program.

Human Kinetics
1607 N. Market Street
Champaign, IL 61820
USA

United States and International
Website: **US.HumanKinetics.com**
Email: info@hkusa.com
Phone: 1-800-747-4457

Canada
Website: **Canada.HumanKinetics.com**
Email: info@hkcanada.com

E7252

To Bill and Angela

CONTENTS

FOREWORD

It was the summer of 2005 at the University of Utah School of Dance, and Colleen Wahl and I were in the first few days of the Integrated Movement Studies (IMS) certification program in Laban/Bartenieff movement studies (L/BMS). It was hot, and most of the movers in the studio were drooping.

But not Colleen.

I remember thinking that she was like the Energizer Bunny seen in the battery ad. She was young and slight, and she moved with dynamic full-out energy across the floor, eating up the space with delightful joy and concentrated enthusiasm. Colleen was totally present, engaged, and invested in both the physical and expressive aspects of her moving. This young woman stood out!

When I met Colleen, I was an adjunct assistant professor in the School of Dance at the University of Utah and cofounder of Integrated Movement Studies and the Laban/Bartenieff certification program at the University of Utah. With an MA in education, certification as a Laban/Bartenieff movement analyst, and professional RSME credentials, I had been teaching certification in the Laban/Bartenieff material since 1981 and had seen many talented students graduate from the IMS program; Colleen, however, caught my attention.

From the beginning of our relationship, I realized that Colleen was committed to taking her understanding of Laban/Bartenieff movement studies to everyone. She expressed many years ago what I now realize was the seed for this book: Colleen's experience with the Laban/Bartenieff movement studies system had freed her movement, had increased her understanding of herself, and had become her inroads into becoming a more creative person; she wanted to share this adventure in increased aliveness with others.

Today, Colleen continues to stand out as a unique mover and shaker in the fields of somatics and movement studies. She embodies the new wave of movement educators and somatic practitioners who are dedicated to paving the way toward a more universal awareness of the role movement plays in how we understand ourselves and others in an ever-changing and increasingly complex world.

She teaches career movement professionals at an advanced certification level; teaches dance and movement theory at the university level; presents at dance, dance medicine, somatics, and fitness conferences; works as a private coach with clients who want to improve their movement skills; and ran a successful fitness studio in New York City. She brings these myriad experiences and ways of understanding people and their movements to the writing of this book.

This is a book for everyone. All bodies move, and everyone is constantly making personal meaning from sensed and felt movement. Movement speaks and is a major way in which we know our world. We create and assign meaning to the movements of ourselves and others, yet few of us have a conscious awareness of the elemental aspects our movement language. What are the components of this language? How do we talk about what we are feeling and seeing in movement?

Colleen's goal is to demystify movement in a fun and engaging manner. Through a sensate and kinesthetic approach to her writing, you will learn about yourself from the lens of movement. You will become more creative at sensing how your own movement informs your health and desires. You will have new inroads into improving your movement capabilities. You will become a more aware observer of others and more consciously know how movement is contributing to the meaning you make in your relationships.

There are many good books about the Laban/Bartenieff movement studies system; however, they are often about only one part of this system. Colleen's book is groundbreaking in that it covers the whole of the Laban/Bartenieff system and is written in a clear and straightforward way that will be engaging to anyone who moves. Colleen has peeled away the jargon. In the book's germinal stages, I remember Colleen saying she wanted to write this book in a way that her father would understand. She has!

One of my favorite things in the book are the sidebars where the reader gets different examples of someone using the Laban/Bartenieff material out in the work-a-day world. I know readers will find these explanations from L/BMS professionals fascinating. Their reflections on their applications of the Laban/Bartenieff system give insight into the multiple possibilities for creative careers in the field of movement.

Colleen is now my colleague and teaching partner at Integrated Movement Studies. We dance and move together, coauthor a movement newsletter, plan trainings, problem-solve on movement issues, and continue to learn from one another as we grow in our understanding of movement and ourselves.

Enjoy learning more about your unique moving self!

Janice Meaden, MA, CLMA, BMC, RSME
Certified Laban/Bartenieff Movement Analyst
Body-Mind Centering Practitioner
Founder of Integrated Movement Studies
Director of the IMS Laban/Bartenieff Certification
Program at the University of Utah
Adjunct Assistant Professor in the University of Utah
School of Dance

PREFACE

Having a body is a fundamental aspect of the human experience. Most people take the movement of their bodies for granted; they don't give it much thought. Yet how you experience the movement of your body and perceive the movement of others' bodies influences much of your life, including your perceptions of yourself and your relationships. Think of an interaction that left you feeling that the person you were speaking with was generous and present. Recall that person's movement and how it may have influenced your perception of him or her. Now think of an interaction in which you felt attacked. Reflect on how the other person's movement may have contributed to your feelings. Movement is part of how you engage with, perceive, and understand the world around you. Yet its multifaceted, ethereal nature makes it very hard to pin down. This book addresses how movement is important in our lives—how it influences our perceptions and helps form our understandings. This text will introduce you to the approach known as Laban/Bartenieff Movement Analysis in a way that is designed to help you organize your perceptions of movement and shed new light on its role in your life.

Laban/Bartenieff Movement Analysis (L/BMA) offers a framework for perceiving human movement in many areas of life. On the most fundamental level, L/BMA recognizes that movement is meaningful: It influences perceptions of ourselves and others. This text aims to develop your knowledge of the Laban/Bartenieff "lens," so to speak, and to cultivate your ability to use it in meaningful ways. Examples of L/BMA's practical applications range from developing a fuller movement palette and fuller range of expression in your moving body, to creating characters and choreography, to coaching and teaching movement, to observing and describing how movement is meaningful.

The framework of Laban/Bartenieff Movement Analysis is also a template for what is possible in human movement. Yet L/BMA does not claim to have encompassed all of what is known. As Laban/Bartenieff theory has developed, those working on it have sought to identify what is most elemental about human movement, often growing and changing the theory as new movement elements have emerged. They recognized that by identifying what is most elemental in movement, the individual parts could be organized and synthesized in new ways, a process that increases the range of movement possibilities and experiences.

The Laban/Bartenieff framework is useful in any context in which movement is important. It allows one to perceive human movement with greater nuance and specificity, to talk about movement with greater clarity and precision, to coach movement with a greater range of possibilities, and to experience movement with a greater variety of options. I originally wanted to title this book *Movement for Your Whole Life* or *Play With L/BMA*. I share this because it demonstrates my view of how the movement perspectives of L/BMA are present in all aspects of our moving lives, from interactions with loved ones, to how we design the places we work, to how we navigate walking through the world. L/BMA addresses movement in its many possibilities.

I have practiced as a Laban/Bartenieff Movement Analyst and have taught the material since I became certified through Integrated Movement Studies (at the University of Utah) in 2006. While teaching Laban/Bartenieff Movement Analysis to graduate and undergraduate students, I noticed that pupils studied L/BMA from diverse perspectives and with varying needs. Some students took the course as part of a dance or movement-studies curriculum. Others did so as part of coursework ranging from athletic training to media studies to art making to music conducting. I wrote this book because I wanted a text for teaching those classes that would lay out an introduction to the Laban/Bartenieff framework and demonstrate the rich possibilities for using it in one's life and career. This book covers the basic categories of Body, Effort, Shape, and Space (BESS), and of Phrasing, including definitions, symbols, and general theory, with an emphasis on how L/BMA can be used in meaningful ways in one's life.

You will read about the diverse experiences of other certified Laban/Bartenieff Movement Analysts as they write about how they use the L/BMA approach both personally and professionally. For example, you will hear from a computer animator on using Weight Effort to bring animations to life, and from a dancer on using L/BMA to quickly pick up phrases in technique class. Throughout the book, activity sidebars use prompts for movement experiences to apply the concepts being discussed.

Part I provides an overview and a historical look at Laban/Bartenieff Movement Analysis, and dives into organizing concepts that frame how you can make it useful in your life. Chapter 1 describes the L/BMA framework, including how it develops one's perceptions of movement. The chapter also provides short biographies of the life and work of Rudolph von Laban and Irmgard Bartenieff and outlines how the approach has continued to grow through the research and efforts of their students. By having a sense of our L/BMA ancestors and their development of the theory, you can gain a better sense of how it might continue to grow.

Chapter 2 looks at L/BMA's Guiding Concepts and Organizing Themes. It focuses on how both are useful to a growing sensitivity to one's body and to an enhanced perception of movement. The Guiding Concepts are a select list of essential ideas that support and are woven throughout the L/BMA framework. The Organizing Themes are presented as polarities, such as function-expression, that will help you consider how to use L/BMA in your world. Also in this section is an introduction to a term I have come to call the "palette," which refers to the goal of accessing the broadest range of possibilities in movement and still feeling at home and whole within oneself. Overall, part I provides an overview look at the values of L/BMA, where they originate, and how they change and grow.

Part II consists of chapters dedicated to each of the concepts that make up the acronym BESS: Body, Effort, Shape, and Space. Another chapter covers Phrasing. This is the version of the Laban/Bartenieff framework used by Integrated Movement Studies; it includes Irmgard Bartenieff's unique contributions as developed by the IMS faculty. Other programs may use slightly different acronyms depending on their interpretations of L/BMA—for example, BEST (Body, Effort, Space, Time) or BREST (Body, Relationship, Effort, Space, Time). The purpose of part II is to provide a basic understanding of the various elements of movement that would likely be covered in a Laban/Bartenieff Movement Analysis course and to focus on how and why each element is useful. Each chapter defines the element and examines how it is useful in movement. Part II includes perspectives from contributors who use Laban/Bartenieff Movement Analysis.

Chapter 3, "Body," emphasizes the Bartenieff fundamentals and discusses the Basic Six. From a foundational overview of each Pattern of Total Body Connectivity, chapter 3 explores movements that become available for the infant at each stage of motor development, and how revisiting these patterns can be relevant and useful for older children and adults. Chapter 3 also reviews what have become known as the Basic Six, the movement experiences developed by Irmgard Bartenieff that bring a functional approach to increasing the ease of the entire moving body.

Chapter 4, "Effort," covers the study of the energetic or dynamic tones present in movement. Through looking at Effort you will learn to consider how the body energetically moves in relationship to gravity and its weighted mass, the passing of time, attention to the environment, and its easeful or controlled feelings. Effort can be a playful and challenging inroad to developing a greater range of possibilities and access as a mover. Effort is highly functional, as when you need to utilize lingering power to open a jar of jam, or channeled delicacy to remove an eyelash from a baby's face. Effort can also be expressive, as in the case of running late for a meeting but not wanting to end a conversation, and bringing in a sense of urgency.

Chapter 5, "Shape," discusses the lens through which you look at the body's form and forming processes. Through Shape you will learn to address movement by asking questions: What is the basic form the body is in? How is the body changing shape in relationship to itself and its environment? In what direction is its form changing? How is the form change supported by the inner "guts" of the body? If you were working with a college football team, you might draw on the Shape category to clarify the tetrahedral nature of the offensive line as the players get in position; then their advancing, rising, and spreading into wall-like forms for fending off the attacking defensemen; and finally creating the border qualities needed to protect the quarterback.

Chapter 6 focuses on Space. Through this category you clarify how the body engages with the spatial world around it, and how you can work with space to challenge and support movement to be more fully balanced and off-balance. For example, the category of Space allows you to recognize that a great deal of your life asks you to move primarily in the forward middle zone around your body (think of writing emails, cooking dinner, driving). With this understanding, you can access tools to help you move through a greater range of the spatial environment around you. Chapter 6 also explains concepts like spatial intent, which addresses how the spatial environment supports and pulls the moving body.

Chapter 7 addresses a less developed aspect of Laban/Bartenieff Movement Analysis known as Phrasing. Through Phrasing, your lens of perceiving movement shifts to be "through time and over time," including how BESS sequences and layers into the complex and multifaceted realities of human movement. This way of looking at movement teaches you to bring Body, Effort, Shape, and Space together to form an integrated understanding of movement.

Part III focuses on how to use what you learned in parts I and II in meaningful ways. Utilizing this material to shed new light on your areas of interest and to expand your perceptive, functional, and expressive skills is challenging and exciting. You will be guided to make changes in how you move in your life to be more effective, easeful, and dynamic. You will become more skilled in movement observation and description. You can teach and coach others in movement with greater clarity and additional inroads.

Chapter 8 discusses things to consider as you use L/BMA in your life. It includes suggestions on how to organize and frame your uses of Laban/Bartenieff Movement Analysis, the process of observing and making meaning from movement, and the complexities of doing so. Chapter 8 is designed to set you up to use L/BMA more successfully and to get more from reading the essays that are contained in chapter 9.

Chapter 9 is a collection of writings by individuals who have used Laban/Bartenieff Movement Analysis in various practical ways. The essays highlight the diversity of application possibilities in careers beyond dance. As you learn about ways in which others are using L/BMA, let their experiences inspire you and open you to new possibilities.

When I teach this material, I loosely structure it in the way shared with me by my mentor Janice Meaden: Do it, name it, identify it in your life, cultivate it in meaningful ways, and, finally, apply it to meet your needs and goals. Use the suggestions for experiencing and cultivating L/BMA throughout the text to inspire your own investigations. Often, once you find the concept in your own life, you discover an inroad to sharing and teaching it. As you read, let the examples and stories of how others use L/BMA become prompts for your exploration and discovery.

My goal with this text is to provide a clear and useful discussion of Laban/Bartenieff Movement Analysis and to guide you to use it in meaningful and satisfying ways. My hope is that you gain increased access to your moving body, expanding your palette of movement possibilities and finding ways to use the Laban/Bartenieff material in whatever applications and interests you have. If you become a soccer coach, use it to develop effective ways to train your athletes; if you speak in public, use it to create strategies for increasing the physical expression most coherent for your message; if you are an observer and interpreter of movement, use it to develop skills to describe and analyze movement in ways that address its complex and personal nature. Let's dive in!

Instructor Ancillaries

Two ancillaries are available for instructors.

- *Presentation package.* The presentation package includes more than 200 slides that cover the key points of every chapter. Instructors can use these slides to facilitate class lectures.
- *Image bank.* The image bank contains all of the figures and tables from the book, separated by chapter. These images can be added to the presentation package, used in student handouts, and so on.

Ancillary products supporting this text are free to adopting instructors. Contact your Sales Manager for details about how to access *HKPropel*, our ancillary delivery and learning platform.

ACKNOWLEDGMENTS

I stand on the shoulders of giants as I share with you the take on the Laban/Bartenieff perspective that I have learned and taught through Integrated Movement Studies. The IMS perspective holds that Rudolph von Laban and Irmgard Bartenieff hoped that the seeds they planted would grow and develop. This book offers a current perspective regarding the growth of the Laban/Bartenieff material at Integrated Movement Studies (IMS). I want to extend a big thank-you to my IMS colleagues and mentors, and to the whole IMS lineage and team, who have developed and clarified this work—their efforts woven throughout the ideas, diagrams, and values in this text, and have been seminal to my development. I especially want to thank Janice Meaden, who spent hours reading and generously giving feedback on this manuscript, and to Janice and Peggy Hackney, who both welcomed me into their homes and allowed me access to their files so I could gain a fuller perspective on this material and its history. I also want to thank my colleague D. Chase Angier, who created the space to allow me to finish this project, and Alfred University for providing funding that made the in-person conversations and archival research with Janice and Peggy possible. And finally, thanks to Bethany Bentley, who so graciously and patiently handled emails and encouraged me when I had concerns; to the contributors, who added so much to this text; to Sydney Celio, whose illustrations brought the book to life; to Peggy and colleagues, who sketched many of the organizing diagrams shared here; to *Point of Departure* by Valerie Preston-Dunlop for inspiring the cover design, to my mother, Kathy Shaughnessy Wahl, for reading and commenting on much of the text; and, of course, to my wonderful husband, Bill, who kept our dog and home together as this book was written.

PART I

FOUNDATIONS OF LABAN/BARTENIEFF MOVEMENT STUDIES

Have you noticed when trying to describe something that happened in movement that there was more going on than you could account for or had language to adequately capture? Or perhaps you have tried to teach or coach movement to others and found that you lacked the language and skill to fully describe the movement. Perhaps you have been unsatisfied with the functional limits of anatomical and kinesiological perspectives, recognizing that there seems to be more that needs to be accounted for. Or maybe you have felt suspicious and distrustful of the prescriptive and highly simplified body-language decoding perspectives that claim to have the answers on what movement means, finding them to be less than true in your life. Maybe you have felt that the movement you do is limited compared to what is possible, and you would like to create greater expressive range for yourself.

Chapters 1 and 2 introduce you to the big picture of Laban/Bartenieff Movement Analysis. Chapter 1 focuses on the many ways L/BMA is useful in the study of human movement, such as describing and observing movement. It also briefly outlines the history of the Laban/Bartenieff framework, including the lives of Rudolf von Laban and Irmgard Bartenieff, and how their interests and skills contributed to the body of work that now bears their names. A subtheme of chapter 1 is that the framework known as L/BMA is in continual development, actively being shaped and made useful by the people who practice it. Chapter 2 outlines the whole of the Laban/Bartenieff perspective, or lens, as it currently exists and discusses Organizing Themes that have been present since Laban used them to develop his perspectives on movement. Chapter 2 also presents an overview of Laban/Bartenieff Movement Analysis, setting you up for part II of the book, which introduces the specific elements of movement.

Overview of Laban/Bartenieff Movement Analysis

"The main objective . . . is to suggest additional modes of perceiving yourself and the world around you, using your live body totally— body/mind/feeling—as a key to that perception."

(Bartenieff 1979)

*M*ovement is fundamental to the human experience. Thus, it is easily overlooked. This text will encourage you to pay attention to how you perceive movement in your world. Once you start paying attention to movement, you may quickly notice that there is much going on in the pursuit of this task. Human movement is complex; even in the simplest of movements multiple elements are present at the same time. Any movement experience is a process involving a person, a context, and a sequence of movement—that is, a beginning, a middle, and an end. What's more, human movement, by its nature, constantly changes—it is ethereal, as soon as you've seen it, it is gone. Laban/Bartenieff Movement Analysis (L/BMA) seeks to improve how movement is perceived by making the processes of observing, describing, and analyzing it layered and precise. L/BMA also enriches the pursuit of moving by increasing movement possibilities and providing options for greater clarity.

Laban/Bartenieff Movement Analysis offers a framework and a language for understanding and perceiving human movement. In the L/BMA framework, the elements of Body, Effort, Shape, and Space come together in Phrases, within a specific context in unique and constantly changing ways to create infinite relationships through and in movement (see figure 1.1). Each of these concepts is examined in more detail in chapters 3 through 6.

When perceiving movement through the various lenses provided by L/BMA, you will learn that movement is multifaceted; thus, there are many possibilities for perceiving it. As you study L/BMA you will notice that you can look at the same movement event in different ways, and with each lens you will gain new information about the movement in the event you are perceiving. The tetrahedron in figure 1.1 has Shape at its center, however, you could shift the tetrahedron in a way that puts Effort, Space, or Body at the center as if you have shifted the lens or focus of your perceptions.

A basic goal of Laban/Bartenieff Movement Analysis is to promote objectivity in movement analysis, allowing the observer to address what is happening free of implicit bias toward certain preferences and interpretive meanings. That said, objectivity, while a noble pursuit, is not a perfect reality. The impulse to create an analytic framework that organizes perceptual processes is arguably in itself a pursuit aligned with value systems and structures that prefer order. Nor are the individual elements of the Laban/Bartenieff perspective perfectly free of interpretive elements; the L/BMA framework is influenced by the understandings and values of those who have worked to develop it and those who use it. Further, L/BMA is not a static or fixed body of work. In the quest for greater clarity and precision, L/BMA has morphed over many generations in ways that afford the student of movement a developed and comprehensive approach to perceiving movement.

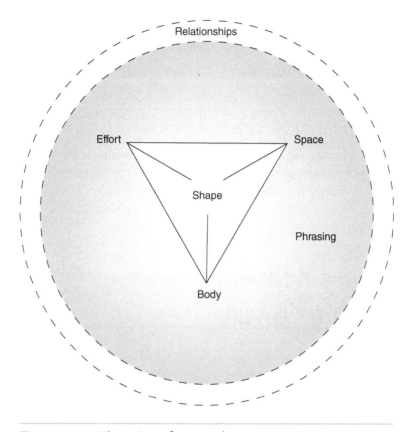

Figure 1.1   The L/BMA framework.

Despite its imperfect objectivity, the Laban/Bartenieff system is useful for the study of human movement. Looking at movement through the lens of L/BMA will impact your perceptions—and encourage you to become increasingly aware of your biases. L/BMA will help you grow more conscious of the associations and preconceptions you bring to movement, such as perceiving delicacy (Light Weight effort) as meek or wimpy, or perceiving power (Strong Weight effort) as aggressive and competitive. As you become aware of your associations, you will see how they shape your perceptions of movement, and you will be able to explore them, enlarging the possibilities for what you glean from movement.

As a maker of meaning from movement, you are at the center of your perceptions; thus, the meaning of movement is not found in Laban/Bartenieff Movement Analysis, nor does L/BMA enable you to read the mind and thoughts of another. Rather, L/BMA lets you claim your impressions of movement based on what is present, what is not present, and how it speaks to you in the context in which it happens. You will find yourself saying (or thinking) things like, "I saw _____ doing _____ in _____ manner, and I experienced it as _____."

What does it mean to analyze movement? The *Merriam-Webster* dictionary defines *analysis* as follows:

1. the separating of any material or abstract entity into its constituent elements;
2. a method of studying the nature of something or of determining its essential features and their relations.

Analysis of human movement through L/BMA is a process of separating movement to its individual elements and then bringing those elements together to form a full picture. By understanding the parts present in movement and then bringing them together, L/BMA makes it possible to perceive movement comprehensively in many contexts.

Perceiving Movement Through L/BMA

The L/BMA framework is particularly useful in contexts in which movement is studied and taught. Practitioners of the many movement studies in which movement matters will apply the L/BMA theories and practices in unique ways, specific to the needs of that discipline and their interests. In any context, the Laban/Bartenieff lens is especially useful for observing, describing, coaching and teaching, making meaning from, and experiencing movement.

Observing Movement

Movement happens quickly and is constantly in flux. As soon one movement ends, another has already begun, making comprehensive and accurate observations of movement difficult. Observing what is happening in movement is a common use of the Laban/Bartenieff framework. Using L/BMA to observe movement allows the observer to be precise and specific about what is happening, it also encourages the observer to recognize how movement calls forth feelings and associations that make it expressive. This is facilitated by the multiple aspects of the L/BMA lens, which enable the observer to comb through movement for its elemental parts and then integrate those parts together towards a larger whole. The ability to be precise in one's observations of movement, despite the movement's complexity, is important to many fields that study and address movement.

Describing Movement

Translating movement into words can feel like juggling two disparate systems of experience. Movement is felt, kinesthetic, and constantly morphing. Language is verbal, intellectual, and relatively durable—words do not change in the same moment they are spoken. Yes, language evolves and words change meaning overtime, but not so fast that we cannot keep up with them. Movement is infinitely faster and more difficult to "pin down"; as soon as you realize what is there, it has passed. Finding words that convey the experienced and changing nature of movement while being precise, accurate, and evocative can be a challenge. In many fields that involve movement, the ability to accurately describe what is happening is essential to conveying how movement is manifesting and how it is important in the context. L/BMA offers a specific lexicon for articulating human movement; explaining these terms makes up the majority of part II of this book. Of course, the L/BMA terminology is probably unfamiliar to those who have not studied this material, so part of using L/BMA is knowing how to translate the specialized language into words that inspire movement, no matter how much or how little L/BMA terminology the other person knows.

Coaching and Teaching Movement

For those who coach and teach movement, the act of facilitating growth and improvement involves many aspects of perceiving movement. The coach or teacher analyzes what is happening in relationship to what is desired, and then communicates that information, confirming what is serving the mover and offering strategies for growth. That information is then integrated into the movement, and then, the cycle begins again, including observing how the new information impacted the movement. This complex process is aided by the clear framework for observation, description, and analysis provided by Laban/Bartenieff Movement Analysis.

Making Meaning from Movement

The biological body is the basis for movement; it produces and makes movement possible, and is itself formed by movement. Yet, the picture of movement in human life is far more complex than that of a biological body moving from synaptic impulses. From the moment of conception, the body is molded by movement, and movement informs the ongoing and shifting perceptions of the self (Bryan 2018). Throughout the human life, movement is meaningful. Movement arises to meet needs: to get closer to what is desired or to create distance from what is not desired, to express inner thoughts and desires, and to accomplish the tasks that maintain and give meaning to life. Laban/Bartenieff Movement Analysis allows those who use it to address the meaningful aspects of movement while honoring the context and sequencing of movement.

Making meaning from movement is different from interpreting movement, and there is a time for both. People are always making meaning from movement, usually unconsciously—for example, someone might interpret how her father moves when he is tired or when he is angry. Making meaning emphasizes the influence of the observer in how movement is understood. Interpretation is about seeking to *understand* someone else's meaning, as if an observer could use movement in order to "read the mover's mind." In the former, the observer is an active participant in making meaning; in the latter, movement is interpreted without recognizing the influence of the interpreter, potentially leading to misinterpretation and misunderstanding. For example, crossing the arms or nodding the head means different things to different people, in different cultures and contexts, and any interpretation one might place upon either of those actions will necessarily change with each mover and each context. I highlight this distinction to emphasize that L/BMA does not provide a dictionary or one-to-one correlation between a movement and "what it means" in any general sense. Movement always happens in a context, and our analysis of any particular movement must honor the particular mover within the particular context, as well as the complexity of what happened and how it happened in movement.

Experiencing Movement

Movement is a constant. Experiencing movement within the Laban/Bartenieff Movement Analysis framework can heighten and refine your awareness of a movement as you do it, and can help you recognize your preferences in movement. It can also help you gain new options in your movement. The specificity of the Laban/Bartenieff framework heightens sensation to bring greater clarity in movement so that you can manifest what you intend. When you bring your L/BMA knowledge to your lived experiences, you will notice new things about your movement, gaining a greater sense of presence, a sense of being "in your body." As you work through the Laban/Bartenieff system you will generate awareness of your personal preferences and patterns for movement. As you learn what you like to do, you can also "style stretch," that is develop movements that you have been less likely to inhabit, thus expanding your range of physicality. You'll increase your expressive range and functional skills.

All of the above—observing, describing, coaching and teaching, making meaning, and experiencing—are ways of perceiving movement. The Laban/Bartenieff framework is fundamentally about creating conscious and effective inroads to the heightened perception of movement. As you use L/BMA to perceive movement in your life, you may feel as though you are learning a new language, and in some ways you are. Your understanding of movement will shift as you apply the Laban/Bartenieff framework to your life. You may notice that you can see movement with greater distinction and that you have new words and approaches to talking about it. You may also notice that you are better able to organize and frame your pursuits around movement, and that you have new options for being creative with your movement goals. Finally, you may notice that as a mover you are more prepared to increase the range of movements you execute and enjoy.

Origins of L/BMA

The body of work associated with Rudolf von Laban has grown and changed since its earliest days. Irmgard Bartenieff was one of those who brought Laban's perspectives to the United States and contributed significantly to the development of its the theory and practices. Her name has been added to the formal title Laban/Bartenieff Movement Analysis used in this text to recognize her specific contributions. The Laban/Bartenieff system has been expanded over the years by many people, and has changed and grown based on the interests and observations of those who work in the field. The following brief accounts of the lives of Rudolf von Laban and Irmgard Bartenieff are meant to recognize and honor the two individuals seminal to what L/BMA is today and their contributions, and to give a sense of the context in which their approaches to movement developed.

Rudolf von Laban

Rudolf von Laban pursued a better way to perceive movement. He sought to elevate dance and movement to a primary art form—one that was valued on its own, not just in relationship to music or as a means of telling a narrative story. Laban felt that if movement and dance could have a written notation record, like music does, it would be considered a more reputable art form. As Valerie Preston-Dunlop writes of Laban's views, "as long as dance gives an impression of the music it cannot be expressive in its own right" (2008, 23). He believed that movement was meaningful, and he sought to develop ways of accessing that meaning. Laban's interests were intimately entwined with the course of his life. His early years of solitude, exploration, and travel influenced his adult pursuits and purpose.

Born in 1879 in Bratislava (in what is now Slovakia) to a wealthy military family, Laban was the eldest of three children and the only son. As a child, he spent much time alone wandering the hills surrounding his home, enchanted by his own whimsical imaginary world. When Laban was a teenager, his father's deployments took the family to other parts of Europe and to the Middle East.

During these travels, Laban encountered Eastern and Western philosophies and traditions; later, he shaped the folklore and stories he was exposed to into plays and puppet shows.

As a young adult Laban entered military training, but left after about a year and a half to pursue life as an artist. He lived in Munich and Paris over the next few years. In Munich, he began studying the practices of Bess Mensendieck, who was interested in movement efficiency and healthy movement. She is considered to have been part of the early physical-culture movement. Laban also studied the work of the music teacher Emil Jaques-Dalcroze, who developed Dalcroze Eurhythmics, which used movement as an inroad to learning music (Bradley 2009, 9). Laban started to observe that present in human movement were organic rhythms; fluctuations that arise out of the human need to exert and recuperate in movement (Preston-Dunlop 2008, 24) toward addressing "struggle for technical mastery of the environment" (Preston-Dunlop 2008, 236).

On a hill called Monte Verita (Mountain of Truth) Laban lived communally, in an environment that suited his pursuits of dance and performance and allowed him to merge his interests in spirituality and community. Here, in 1913 Laban opened a "School for Art" in Ascona, Switzerland, and met and worked with Mary Wigman, who was seeking a movement-centric (as opposed to music-centric) approach to dance. Laban also experimented with movement choirs, a community dance form in which participants express themselves to varying degrees by weaving together individual and group dances.

During the First World War, Laban's time as a permanent member at Ascona ended, and he moved to Zurich. There, he and Wigman experimented with the basic ideas that would grow into the theories known as Choreutics and Eukinetics (which loosely refer to Space Harmony and Effort; see chapters 6 and 4) having fairly fully fleshed out by 1981 (Preston-Dunlop 2008, 49). Over the next few decades Laban was very productive. He wrote the book *Die Welt des Tanzers* (The World of Dancers) and developed the system of notation called **Labanotation** (see figure 1.2). He became the ballet master for the National Theater of Mannheim, and he opened schools to train dancers in his techniques throughout Germany, Switzerland, Austria, Serbia, and Italy. Among the main focuses of the curricula were Choreutics, Eukinetics, and movement choirs.

There is much speculation about Laban's relationship with the Nazi party during his time in Germany, which was arguably the height of his

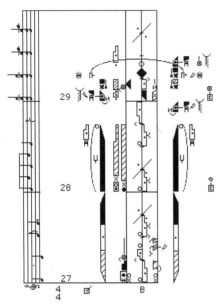

Figure 1.2   Labanotation uses a staff with symbols designating movement direction and level, as well as leg and arm gestures, all in relation to music.

career. For a theater opening taking place during the 1936 Berlin Olympics, Laban was invited to choreograph the opening dances for a festival including a massive movement choir. However, the performance was cut after Goebbels heard Laban's speech to the performers and deemed it contrary to Nazi values. Of the speech, Goebbels said, "It is all dressed up in our clothes and has nothing whatsoever to do with us" (Preston-Dunlop 2008, 196). Most of Laban's work and archives were subsequently destroyed by the Nazi party, leaving little record of his creative endeavors.

Dejected, Laban fled Germany and wound up at Dartington Hall, a refuge for exiled artists and scholars on England's west coast. During a bout with depression, he met Lisa Ullmann, who encouraged him back to health and helped advance his ideas. Together they wrote the book *The Mastery of Movement*. He also began collaborating with the management consultant F.C. Lawrence to apply his understanding of movement to efficiency in the workplace. Working from ideas associated with Taylorism, a system of analyzing and teaching movement in industrial settings to achieve optimal productivity, Laban and Lawrence paired workers with tasks that were compatible with their movement preferences. With Lisa Ullmann, Laban opened the Art of Movement Studio. He died in 1958, after having seen his work grow into new fields and areas of study.

Laban was an inspiring yet challenging visionary and teacher. He is known to have been moody and changeable, both deeply encouraging and intensely exacting. He could be a perfectionist, and he was criticized in turn for being too rigid and too loose. His personal complexity is paralleled by the layered foundation he created for new versions of dance and movement (Bradley 2009, 36).

Irmgard Bartenieff

Irmgard Bartenieff, born Irmgard Dombois, was a student and colleague of Laban's who in 1936 fled Nazi Germany with her husband Michail Bartenieff and came to the United States (Tobin n.d.). She is the primary channel through which Laban's ideas on movement were introduced to the United States. Through Bartenieff's contributions, Laban's work became known as Laban/Bartenieff Movement Analysis, which represents a synthesis of Laban's notions of Effort and Space with Irmgard's whole-body study of movement.

Prior to arriving in New York City, Bartenieff had been a dancer in the company she and her husband ran, but newly arrived in the United States, she found little time for artistic pursuits (Tobin n.d.). In 1943, she graduated from New York University with a degree in physical therapy; she was employed by several hospitals in the area, most notably the Willard Parker Hospital, where she worked with patients recovering from polio (Bartenieff and Lewis 2002). This work contributed significantly to the development of her theories, which she used to rehabilitate movement capacities in adults stricken with polio.

Bartenieff continued her relationship with Laban. She traveled to England over several summers to collaborate with him and further her understanding of Effort. Through these visits Bartenieff's understanding of Effort/Shape (later Labananalysis, and later still Laban Movement Analysis and now, in this text, Laban/Bartenieff Movement Analysis) solidified, as she brought the theories and practices to the United States and shared them with her students.

Bartenieff's practice as a physical therapist was shaped by her Laban-based training. She was a remarkable motivator who could get patients to stand who previously could not stand, using cues such as touch, vocalization, and imagery—an untraditional shift that brought remarkable results. Equally, the knowledge of anatomy and kinesiology, as well as her understanding of the developmental motor progression that she gained from her studies as a physical therapist allowed her to bring a whole-body component to Laban's study of movement. She emphasized internal body connectivity and full-bodied expression.

Bartenieff's work deeply influenced the field of dance therapy and was foundational for somatics, a philosophical and practical approach to movement that focuses on the whole, sensate, becoming person. Bartenieff was a charter member of the American Dance Therapy Association (founded in the mid-1960s) (Hackney, 2002); her body of work remains fundamental to the study of dance and movement therapy. In 1978 she founded the Laban Institute for Movement Studies, now the Laban/Bartenieff Institute for Movement Studies. Her pamphlet *Notes from a Course in Correctives,* published in 1974 by the Dance Notation Bureau, features five lectures and exercises focused on essential movement skills. In 1979, with coauthor Dori Lewis, she published the book *Body Movement: Coping with the Environment,* the first and among the most comprehensive accounts of Laban/Bartenieff Movement Analysis.

Irmgard Bartenieff died in 1981. Her methods, advanced by generations of students, continue to resonate with those studying movement. She promoted the idea that movement is a process of constant change and the importance of paying "attention to movement—bodily and mental—which is obviously at the basis of all human activity" (Hackney 2002, 4). She was known as a creative and inspiring teacher who had a skill for seeing below the surface of a movement and encouraging greater support, integration, and inner connectivity (Hackney 2002).

Continuation and Evolution

Both Laban and Bartenieff had a talent for recruiting people to their visions and encouraging others to develop and further their own ideas. Both fostered strong communities, which is a significant reason why their work remains prominent. The legacy of sharing and advancing these ideas lives on as practitioners continue to adapt them to specific areas of research.

The individuals who today work with Laban-based frameworks for movement make up an international community. In the United States, the influence of Irmgard Bartenieff is especially present in the pursuits of somatics and dance therapy. Peggy Hackney and Bonnie Bainbridge Cohen in particular have advanced these aspects of her work. Others, such as Warren Lamb and Carol-Lynne Moore, have taken Laban and Bartenieff's work in other directions, such as the workplace. Laban Movement Analysis and Bartenieff Fundamentals are offered at universities and community colleges as undergraduate and graduate courses, and several graduate-level certification programs exist for those interested in in depth study.

Summary

The Laban/Bartenieff framework has grown to influence the study and understanding of movement across many fields. The following chapters discuss L/BMA as it is currently taught in many U.S. schools, but the ideas started by Rudolf von Laban and expanded by so many after him will continue to grow and change as new students discover and promote it. After all, both Laban and Bartenieff resisted the rigidity of thought and the dogmatic adherence to tradition that could stifle the growth of the seeds they had laid down.

Further Reading on the History of L/BMA

Bainbridge-Cohen, Bonnie. *Sensing, Feeling, and Action: The Experiential Anatomy of Body-Mind Centering.* North Hampton, MA: Contact Editions, 2012.

Bartenieff, Irmgard, with Dori Lewis. *Body Movement: Coping with the Environment.* New York: Routledge, 1980.

Bradley, Karen. *Rudolf Laban.* New York: Routledge, 2009.

Dörr, Evelyn. *Rudolf Laban: The Dancer in the Crystal.* Lanham, MD: Scarecrow Press, 2008.

Laban, Rudolf. Translated and annotated by Lisa Ullmann. *A Life for Dance: Reminiscences.* London: Macdonald & Evans, 1975.

Moore, Carol-Lynne. *The Harmonic Structure of Movement, Music, and Dance According to Rudolf Laban: An Examination of His Unpublished Writings and Drawings.* Lewiston, NY: Edwin Mellen Press, 2009.

Preston-Dunlop, Valerie. *Rudolf Laban: An Extraordinary Life.* London, UK: Dance Books Ltd, 2008.

CHAPTER

2

Guiding Concepts and Organizing Themes

"Open your eyes and your body to the possibilities of body movement."

(Bartenieff 1979)

I n chapter 1 you gained a sense of what Laban/Bartenieff Movement Analysis is, what it seeks to do, and how its development over time has been influenced by the needs and interests of those who work with it. Chapter 2 introduces you to the Guiding Concepts and Organizing Themes that form the approach to movement used by L/BMA.

As discussed in chapter 1, Laban/Bartenieff Movement Analysis seeks to describe and make meaning from human movement. In any moment of human movement, human desires and needs organize the body to influence the outcome of the action. I recall learning in exercise-science classes that the muscles are responsible for movement. This was confusing because of what was left out. Yes, muscles and nerves are the biological mechanisms of movement, but movement in its most fundamental sense emerges from the impulses to meet needs for safety, food, sensation, curiosity, comfort, love—for example, going toward or moving away from something. Infants and toddlers do not think about muscles as they learn kinesthetically about themselves and their world. Likewise, except in cases of pain or injury, most adults do not move through their lives thinking about how their muscles produce movement; they move because of and in response to their needs. Laban/Bartenieff Movement Analysis recognizes the underpinnings of desire, intention, and expression as relevant to the study of human movement.

The quest to account for what is happening in movement, including action, experience, and perception, can quickly become confused. Words do not always seem able to adequately capture the ethereal domain of human movement. Language and movement can feel so distinct from one another: movement too complex, words too linked to other ideas. Or is it the other way around—language too complex, movement too linked to other associations? In L/BMA, the words and their associated symbols *represent* elements of movement. The word is not more important than the movement; the word and symbol are in service to the movement, and the movement is an entity unto itself.

Even as Laban/Bartenieff Movement Analysis has developed into a wide-ranging body of work, it has continued to follow certain Guiding Concepts and Organizing Themes that have anchored it throughout its history. Other Laban and Bartenieff-based texts have used various terms for the following concepts including overarching themes and principles. The terms used here were selected to most accurately support the goal of applying L/BMA to your areas of interest.

The writing and teaching histories of Rudolf von Laban and Irmgard Bartenieff contain references to how each used these bigger ideas to inspire their perspectives. Laban wrote, for example, about the rhythms of Stability and Mobility that apply to studying movement. Bartenieff taught students to organize their inner intent in order to manifest movement outwardly. This chapter reviews the larger themes present in L/BMA; chapters 3 through 7 deal with specifics of Body, Effort, Shape, Space, and Phrasing.

Guiding Concepts

Certain abstract ideas are so embedded into the Laban/Bartenieff framework that they almost seem like givens. Referred to as Guiding Concepts in this text, they give structure to L/BMA and affect the approach used to perceive movement. The Guiding Concepts discussed below include the elemental framework of L/BMA, polarities that permeate the L/BMA viewpoint, the relational nature of movement, and the understanding that movement is a personally unique experience.

The Elemental Framework of Laban/Bartenieff Movement Analysis

The developers of Laban/Bartenieff Movement Studies created a framework for perceiving movement that is based on the most elemental aspects of human movement. There are a great many possibilities for human movement, some of which are likely still unknown; thus, the framework of L/BMA reflects the vast range of what is possible. Like a painter whose palette consists of a wide array of tones and hues that is made even more vast by mixing paints, L/BMA offers a palette of movement possibilities that becomes increasingly complex as elements are combined and mixed.

Over time the body of work associated with L/BMA has developed increasing specificity and nuance. The Laban/Bartenieff framework, including BESS and Phrasing, seeks to embrace the whole of what is possible in human movement by identifying what is present and observable in movement. This quest to identify and name the full palette of movement possibilities has caused the system to change over time. For example, American dance in the 1970s began to perform different aspects of movement than what had been seen in earlier generations of dancers and choreographers, including an increased sense of buoyancy and new torso articulations. As these new options appeared, Laban/Bartenieff Movement Analysis adjusted to accommodate them.

Similarly, L/BMA challenges you to expand your range of movement, asking you to move in new ways and to pursue greater specificity and complexity in your movement abilities. Part of getting to know an aspect of movement within L/BMA is physically experiencing it in order to gain access to the fullest palette of possibilities. Some elements of movement will feel familiar and easy to do, and others will feel new or less known. While performing each element of movement, you will notice that personal associations and understandings arise. For example, you may become aware of associations such as bound Flow and having it together, or quick Time and aggression. Notice these—they are fodder for further learning.

As you expand your range to include lesser-known movements, you will notice how the elements present in movement layer together. Say, for example, something from the Effort category frequently comes with something from the Shape category. In any movement, multiple elements exist at any given time. As you explore and track them, you may notice personal preferences for certain elements that tend to combine together. Gaining access to a greater variety of movement possibilities is enriching—it opens new opportunities for expression, increases function, and challenges assumptions associated with movement.

Polarities

Polarity spectrums permeate the Laban/Bartenieff framework (see figure 2.1). A **polarity spectrum** is made up of two distinct ends, which are occupied by opposites, yet exist interdependently in service to a shared purpose. The spectrums that lie between the opposites offer nuance. One group of polarities is discussed in this text as Organizing Themes, introduced below, which are larger constructs of movement used by Laban and consistently present in the perspectives on movement he inspired. Other polarities are present throughout the L/BMA framework, including Effort factors and Shape qualities, discussed in chapters 4 and 5.

Although polarities are opposites, they are interdependent and support a common goal. One without the other is incomplete, and together they are more than the sum of their parts. Say you want to develop in one area, considering the other end of the polarity and working through the whole spectrum will bring you increased options and inroads for growth. You may find that you want to further explore polarities in movement. One strategy is to get to know each end—to see what perspectives it uniquely brings. Next, explore the gradations and relationships between the opposing poles, noticing what they bring to your understanding of the larger whole.

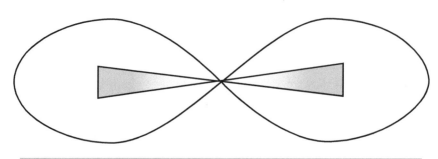

Figure 2.1   Polarity spectrum.

The Relational Nature of Movement

Relationship means a connection between ideas or parts. Things come together; there are likenesses and tensions; there is an association. The relational nature of movement resonates with many aspects of perceiving movement. Movement involves ever-changing physical and sensory relationships within the body. Movement also creates relationships between the body and its environment. Personal and cultural meanings emerge as you perceive movement in ways that influence your relationships within yourself and with your world.

Broadly speaking, relationships are formed and dissolved through movement. Relationships and connections occur throughout the body. The knee moves in relationship to the act of standing up or sitting down; the eyes and head move in relationship to tracking a leaf falling from a tree; the movement of the head triggers a change in how the weight of the body relates to its base of support.

An action considered simple, like moving from sitting to standing, actually involves change in many relationships: the angle of the hip, knee, and ankle joints, different muscular activations, new relationships to gravity and the spatial world, shifting the base of support from the bottom of the pelvis to the feet. It affords new access to mobility and locomotion, and a different perspective.

Relationships are present throughout the L/BMA framework. As you study the Laban/Bartenieff framework you will learn about different elements of movement. At first, each of these will be learned as a separate entity. Through movement, you will notice that individual elements have relationships to other elements: some will be polarities, some will fall into the same categories, some will frequently come together with elements from other categories.

You will also notice relationships between the Laban/Bartenieff framework and your personal perceptions of movement. For example, when you become familiar with strong Weight effort, you may relate it to contexts and emotions in which it arises, such as aggression, celebration, or power. Your relationship to different elements of movement in L/BMA will inform your associations and interpretations of movement. Some of these associations will be understandings unique to you; others will be shared by others who have similar understandings.

Different cultures have unique relationships to movement. A hip-hop dancer will likely have a different relationship to movement than a corporate sales team does. There are likely to be said and unsaid values about movement specific to each culture, including movements that are encouraged and others that are discouraged. What is and is not valued in movement influences how a culture perceives movement, and even what is perceived as possible. As you learn the L/BMA framework you will likely view it in relationship to different movement cultures and values. It is in these associations that the study of movement is made meaningful and relevant to your life.

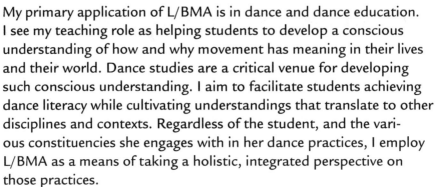

L/BMA in Your World: Teaching L/BMA

Frederick Curry, MA, CMA, PMA-CPT

My primary application of L/BMA is in dance and dance education. I see my teaching role as helping students to develop a conscious understanding of how and why movement has meaning in their lives and their world. Dance studies are a critical venue for developing such conscious understanding. I aim to facilitate students achieving dance literacy while cultivating understandings that translate to other disciplines and contexts. Regardless of the student, and the various constituencies she engages with in her dance practices, I employ L/BMA as a means of taking a holistic, integrated perspective on those practices.

As a teacher, L/BMA grounds me. It helps me remain empathetic by constantly reminding me of positionality and that all perspectives are, to a certain extent, relative and partial. BESS is a wonderful metaphor for this positionality—my experience will differ functionally and expressively depending on my intent. For example, the way I move and feel in a situation would differ if I entered into it with the intent of engaging in co-creative meaning making versus "wanting to get it over with as quickly as possible." L/BMA helps me value, invite, and cultivate my own and students' personal experiences and desires as data to support collective movement and intrapersonal and interpersonal insights.

I find that the L/BMA Organizing Themes are both an effective container for, and clarifier of, content. In integrating them into my classes, I tend to use part-whole when addressing Body; stability-mobility when addressing Space; exertion-recuperation when addressing Effort; and self-other when addressing Shape. I find that the Organizing Themes are a consistent mechanism for students to make connections and to make meaning of their movement experiences.

In education, L/BMA supports critical thinking, collaboration, and student-centered learning. It addresses cognitive, emotional, and psychomotor aspects of learning. Core concepts from L/BMA both inform and illuminate contemporary teaching and learning frameworks, including the National Core Arts Standards for Dance. L/BMA supports the creative processes through which dance making and learning are achieved.

Personal Uniqueness

The movement experience is individually unique. You may have been told, "I could tell it was you from your walk." No two people execute or experience movement the same way. Like your signature or fingerprint, or indeed your physical body, the way you move is a mark of your distinctiveness. The uniqueness of how you move is shaped by many factors, including your experiences, your perceptions, and your body.

As you gain knowledge and understanding of movement through the L/BMA lens, your comprehension of how movement is unique to you will grow. You will come to recognize elements of your individual style, such as how your feet feel in contact with the ground and your preferences for certain energetic expressions. You will also come to recognize others' uniqueness in movement, including their preferences and styles. And as you heighten your sensitivity to movement in all aspects of your life, you will begin to recognize how movement influences your impressions of others.

Organizing Themes

Themes are main subjects and ideas that recur regularly in a body of work. As you study movement through the L/BMA lens, themes emerge through repeated ideas and motifs. The Organizing Themes outlined below were first used and developed by Laban as part of his perspective on movement. He used them to describe and inspire movement, and they are present throughout his writings. For the purposes of your inquiry into human movement, the Organizing Themes shed light on the roles of movement in human life and may inspire you to expand how you approach movement and your inquiry into it.

Think of the Organizing Themes as polarity spectrums that are useful to expanding your perspective on movement. Each Organizing Theme comprises two ideas about movement that at first appear to be opposites of each other, such as function and expression. When you apply an Organizing Theme to your movement inquiries, you expand and clarify your approach, and what seemed like opposites may increasingly inform and serve one another toward a common purpose. In the case of function and expression, you might first approach movement functionally, describing the action, the muscles and joints involved, or what a movement does and how it is useful. Increasing your perspective to include expression would mean introducing imagery, sound, or evocative play to your perspective. Working from one end influences and changes what is known about the other end, and affects change in the larger whole. In the case of function and expression, expressive inroads can improve functional skills, and functional knowledge can lead to new expressive possibilities and the whole moving system is changed as a result.

As part of your work with the Laban/Bartenieff approach, use the Organizing Themes to consider new perspectives and to add new facets to your understandings of movement.

Inner-Outer

This theme emphasizes movement as an interplay between the inner, which includes sensations, impulses, and internal motivations, and the outer, or the physical manifestation of movement (figure 2.2). The inner influences the outer, and vice versa (Hackney 2002, 44). They reflect and influence one another.

Laban recognized how inner impulses influence and produce movement, and how, in turn, the physical movement affects the inner environment. Organizing movement around the theme of inner-outer embraces the full spectrum of movement as an outward response to inner needs. It also encompasses the understanding that subtle changes in the inner affect movement and the lived experience of the moving body. By exploring movement from this organizing theme, the interplay between what is felt and what is seen comes to the forefront.

Inner-outer is already popular theme in mainstream movement disciplines. For example, yoga uses inner-outer by linking movements and postures to inner experiences and feeling states. It is also a popular theme in athletics, when coaches encourage athletes to visualize as a way to prepare for a match, or to get moving, suggesting that action will bring motivation and a change in the willingness one feels toward training.

Part-Whole

The body is a whole entity made of many distinguishable parts. Similarly, any movement statement can be seen as a whole that is made of many parts. The Organizing Theme of part-whole encourages you to take in the whole, and then zoom in to a part to get to know it clearly. Or, you can hone in on the details

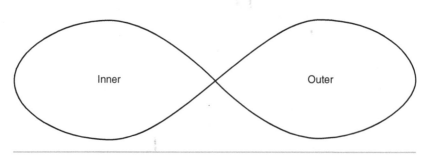

Figure 2.2   Polarity spectrum for the theme inner-outer.

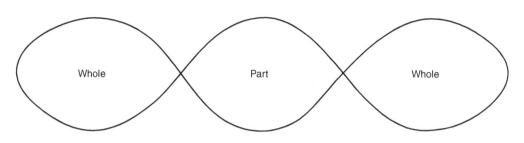

Figure 2.3   Whole-part-whole.

and specifics of a movement, and then integrate the knowledge of the part into your perspective on the whole so that the new information affects your overall experience or understanding of the bigger picture.

Another useful model of this Organizing Theme is:

Whole-Part-Whole

The whole-part-whole model describes the process of seeing the whole of something, the big picture, then narrowing in on specific aspects that would be useful to further investigate, and after diving into details, zooming the focus back out, seeing what has changed in the whole (figure 2.3).

However you choose to sequence it, the Organizing Theme of part-whole highlights the relational nature of movement. Gaining new understandings of one aspect of movement can permeate and resonate into many other aspects. As the famous saying in the L/BMA world goes, "Change in one part changes the whole" (Hackney 2002, 39).

Function-Expression

Human movement is both functional and expressive. The result of functional biological processes, movement accomplishes a task, addresses a need, expresses an inner drive, reveals intent. The infant latching to its mother's nipple, the toddler seeking affection then running away again to play, the adult warmly embracing or brutally punching another. Movement involves the complex coordination of a functional, biological body, but it also involves feeling tones and expressive impulses that make movement a primary mode of communication. Laban wrote extensively about movement's expressive nature, and much of his work sought to highlight this aspect of movement, "Movement is first and fundamental in what comes forth from a human being as an expression of his intentions and experiences" (Laban 1975 *Life*, 87).

Movement can be approached from either end of this spectrum. Specific movement cultures have different preferences for approaching movement from

L/BMA in Your World: Mentoring Artists
Alexandra Beller

I use whole-part-whole in artistic mentorship with emerging artists. I ask about their desires for the near and distant future. There is often a median size to their focus. "I want to dance for a big touring company." "I want to show my work at NYLA." "I want to be making all my money through dance." These goals are usually tangled up with a multiplicity of issues that include some essential ideas, such as personal challenges, artistic expression, and desire to communicate, as well as some less efficient motivators, such as vanity, adherence to a fixed idea of success, or family pressure. By changing the aperture of our focus—going really wide, and then really micro, and back—we are often able to come up with both a tangible, actionable to-do list and a set of spiritual and ethical goals that feel authentic.

   I start by getting expansive. "I want to tour in a big company." "Why?" "Because I want to be dancing every day." "Is that the only reason?" "No, it would also make me feel successful to family and friends." "Let's separate those ideas and start with dancing every day." (Later, we will look at "success" and get expansive with it, then micro.) "Let's list all the circumstances in which you'd be dancing every day—rehearsal process, teaching, taking class, etc.—and then go smaller. Take class as our first option. What would you have to do to take class every day?" Here we go smaller and smaller, down to the most basic, actionable steps, like, "Update my reel for dance performance to be able to apply for an internship at x studio." Eventually we look back at the largest ideas—success, expression, contentment, empathy, communication, activism, etc.—and see if we have made tangible structures for accomplishing them.

functional or expressive inroads that affect the values placed on movement. In some instances, movement is referred to anatomically and cued around the biological functions of the body—for example, a personal trainer might say to a client, "The iliopsoas flexes the femur in the pelvis," or, "Try an arm circle to activate your scapula humeral rhythm," or "This makes your posterior chain strong for shoveling snow." In other cases, the expressive aspects of movement may receive greater emphasis—for example, "Sense into the strength of your warrior pose," or, "Her posture made me think she is open to new ideas." To approach movement from a larger perspective, integrate the two ends of the function-expression polarity—for example, by using functional knowledge to develop expressive abilities, or working expressively to achieve new functional skills.

Simple-Complex

The Organizing Theme of simple-complex is about perceiving movement at different levels of complexity. Movement can be described in the most simple terms, such as "The body opens, the body closes." It can also be described in ways that honor its great complexity at any moment. Take the action of folding all your limbs into your torso and hugging your arms around your knees, as though you were curling into a ball. This could be described most simply as closing the body. It could also be described comprehensively, using terms that address the energetic tones, the changing relationship to gravity, the spatial environment, and the anatomical relationships. It could be described using metaphors and images like "recoiling" or "hollowing the guts" or "with urgent tension that clamps the arms around the legs in protection."

Another model for simple-complex is:

Subtle-Simple-Complex

The addition of *subtle* suggests the role of sensation in movement. The concept of subtlety honors movement that is felt but maybe not yet seen, the realm of connectedness and sensitivity that later develops into complexity in full-bodied movement. Seeking sensation as part of movement is like noticing the faint whisperings of a new possibility, or following nearly imperceptible pathways of movement that later become complex virtuosic sequences. Oscillating between simple and complex, or building a class around shifting from subtle to simple to complex, organizes the movement experience—from the most simple unifying clarity to its fully lived complexity.

Stability-Mobility

The Organizing Theme of stability-mobility addresses the relationship between the solidity that emerges from stability and the suppleness found in mobility. This relationship is readily observable in several aspects of human movement.

Laban found this theme especially relevant in the Space harmony scales he created as they invigorated the rhythmic fluctuations of stability and mobility. In these scales stability and mobility rhythmically fluctuate in movement sequences. Such fluctuations are present in other movement trainings, such as throwing a shot put. First the athlete stabilizes and anchors his body into the ground, and then he mobilizes his whole body around sending the shot put into the air. Or the ballet dancer grounds and stabilizes in preparation for a series of pirouettes, returning to stability as she roots her feet into the floor afterward.

Rhythms of Stability-mobility are present within a body at the same time. You emphasize stability in some parts of your body in order to find mobility in others, such as anchoring a foot and leg on one side in order to mobilize and find freedom in movement on the other side. Think about taking a step, or a rock climber who stabilizes two handholds and a foothold in order to reach for a faraway foothold. The rhythmic fluctuations of these two polarities produce the exciting and thrilling possibilities of the body flying through space as well as the satisfying sense of being anchored, centered, and grounded. You use one to support the other and enhance the whole.

Exertion-Recuperation

The theme exertion-recuperation emphasizes the constant fluctuations inherent in movement and the need of the human body to live out those fluctuations. *Exertion* in this context means more than the expending of energy as one would do when participating in a sport. It also means an ongoing investment in aspects of movement. Recuperation is a shift or change in movement that brings the body relief from previous exertion. Recuperation does not need to be a fully opposite investment; but involves small, subtle shifts that change some elements of movement. You can think of it like the rhythmically shifting river of movement that fluctuates constantly, exerting and recuperating to keep you adapting to the demands of your world.

Laban especially used the theme of exertion-recuperation when he worked with F.C. Lawrence in factories. They noticed that workers needed opportunities to recuperate from the physicality of their jobs, and not just by being passive and at rest, but by actively shifting their energetic investment in movement to recuperate from the energetic demands placed on their bodies by the tasks of their jobs. To apply the concept to an office setting, if you sit with your attention urgently focused on a task, after a while you might crave recuperation that allows you to divert your attention to encompass the whole of your environment and dwell in your bodily sensations before returning to detailed and laser-like focus.

Summary

Laban/Bartenieff Movement Analysis is unified by certain Guiding Concepts and Organizing Themes. The Guiding Concepts include the elemental framework of L/BMA, polarities that permeate L/BMA theories and practices, the relational nature of movement, and the idea that movement is a personally unique experience. Certain polarities, referred to in this book as Organizing Themes, are especially important. They help the student of movement expand the range of their perceptive options and provide inroads to address movement in many contexts.

PART II

THE LENS OF LABAN/BARTENIEFF MOVEMENT STUDIES

Human movement is often described with words that are action oriented, such as *hop, fall,* or *twist.* When considering movement through the lens of Laban/Bartenieff Movement Analysis, however, the action of the body is only one part of what is talked about; it is the *what* happens. More is occurring in any given movement than an action; there is also *how* it happens. It is the *how* that colors a movement with expressive and meaningful tones or styles and in ways that impact the function of the body.

The L/BMA term for *what* happens when a body moves is *basic body actions.* These include stillness, pause, flexion, extension, jump (air time), gesture, balance, off-balance, twist, turn, scatter, and gather. An action like a hop can be performed in a variety of ways. The hop can go in many possible directions: forward, backward, sideways. The hopping body can shape itself into many possible forms, such as one resembling a long, rising pin, or a tightly wound and retreating ball. It can also hop in a range of dynamic or energetic tones, with nervous, punchy urgency, or groggy, soft lethargy. Again, the action is *what* happens. To address *how* it happens, L/BMA considers movement from a framework of four main categories—Body, Effort, Shape, and Space (BESS)—and how they come together in Phrasing.

Each of these categories highlights a specific aspect of human movement from which to recognize what and how movement is happening. Within each category are individual elements that represent the most fundamental aspects of movement. In actual life, these elements sequence and layer together to form the complex processes that are movement.

Part II of this book discusses these overarching categories and outlines the elements within each. As you learn to work with movement through the L/BMA lens, you will learn to identify what you are seeing from one of the categories before layering information from other categories. The complexity of human movement makes this a challenging task. Early in the learning process, do your best to maintain your perspective within one category to gain insight regarding what it contributes to your understanding of movement. As your proficiency grows you will begin to see what each category distinctly offers the study of movement, and in time you will be able to integrate and layer the categories to form a discerning awareness of what is happening in movement.

When learning about each category, practice identifying its applicability to your life and the value and possibilities it offers. You may notice that you like and feel familiar in some elements of BESS, while others feel foreign. That is wonderful! You are getting to know your preferences and personal style. Studying this material often prompts people to *style stretch,* to go to new places in movement, a process that brings increased possibilities in movement as it is consciously cultivated. To further support your journey, read the sidebars. They contain commentary from certified Laban/Bartenieff Movement Analysts on how different aspects of Body, Effort, Shape, and Space have been meaningful in their lives and careers, in the field of dance and beyond.

CHAPTER 3

Body

"As we claim the full development of our bodily connections through movement patterns, and recognize the role they play in forming who we are as feelingful, spirited, thoughtful human beings, we will increase our options for a lively interplay with our world. We will feel more alive."

(Hackney 2002, 17)

n Laban/Bartenieff Movement Analysis, the category of Body focuses on the actual physical body—the tangible, graspable body you live in, complete with its muscles, bones, and sinew. This category is commonly considered for its use in developing functional movement skills. This is accurate, but only part of the picture. Body is also expressive, creative, and personally meaningful. Working through Body's creative, imagistic, and expressive nature enhances function and brings new possibilities to and understandings of the moving body. This chapter is written to honor both.

The Body category addresses how the body is organized, provides information on the initiation and sequencing of movement, and fosters increased efficiency, ease, and expressivity of movement. The following discussion is organized into three main classifications: foundational information about the Body category, Patterns of Total Body Connectivity (PTBCs), and the Basic Six. Each of these aspects of Body sheds light on developing movement skills and connections within the body in specific ways. Taken as individual pieces, they offer snapshots of information on how movement is organized. Taken as a larger whole, the Body category provides ways of describing, organizing, progressing, and refining movement skills.

Foundations of the Body Category

Many people working with Laban/Bartenieff Movement Analysis have contributed to and helped shape the Body category. Tracing its complete history is beyond the scope of this book, but I will provide some historical context.

The roots of the Body category lie in Irmgard Bartenieff's work with Laban's Space and Effort theories to bring fuller functional and expressive movement capacities to adult movement. Bartenieff's formal contributions to the field of Laban/Bartenieff Movement Analysis include her pamphlet *Notes from a Course in Correctives* and the book *Body Movement: Coping with the Environment,* cowritten with Dori Lewis. They also include her movement experiences (the Basic Six), and the integration of Effort, Shape, and Space into the study of Body. As a physical therapist, a dance therapist, and a student of Rudolph von Laban, she became known in the 1960s for her work with adults who had polio (Hackney 2002, 6-7). Using her skills combined with her working knowledge of Laban's Space and Effort theories, she was able to mobilize her patients in ways that others had been unable to.

In her pamphlet *Notes from a Course in Correctives,* Bartenieff outlines possibilities for sensation and perception, imagery, kinesthetic awareness, and movement that will improve posture and alignment. She describes using Laban's ideas of Space and Effort as vital to achieving these goals. She also considered the progression of movement in one's life. In the following passage, she alludes to how her work follows stages of human motor development:

Locomotion seems to be built in on every level from lying to stand-ing. Locomotion . . . gradually assumes orientation toward outside space. . . . In lying, there is wriggling and rolling where wriggling has a headward-tailward orientation. Crawling patterns as well as early swim-ming patterns, involve progression with the use of our four limbs . . . unilaterally . . . or contralaterally. . . . In man, right and left distinction as well as asymmetrical use of limbs is further refined by the separate, though simultaneously occurring development of the upper limbs for reaching, grasping and their coordination with vision and hearing (Bartenieff 1977, 2).

Also included in the pamphlet are five specific movement experiences, or exercises, that guide the reader to find basic movement connections. These movements are focused on "core" ("lower spine-pelvis-hip-thigh") patterns and their relationship to the upper body (Bartenieff 1977, 2). The five core exercises have since grown into six prototype movements known as the Basic Six. Initially performed supine (lying face up), they increase in complexity and difficulty, especially if you choose to explore them in other relationships to gravity, such as sitting or standing. In *Notes from a Course in Correctives* Bartenieff offers a model for progressing movement learning and demonstrates how to layer the complexity of these patterns.

Bartenieff did not work explicitly with the patterns of motor develop-ment, but she likely studied them in her training as a physical therapist and considered them in her practice. As Peggy Hackney explains in her book *Making Connections: Total Body Integration Through Bartenieff Fundamentals,* the first version of Bartenieff's book *Body Movement* (which before publication she titled "The Art of Body Movement as a Key to Perception") included a since deleted discussion of how her work was "based on a thorough understanding of the early patterns of neurological development, includ-ing the early reflexes, righting reactions, and equilibrium responses, as well as the importance of breath, core-distal connections and patterns in spinal, homologous, homo-lateral and contra-lateral movement" (Hackney 2002, 8).

The terms used later in this chapter to describe humans' developmental movement patterns come from Peggy Hackney, student and protégé of Barte-nieff. As Peggy explains it, she chose to use them because

- Bartenieff used these words to teach fundamentals, and as part of Bartenieff's lineage Hackney felt this was a way of honoring her,

- they are understandable to those less studied in movement, and

- they are being used to describe movement patterns in adults, not just developing infants.

(Peggy Hackney, email exchange with Helen Walkley (February 23, 2014, shared with author).

The movements of the Basic Six are embedded within the larger framework of the Patterns of Total Body Connectivity (PTBCs), which in turn are based on the developmental movement patterns of infants, or the basic neurological patterns (based on the work of Berta and Karl Bobath). They provide ways of looking at how movement is organized in the body. The underpinnings of motor development in the Body category have been written about extensively by many authors, especially Peggy Hackney, Bonnie Bainbridge Cohen, and Linda Hartley. As with many of the theories and systems associated with Laban's work, the Body category continues to grow as new information comes to the fore through research in fields like somatics, physical therapy, embryology, and exercise science.

Before diving into the meat of the chapter, let's define some basic terms. Understanding them can bring more nuance to your observation, description, and execution of movement.

Postures and Gestures

Describing a posture or gesture is one of the most basic aspects of movement. Is the movement a gesture—for example, the movement of a limb? Is it a posture, a physicalized stance? Linguistically these words have a different sense of weight and are often used colloquially to suggest the degree of investment: a gesture is less firm or committed, while a posture carries a sense of greater importance. In movement studies, however, the linguistic link does not necessarily hold up in movement; a gesture is not less important than a posture.

In the context of Laban's work, a **posture** involves movement of the whole body. When there is change in one part, like a weight shift, it affects the entire body; the stance has shifted.

A **gesture** in the Laban tradition is considered a movement of the limbs, usually small, that does not impact the whole body. Gestures are often seen as indicative and revealing of an inner understanding or logic.

A **posture-gesture merger** is when the posture and the gesture are congruent, as though they are linked and have come together with equal importance (Fernandes 2015, 133).

Understanding postures, gestures, and posture-gesture mergers can be a first inroad toward becoming more nuanced in your comprehension of movement. The distinction that emerges from this information allows you to ask questions about what parts of the body are participating in the movement and how movement choices influence and affect the overall experience of the movement. These concepts are useful for exploring and developing characters, as well as for understanding movement generation through experiences such as beginning with a gesture and taking it into a posture, or working from a posture to finding accompanying gestures.

Body Attitude

Body attitude refers to a person's habitual constellations of movement and body alignment (Hackney 2002, 233). As you observe or consider movement, you may notice particular tendencies, including repeated postures and relationships within the body, that seem to be "of this person," or "of this person right now." Beyond observing movement, developing characters or choreography from the perspective of body attitude can take you to unexpected creative places. By trying on a different body attitude than your personal baseline, you may find that a new world of movement choices and perceptions arises.

Body-Part Phrasing

Another basic aspect of movement is body-part phrasing, which describes the sequencing of movement through the body. Body-part phrasing is a useful concept when describing movement because it gives you a framework for recognizing how the body is participating in the movement and how movement is sequencing through the body.

Consider exploring body connectivity (explained later in the chapter) using different body-part phrasings than you normally would use. What does it bring to your experience? What connections emerge from new phrasing options?

Simultaneous body-part phrasing is when all active parts of the body move at once. **Successive body-part phrasing** is when movement in one part of the body flows to an adjacent part of the body. **Sequential body-part phrasing** is when movement in one part of the body flows into another, nonadjacent part of the body (Hackney 2002, 219).

There may be a movement you do frequently using a consistent sequencing of body parts: throwing a football or getting out of bed, for instance. In these examples, a different choice of sequencing could impact the action functionally, change the feeling of the movement, and bring a different expressive life to it. When throwing a football, switching from simultaneous to successive phrasing along the diagonal can improve the spiral of the ball and bring greater accuracy to a pass. Getting out of bed in the morning with simultaneous instead of sequential phrasing could generate feelings of "I am here, all of me, all at once" to initiate your day. Or perhaps successive phrasing to get out of bed allows you to feel like you have eased yourself into the day and can generate a feeling of budding alertness. Sometimes exploring body-part phrasing will reveal useful and effective sequencing that you are already utilizing, and at other times it will give you options to improve sequencing.

Body-part phrasing can be a metaphorically meaningful approach to looking at how you move through projects and transitions in your life, not just those primarily centered around physical activity. When I set out to write this book, I was clear that it would be both a sequential and a successive process. There would be times when I wrote in a successive pattern, moving from one section to the next adjacent section, and other times when I would jump from one part to a nonadjacent part to make sure I was weaving material together coherently throughout the text.

The information provided so far in this chapter forms the foundation of the Body category. It encourages you to consider how different parts of the body participate in movement in relationship to the whole body. The remainder of the chapter dives into the details of the Patterns of Total Body Connectivity and the Basic Six aspects of the Body category.

Patterns of Total Body Connectivity

The **Patterns of Total Body Connectivity** (PTBCs) are based on the neurological movement progression, often called motor development, or the basic neurological patterns that the infant goes through in the first approximately fourteen months of life. Generally, the infant is physiologically mandated to execute these patterns. These patterns develop functional capabilities, which creates the opportunity for increased psychological expression and organizes the developing brain. In other words, as physiological development allows new sensations and experiences of the world, psychological understanding changes.

While all humans are mandated to progress through these neurological patterns, interferences, glitches, and individualized patterns of development may prevent them from being fully experienced and expressed. Revisiting the PTBCs as an adult can be useful to enhance movement skills for a diverse population ranging from those with developmental uniqueness (delays) to those seeking physical virtuosity (refined movement skills). Further, they offer the student of movement a framework for how movement is organized in the body.

There are six Patterns of Total Body Connectivity, each with a corresponding symbol, a palette of movement experiences. The patterns are listed below.

1. Breath
2. Core-Distal
3. Head-Tail
4. Upper-Lower
5. Body-Half
6. Cross-Lateral

As you read over the list above you may want to map or imagine on your own body the relationships the pattern is referring to. For example, for the third pattern, head-tail, send your attention to your head and your tail (your tailbone or imaginary vestigial tail). Notice the soft through-line of your spine, the movement possibilities this attention conjures, and the sensations that arise. Do this for each pattern. What did you notice as you explored the relationships listed above?

Each pattern represents a way of organizing the self in the world and offers different possibilities in coordinated movement. Deliberately returning to these patterns after infancy and toddler years can be both challenging and enriching, and can bring greater possibilities to your movement. The focus of the following discussion of the PTBCs is to connect where they emerge in the baby with how they can be useful in adult life and how studying them enhances the adult movement experience.

Breath Patterning

As the first Pattern of Total Body Connectivity, breath (see figure 3.1) is the baseline from which all other movement patterns develop. It is fundamental to life and among our first experiences upon entering the world. Before an infant's first breaths, the fetus practices the movements of breathing in utero, as the mother breathes for the fetus by sending oxygen through the umbilical cord.

For an infant, breath affords sensation of the inside of the body, including the body's inner volume. Through breathing you feel the internal body growing and shrinking through the swelling of the inhalation and the contracting of the exhalation. The gentle expansion and contraction of the breath's rhythm provides the basic material of human life, oxygen, and the important release of carbon dioxide.

Breath patterning assists the coordination of the internal body that is vital in human movement. Functionally, every inhalation and exhalation is a complex event. Upon inhaling, the five lobes of the lungs expand to engulf the heart and welcome oxygen. The diaphragm is pulled downward toward the pelvis by the central tendon, filling up like an inverted hot-air balloon (see figure 3.2). Oxygen is taken into the body via the lungs, where it is transferred through small air sacs called alveoli into the blood, which is pumped throughout the body by the heart—a process that allows every cell in the body to respire. Carbon dioxide is released via exhalation, eliminating waste products. As you exhale, the central tendon releases, the diaphragm contracts upward, and the pelvic floor moves up, back, and in. Deliberately bringing your awareness to your breath as support for your movement is a precursor to whole-body coordination and virtuosity in movement. This is true

Figure 3.1   Breath symbol.

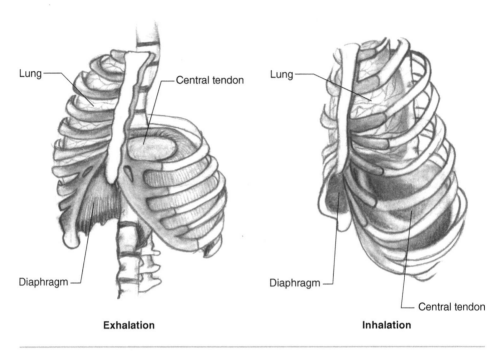

Figure 3.2   Lungs, diaphragm, and central tendon, at the height of exhalation and inhalation

Illustrated by Sydney P. Celio.

for movers of all levels as breath allows the entire body to be supported from within in complex coordination.

As long as there is life, breath is present; it is the baseline of life force, the river on which all movement and expression runs. As an adult, revisiting the breath pattern is a useful way of connecting with sensation. Tuning into sensation within the body offers a way of becoming present within yourself and identifying what is needed in the moment. As a way of checking in with yourself, you can revisit the breath pattern when you are overstimulated, exhausted, or stressed; observing your breath can sooth what feels overwhelming. You may notice your breath changing with your emotional states. Agitation may shorten or truncate the breath, and rest may deepen it. You can alter and shift "emotional tone" by inviting the breath. The breath pattern is a reminder that you have the choice to affect your feelings and thereby your responses. Paying attention to the sensation of breath with its wave-like, rolling inhalations and exhalations can release muscle tension associated with stress.

Notice how the breath pulses inside of your body. Sensing the breath may bring you home to yourself. Many spiritual and centering practices, like meditation and stress reduction, use a focus on the breath as a key principle because it brings centeredness. It is a way of returning to a fundamental aspect of being alive. When stressed or feeling distanced from yourself, connecting to the breath can help you reconnect to yourself and feel calmer and more present.

Breath also provides access to the sense of yielding, bonding, and being with that will be discussed in depth later in this chapter. Imagine that as you attend to your breath you can soften the surfaces of your body and bond with the surfaces of support around you.

Breath brings with it a sense of the connection between one's inner and outer worlds, an experience that can be life-giving and profoundly essential. The exchange of oxygen and carbon dioxide changes the torso as it expands and contracts. Allow this internal to growing and shrinking to support and fill your movement. **Breath support** is a concept used by Irmgard Bartenieff to illustrate the breath's ability to support and enliven full-bodied movement.

Visiting the breath pattern can provide another way of getting ready for activity. Breath supports movement. To accompany and support movement, the breath can be activated and vigorous, or soft, sustained, and elongated. Beginning an activity by getting the breath going is like preparing the insides of the body for what will later become activated outwardly. By using breath as part of a warm-up, you activate sensations of the internal three-dimensional support for movement, and you recruit the tissues of the body to be responsive and pliable.

For many adults who lead sedentary lives, the torso can feel tense and stuck, while their attention is directed outward. Attending to the flow of breath by directing attention inward can help them find movement and ease in the torso. When tension headaches or fatigue arises due to limited and contained movement, a person can deliberately deepen the flow of breath to nourish tissue and find new movement potential throughout the torso. To help you visualize the flow of breath, imagine a surfer riding a wave into shore. Like the wave that catches the surfboard, "catch" your exhalation and "ride" its undulating pattern through your body, noticing how and where it moves. You can also explore the feeling of being filled and expanded by the inhalation.

Bringing breath patterning into the forefront of your movement gives you the opportunity to let breath guide and initiate and influence the movement. In this way, the breath stimulates support of the core, the supple undulations of the spine, and massages the connection between upper and lower body. Fully receiving the exhalation allows for the area around the belly button to gather and hollow inward toward the organs, providing the first inklings of what will come next in movement.

As an expression of inner life, breath patterning has an audible nature, revealed in sounding and speaking. Every verbal or sounded expression rides on the breath; we can either use it fully or diminish and stunt it. An example of breath support in sound is the grandeur of passionate song or chanted liturgy; an example in which breath struggles to support us is hyperventilation. As the expression of inner life, another person's use of breath allows us to perceive the states of his or her thoughts and feelings. Listening to someone talk and sensing the congruence between breath, voice, and body gives the sense that they are coming from a grounded, centered, and committed place. We sense them as believable.

Finally, breath patterning supports big, exuberant, and virtuosic movement. It increases the strength of a boxer's punch or the quick burst of a swimmer's takeoff. The horseback rider uses her breathing to control and communicate to the horse, and the dancer exhales as he prepares to turn.

Explore the Breath Pattern

Check in with your breath. No need to boss it around. Bring your attention to what is currently happening with your breath, and allow it to change as it will. Notice the movement your breath is inspiring in your body. Can you send breath to areas that feel tight or bound up to change the tension of your tissues? Follow and ride the breath pathway like you might follow and ride a wave. Notice where in your body the organs and tissue grow with your breath, and where your internal world is softening or shrinking. Take some time here, and notice how you feel and what this experience has brought. Try singing or sounding the song of your breath. Have your feelings shifted? Where might actively focusing on your breath patterning be useful for you? How might your awareness serve you in your daily life?

KEY POINTS FOR THE BREATH PATTERN

- Connecting to breath is a way of connecting to and centering the self.
- Breath brings oxygen to the blood and tissues, and releases carbon dioxide waste.
- Breath is the infant's first experience of the inner volume of the body.
- The end of the exhalation, when the breath empties and the diaphragm floats upward, sets up the core-softening necessary for the next pattern.
- Breath support enlivens movement throughout the whole body and promotes complexity and virtuosity in movement.

Core-Distal Patterning

The second Pattern of Total Body Connectivity is known as core-distal patterning (see figure 3.3). Moving one's focus from the rhythmic wholeness of breath patterning into core-distal patterning means bringing the entire body into awareness; there is a deeper sense of the body's center (its core) and its farthest edges (its distal structures)—and of the pathways of flow connecting the center with the edges.

Core-distal patterning is based on differentiation of the center of the body from the distal edges. The **core** is the deep guts of the body. The **distal** edges are the body's outermost parts: the head, the vestigial tail, the fingers and toes (see figure 3.4). The infant gradually becomes aware of how the center (core) and edges (distal structures) connect, and thus gains a burgeoning sense of the self as a whole being in relationship to the outer world. If there were a mantra for this pattern it could be: "Me to World, World to Me."

Like the arms of a starfish, the limbs in core-distal patterning are organized around a pliable and supportive center; in the starfish the center is a mouth, and in the human it is the navel. In both, the center is adaptable, flexible, and strong. Anatomically, the core consists of several muscles, especially

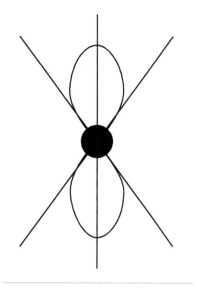

Figure 3.3   Core-Distal symbol.

the pelvic floor, transverse abdominis, rectus abdominis, internal and external obliques, erector spinae, and diaphragm (see figure 3.5). However, in the study of movement patterning, the core also encompasses the digestive organs and the deep guts contained by these muscles as its voluminous inner contents.

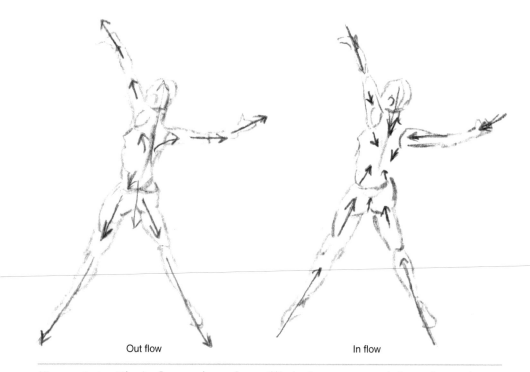

Out flow   In flow

Figure 3.4   The in-flow and out-flow of limbs into core , and through to other limbs, and core out to the world.

Illustrated by Sydney P. Celio.

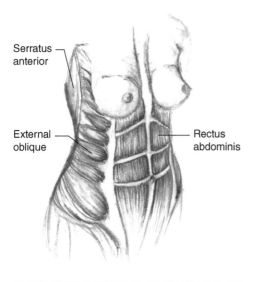

Serratus anterior

External oblique

Rectus abdominis

Figure 3.5   Muscular anatomy of the core.

Illustrated by Sydney P. Celio.

Core support, a concept first used by Irmgard Bartenieff, is encompassed by the theory of the core-distal Pattern. **Core support** highlights the body's center as its alive, supple, and dynamic support system. Core support is not about holding the center rigidly or stiffly to create a hardening within the body. The hardened or held core does not offer the pliable, adaptable qualities that provide deep inner support of the body's center. Nor is core support the totally released, passive relaxation of the center. It is a deep, inner lifting from the base of the pelvis along the line of the iliopsoas toward the diaphragm that allows the core to be simultaneously soft and engaged from deep within.

The discoveries from breath patterning—how the breath fills and empties from the core, impacting muscles as deep as the pelvic floor—are precursors to experiencing core support. To find core support, explore making deep, guttural yet easeful exhalation sounds that promote a hollowing engagement of your core. Notice the deep anatomical support you experience at the end of the exhalation, when the central tendon releases and the diaphragm contracts in, back, and up. Consider the image of a flexible container lifting from the pelvic floor and gathering the guts inward and upward toward the back of the heart from all directions. This activates the central structures deep within the core, instead of muscularly pulling the body wall in, to create support for movement at the center of the body.

As mentioned, the distal aspect of core-distal patterning involves the farthest ends of the limbs. In the PTBC perspective, there are six limbs: two arms, two legs, a head, and a vestigial tail. Like the tentacles of the starfish, human limbs actively seek information about the outside world. Each provides a pathway from the center of the body to its farthest edges and out to the world.

Core-distal patterning is also about the pathways of connection or flow inward from the distal edges to an enlivened core, and through the center to other parts of the body and out to space, like laser beams that radiate into and out of the core. You can open pathways of connection by rocking along kinetic chains. Functionally speaking, **kinetic chains** are the joints and muscles that are affected by each other during movement. When one part changes or moves, it creates a ripple response along the kinetic chain.

In the perspective of Patterns of Total Body Connectivity, kinetic chains offer pathways that foster connection between parts of the body and enhances your sensation connection. Rocking or messaging from one part of your body to another is a way of activating the kinetic chains and finding pathways of flow through the body (see figure 3.6). Rocking is a rhythmic push and release that sends a message through the body, from one place to another, and encourages you to notice the sensations of connection between parts of the body and the sense of a through-channel of movement that connects one part to another. As you rock, "give the energy a place to go"—that is, be clear about the spatial pathway you are messaging through your body. Rocking and sending messages along kinetic chains allows the whole body to participate in a movement experience and encourages movement that is easeful, connected, and integrated.

Figure 3.6   A sample kinetic chain from the inner edge of the foot to the core.

Illustrated by Sydney P. Celio.

Another way to experience the inflow and outflow of the core-distal pattern is to imagine your center as a lake and your limbs as tributaries that can drain either into the lake or into outlets through which the water flows to irrigate the environment. If there is holding or constriction in parts of the body along the path between edge and center, the message does not get in or out. You can use your hands to trace the pathways from center to limbs and limbs to center on your body.

It is useful to imagine aspects of the last trimester of pregnancy and the birthing process as providing early visceral information that sets up later core-distal adult movement. In the last trimester the fetus pushes against the uterine wall, the feet and hands pressing against their container. This compression experience sends kinesthetic messages inward, encouraging the fetal body to "sense itself"—perhaps conveying the message of "me at my very center."

Later, as part of the infant's motor development, core-distal patterning is evident when the infant extends its limbs, opening to the spatial environment, the earliest inklings of a reach. Unlike in the uterus, where the limbs were contained by the uterine wall, they now find space. What had been inflow now has the possibility of outflow as the limbs elongate into the environment. The infant's pushes do not hit a container, they extend into the new world of space, from the core to the edge and beyond. As the infant matures, the rhythms of in and out found in core-distal patterning are biologically mandated and practiced. You will see this as infants stroke the air and the space around them as if their six limbs had a tentacle nature, exploring, massaging, and squirming to get to know their new world. When you watch an infant in this early pattern you will notice that nothing happens at the distal edge that is not supported by the core, and as the core center of the baby adapts, the edges are in synchronization.

As an adult, the core-distal pattern takes on significant meaning and metaphor. The adult's core is adaptable. It can be strong, rigid, fluid, dynamic, supportive, or at rest. Having access to a range of expression and kinetic options allows the adult's core to support whatever is most right in any moment. As the center of the being, intuitive gut knowing, the core brings aliveness and vitality.

Through the support of the core, you move into the world knowing that every part of your body is connected to and through the alive center. And this aliveness is constantly feeding information out to the edges, where you can connect to the world. The messaging of inflow and outflow goes both ways: What happens at your edges, where you meet the world, comes into you, and you know how to adapt at your very core. Working with the core in this manner allows you to be aware of how the whole of you is invested in something, and how to be in the body in a supported and easeful way that feels good. When does the core need to release? Or stand up for itself? When does it need inner strength? When does it need nourishment or rest?

The core-distal pattern surfaces frequently in the adult life. It happens when you first awaken in the morning as you elongate your limbs and yawn. It is present in the actions of a jazzy club dancer who organizes her movement around a dynamic, swaying center. Group exercise classes often start and end around core-distal patterns executed to the beat of popular music. This is to warm up the participants, who are instructed to extend their limbs out into space and fold them inward again. You can imagine the drawing inward of the limbs when performing a plié at the ballet barre, and then radiating out as you straighten the legs and extend the arms into second position.

Revisiting core-distal patterning as an adult increases awareness of the center of the body and its most distant edges. Rocking along the pathways of flow, as described earlier in this section, brings coordination and connection between the center and the edges. It teaches the adult to sequence movement through kinetic chains. And it helps him or her find internal support from his or her deepest center. Many complex movements require the

L/BMA in Your World: Core-Distal Patterning

Molly S. Jorgensen

Core-distal patterning helps me to find balance between my career (or the ways in which I make money) and my family. I identify as a dance artist, somatic-movement educator or therapist, and choreographer. I'm also a mother to four beautiful children, a wife, a sister, and a daughter. I love both the movement ideas that core-distal patterning reveals to me and the personal psychological correlations I have made. *Core* is a buzzword used in many different contexts in the world today. What does it mean? Do we have a core the same way an apple has a core? Core-distal patterning has helped me to understand that I can move physically in all directions and reach fully into my **kinesphere** while maintaining a sense of balance and control within my movement. From a psychological and even spiritual perspective, core-distal patterning has allowed me to understand that all parts of me have a relationship to the whole of who I am. If I can live from a place of "core" purpose, and if I know what is "core" for me, then I am able to extend myself in many different directions without mentally and emotionally falling apart, because I know where to return to if I find myself getting lost. I know where my home is.

sending of movement from one body part to another through an enlivened core. Think of the downward dog in yoga. From there, you lift a leg, reaching with your toes to "flip your dog," and then reaching with your fingers to return to downward dog. Or imagine the running back as he takes the pigskin into his abdomen, folds in around the ball to protect it, and sprints down the field.

When your body feels compartmentalized and tense, enlivening the core and engaging the body around your enlivened core can help your body feel connected and whole. It can enhance your connection to your guts and your sense of being centered—your sense of what is at the core, what is important, and where you stand with it. Speaking and moving from your entire body allows feelings of supported wholeness. Nothing gets left out; all parts participate. You are whole.

Exploring the Core-Distal Pattern

This movement experience has you shift between being a starfish on your back and a ball on your side. Begin by lying on the floor on your back in an X shape, so that your legs extend easily from the hips. They should not be too far apart as this will cause you to grip the front of the hips and thighs and anteriorly tilt your pelvis, diminishing your access to your deep core support. Breathe deeply so your breath supports the movement. At the end of an exhalation, as you experience the release of the diaphragm's central tendon and the gathering of your deep center, allow all six of your limbs to fold into a ball-like shape as you roll over to one side (see figure 3.7). Imagine that the limbs are like rivers flowing into the lake of your center. Next, switch the direction of the flow, allowing the center to reach toward the ground as though the lake at the center of you is flowing into the rivers of your limbs, returning you to the starfish position on your back.

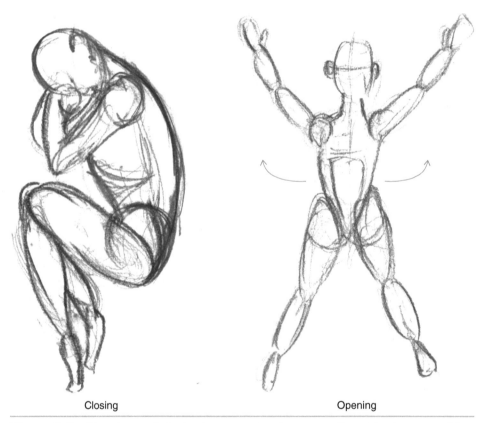

Closing   Opening

Figure 3.7   Opening and closing in a core-distal pattern of total body connectivity. Illustrated by Sydney P. Celio.

- The core-distal pattern is about finding the center and the edges of the body and sending the limbs into the environment.

- It brings awareness and differentiation of the body's boundaries, the "me," "not me," and "me" "world."

- Pathways of flow in the body, including inflow and outflow, set up relationships between parts of the body and promote possibilities for more complex sequences of movement.

- Core support is a concept describing an adaptable, alive center of the body that dynamically radiates inward and outward to support the whole body.

Head-Tail Patterning

The third Pattern of Total Body Connectivity, head-tail patterning (see figure 3.8), highlights the developing awareness and articulation of the central through-line of the body: the spine. The spine is the bony structure that encapsulates the nervous-system, including the spinal cord and cerebral spinal fluid and forms the vertical core of your being. It is a snake-like axis that can be fluid and supple or firm and sturdy (see figure 3.9).

The head-tail pattern is characterized by two distinct ends that are brought into relationship with each other along the pathway, or through-line, connecting them. Irmgard Bartenieff regularly referenced the head end or the tail end of the spine to cue movement.

Movement sequences between the two ends of the head-tail forming a through-line of connection that echoes the metaphoric and physical ability to "follow through"—to initiate a movement at one end and to send that impulse all the way through to the other end. You can root and push with the tail to send an impulse through the vertical core and out the sinuses at the top of the head. Or you can reach the head to the right and let the message travel to the tail, causing the tail to move in response. Allowing an impulse to move all the way through feels like a massage for the inner body.

Allowing the head-tail pathway to express its full range of three-dimensional adaptability feels wonderful to the body. You can move the whole spine at once, or one vertebra at a time, letting the impulse ripple through successively to the other end. Or you can move one part of the spine followed by a nonadjacent part in a sequential phrasing. This exploration of sequencing

Figure 3.8   Head-tail symbol.

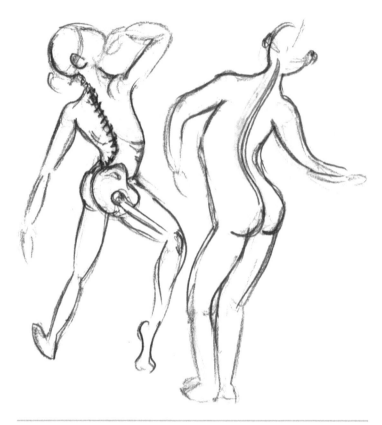

Figure 3.9   The spine has the capacity to be both strong
and bony and supple and soft.
Illustrated by Sydney P. Celio.

through the spine may help you feel the "throughness" of your inner body and
notice that an initiation can travel through the body's structures.

In the earliest developmental phases of the fetus and the newborn infant,
the head-tail pattern is expressed as soft and wave-like. It undulates, squirms,
roots, falls, and wiggles. All of this activity along the head-tail pathway
strengthens and mobilizes the vertical core, preparing the developing baby for
the challenging new relationships to gravity that will emerge as the body adapts
to a vertical stance. As the human relationship to gravity changes from lying
on the floor to quadrupedal (hands and feet or knees on the ground), to the
vertical relationship of standing, changes at the head and tail ends influence
and make this progression possible. As the developing body gains verticality,
the senses of the head end move higher in the spatial world, and changes at
the tail end and in the pelvis cause the hip flexors to lengthen, allowing the
pelvis to shift the torso and upper body into uprightness.

The senses at the head end allow the infant to send attention outward,
into the world. The desire to see, eat, hear, and smell the world mobilizes

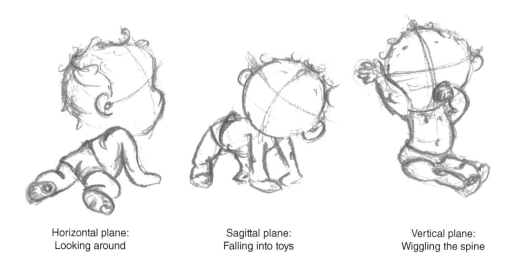

| Horizontal plane: | Sagittal plane: | Vertical plane: |
| Looking around | Falling into toys | Wiggling the spine |

Figure 3.10   Infant movement in all three planes that emerges from head-tail patterning.

Illustrated by Sydney P. Celio.

the infant's head. When a baby smells milk, the mouth reaches toward the source of that milk, turning the head and causing a ripple response through the spine to the tail end.

As the head end facilitates attention, the tail end facilitates intention and the ability to mobilize into and through space. The tail roots, pushes, and activates from the intention to go—to get somewhere—triggering the first sensations of propelling the body into space. Imagine a fish whose eyes seek and whose tail propels it through water.

When infant movement progresses through the head-tail phase of motor development, the little body gains access to all three planes of motion as a mobile, moving being (see figure 3.10). The infant can wiggle its spine into the body of its parent through the vertical plane, fall into its toys in the sagittal plane, or watch someone walk by and follow them with the eyes by rotating around the horizontal plane. This is all exhilarating and mobilizing! Through the developments made at the head-tail phase, a baby's access to the three-dimensional world is enhanced and they are prepared for their next big movement challenges.

Through repetition and increasingly challenging movements, the suppleness of the exploring, mobile spine begins to gain strength and stability that allows the body to progress toward vertical. The three-dimensional adaptability of the mobile spine continues as the spine develops stability. The strong and stable spine rotates horizontally, flexes and extends sagittally, and laterally. It also spirals, combining more than one plane of motion at a time, as if while sitting at a desk you were to rotate and flex toward the floor on the right side of the desk to pick up a shoe.

Initiation in Physical Therapy

Andrea Cordova Caddes, DPT, CLMA

Irmgard Bartenieff said that initiation determines the course of the movement phrase. As a physical therapist, I think it is important that patients understand where a movement should initiate from in order to efficiently activate the kinetic chain. I see a lot of compensatory patterns when people do not understand effective body-part sequencing. I teach people to become more mindful of their bodies to ensure that all parts of the body are working harmoniously. I believe that harmony within the body is about balancing the long, weak structures with strengthening exercises and the short, tight structures with stretching and release work. Finding this exertion-recuperation rhythm in muscle activation is dependent on body-part sequencing. I spend a lot of time educating patients about the initiation of the movement and why it is important to get the whole body working together with an optimal length-tension relationship in the muscles.

At the head-tail stage of motor development, the **basic neurocellular patterns** used in Body-Mind Centering of yield/push and reach/grasp/pull become available to the infant (Bainbridge Cohen, n.d.). These movement patterns are how the infant learns to pursue desire and achieve satisfaction of its needs. They are essential for setting up the locomotion patterns that develop in upper-lower patterning, and then grow more complexly phrased in body-half and cross-lateral.

Yielding, a term integrated into movement understandings by Bonnie Bainbridge Cohen, occurs as part of the developmental progression. **Yielding** is a movement quality that involves connecting to and bonding with someone or something. **Pushing** is a movement quality that involves activation into something to move away from or toward someone or something. First, the developing infant connects to its caregiver for safety, then it pushes away to establish independence. A baby may burrow its head into its mother's body, settling into the safety provided there; later in its development it will test its independence by pressing away from her, setting a boundary.

Yielding and Pushing: Patterns of Grounding into Self

- Yielding is about letting your energy flow "out and in" so you are able to connect and "bond" or "meet" with someone or something. Through yielding, you are able to "be with." It is present in the breath pattern of total body connectivity.

- Pushing is about sending your energy "into" something or someone so you can press against it in order to propel yourself. It can move you away from or toward something or someone.

Reaching, grasping, and pulling are driven by the desire to take possession of whatever is necessary for feeding and survival. The infant reaches out and wraps its fingers or toes around something to pull it toward itself or itself toward something. The **reach** is an elongation into the environment, while the **grasp** is an engulfing or wrapping around, and the **pull** is an active bringing of the object into oneself or the self toward something. When the infant seeks the nipple to suckle, it is an example of the reach, grasp, pull pattern at the head end. The tail end has its own version: from a stimulation the tail will reach, follow, and shift toward that stimuli.

Reaching, Grasping, and Pulling: Patterns of Moving into Space

- Reaching is about desiring something that is beyond your bodily boundary and elongating yourself into space to make contact with it.
- Grasping is about connecting with and taking hold of something. It directs the energy of the reach back toward the self.
- Pulling is about either bringing what is desired and what is outside yourself to you and you to it, or removing yourself from what might be scary or unwanted.

Integrating Y/P, R/G/P

- Together, yielding and pushing are about coming into yourself, while reaching, grasping, and pulling are about elongation into space (figure 3.11).
- The cycle refreshes and renews by returning to the state of rest provided by yielding.
- Phrases of Y/P into R/G/P are present in head-tail, upper-lower, body-half, and cross-lateral Patterns of Total Body Connectivity. The basic neurocellular patterns phrase through the body in different ways in each of these Patterns of Total Body Connectivity in order to organize movement in the body according to that PTBC. For example, at the head-tail phase, Y/P and R/G/P are organized around the head-tail through-line of the body.

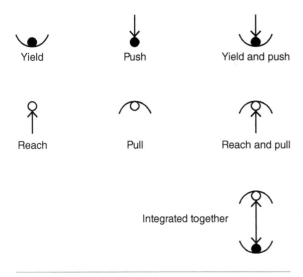

Figure 3.11   Integrated yielding and pushing and reaching and pulling patterns.

In the infant, head-tail patterning and early experiences of yield, push, reach, grasp, and pull are precursors to locomotion.

- Rhythmic yielding and pushing of the tail create a rocking and undulating of the spine. The ability to drive and push through the tail shifts the pelvis with intention.
- Reaching through the tail initiates the pull to sitting or standing.
- Softening and yielding of the eyes, mouth, ears, nose, and tissues in the face allow the infant to experience sensations and desires.
- A reaching out of the mouth and grasping food brings satisfying and nourishing sensations.
- A pushing from the head end into the floor or into a parent's body brings sensations of compression and feelings of containment.

For adults, head-tail patterning is important in many day-to-day activities. The central through-line of support from head to tail organizes and supports desires and needs with options for flexibility and durability. Head-tail patterning allows the adult body to be fluid and malleable from a juicy midline or to be steadfast and committed from a strong "backbone."

During long hours of sitting, when the body feels immobilized, deliberately engaging in movements related to head-tail patterning can offer fluid relief. You can actively root through your tail to ground into your base of support and let the impulse flow through your dynamic, vertically aligned center. This rooting lets you reinvest in sitting and feel your insides float on top of your tail. If rooting through your tail is not sufficient, you can shift to supple mobility. Engaging in undulating, wave-like, successive movement along the spine heightens awareness of the throughness of the spine and increases sensitivity to the possibilities for movement between the two ends of the vertical core. It nourishes the connections along the spine, enhancing the potential for movement and adaptability.

When you need to motivate yourself to get moving, to get something done, reaching through your tail makes it easier to mobilize into the world (see figure 3.12). Try reaching the tail to forward high as the impetus to rise out of a chair. Or if you stand on your left leg, you can reach your tail toward

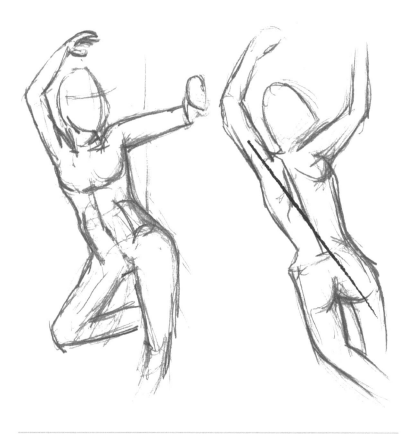

Figure 3.12   Head-tail movement pattern. When the head moves, the tail responds.

Illustrated by Sydney P. Celio.

your left heel to shift your weight over to the left side. Driving the tail toward the ground initiates the action of a weight lifter's dead lift. Shifting the tail toward the other leg is the beginning of a golfer's swing. Pulling your tail to the leg you stand on is the basis of the propulsion of a weight shift. The tail is like a rudder that initiates and directs movement, launching an action that will propel you to a new place in the world.

For the adult, the senses located in the head take in information about the world. When the world calls your attention outward and into its offerings, it can be soothing to take moments to soften these senses, easing the head-tail connection and yielding to internal sensations. You can explore this by relaxing your eyes and mouth and nose as though they no longer seek to connect to the outside world; their relaxation lets you check in with your inner experience. When rested or called to the outside world, like the antennae of an insect, the senses can emerge again to attend to outer affairs. This phrasing of in-out is fundamental to recuperating and refreshing the adult who is "out in the world."

Finally, activating the head-tail pattern affords a way of warming up the **central vertical core** of the body. Yoga's cat-cow, a flexion and extension in the sagittal plane of the spine, activates ease and mobility along the head-tail continuum, getting the practitioner ready for the bigger movements of wringing and twisting and folding and unfolding and squirming and undulating through the spine. Imagine if the cat-cow explored all three planes, all body-part phrasing possibilities, and the full range of spiraling, preparing the practitioner for a much greater range of spinal mobility. The warm-up described in the following sidebar will benefit almost any activity, getting the body's central axis ready for more full-bodied movement.

Exploring the Head-Tail Pattern

As you sit, let one end of your spine move, seeking curiously out into the world. Notice what happens to the rest of your spine. It can stabilize and brace against the movement, or it can respond, like a teeter-totter. As the head moves up the tail moves down, as the tail moves right the head counterbalances. If the head and neck rotate to the right, the tail twists in the opposite direction. Like an undulating reed or a gentle wave, responding movements ripple along the soft tissue of the digestive tract, which rests along the front of the spine.

KEY POINTS FOR THE HEAD-TAIL PATTERN

- Anatomically, it follows the spine, nervous system, and digestive tract.
- Undulating, flexing, and rotating along the head-tail pathway affords access to three planes of motion—vertical, sagittal, and horizontal.
- Emotionally and physically, the head-tail axis can be soft and supple, supportive, or steadfast and rigid.
- The head-tail pattern sets up the movement patterns known as yield/push and reach/grasp/pull. These movements underpin locomotion in the next stages of development.

Upper-Lower Patterning

The next phase in infant motor development is known in the PTBCs as upper-lower patterning (see figure 3.13). The physical knowledge and skills established in the head-tail phase now grow to encompass limbs; the head end gains awareness of and use of the arms, and the tail end gains awareness of and use of the legs (see figure 3.14). The differentiation of the upper and lower body from one another is the basis of upper-lower patterning. This differentiation allows coordinated sequencing from upper to lower and lower to upper to facilitate locomotion—the body traveling through space. In the earlier patterns you established a sense of movement traveling through the space in your body, now you get to travel your body into space! Movement takes you into the spatial world so you can get to what is desired or get away from what is not desired. You propel yourself through the world, shifting your weight to a new base of support.

The differentiation of the upper and lower halves of the body is developmentally apparent in **homologous movement**, which is the symmetrical movement of the entire upper half of the body or the entire lower half of the body—for example, throwing both arms upward simultaneously (Hackney 2002, 113). The developing body has not yet learned to

Figure 3.13   Upper-lower symbol.

distinguish right arm from left arm, so the impulse for an arm to push means the whole upper body pushes. The same is true for the lower half of the body: The impulse to push in the lower body means all three lower limbs (legs plus vestigial tail) push. The three limbs of the upper body (right arm, left arm, and head) lead this motor learning, developing the patterns of yield, push, reach, and pull first. The three limbs of the lower body follow, developing from the learning first laid down by the upper body.

The basic differences between upper and lower become apparent during this pattern. The upper body is more mobile. It is capable of reaching, grasping, and pulling with precision and dexterity. The lower body is more stable. It facilitates grounding and pushing that move the body into the world. The infant's developing sense of the movement preferences between upper and lower allows it to further differentiate movement and gain new ways to access the world. The upper body reaches and brings desired items into the body, especially the mouth. Lower body grounds, activates, and mobilizes the weight of the body. These differences do not preclude the other end from also developing the less available capacities—such as the lower body being

Figure 3.14   The head and tail ends gain coordinated use of the arms and legs in upper-lower patterning.

Illustrated by Sydney P. Celio.

dexterous and mobile, or the upper body being grounded and capable of locomotion into space.

Once the differentiation between upper and lower is established, the young child begins to notice that what is happening at one end influences and coordinates with movement at the other end. A push from the upper body can sequence through and affect the lower. The toes can curl under and push back, or the toes and tail can reach, causing the body to scoot backward. Note: Scooting backward with a push from the arms to set a boundary is usually the first phase of locomotion; later the legs begin to push the child toward what interests her.

Propulsion, the ability to mobilize the body into space, is made possible by the new movement developments in upper-lower patterning (see figure 3.15). From the differentiation of and connection between upper and lower comes the ability to propel yourself to a new place, to shift your weight, sending the whole body from one base of support to another, a process Irmgard Bartenieff referred to as pelvic propulsion. The longing to get to a new place is the impetus for the weight shift. In order to shift, some parts of the body have to first ground or anchor into the earth or another support to gain stability. Getting going into space happens in sequences—for example, grounding and stabilizing and then pushing the upper body, followed by reaching with the lower body to scoot backward. Or grounding and stabilizing the lower in order to reach, grab, and pull from the upper. With a grounded lower body comes the ability to reach so many new things! It is as if the expanded possibilities in movement have granted the body access to a much bigger world around it.

As an infant gets ready to creep through space, she will test her relationship to the ground by "revving her engine," rocking back and forth in the sagittal

Figure 3.15   Crawling and creeping from upper-lower organizations.
Illustrated by Sydney P. Celio.

plane on all fours. Rocking from the grounding rhythm of yielding and pushing sends messages through the body, preparing it to take new risks. As the infant grows confident in the grounding and stabilization of her lower body, she will lift a hand from the floor, allowing her to reach forward into space, plant her feet, and scoot forward from the lower body, first crawling and then creeping when the belly comes off the ground.

The patterns of yield/push and reach/grasp/pull, referred to as the basic neurocellular patterns (see discussion earlier in the chapter), begin to develop into sophisticated sequences to achieve locomotion through space. As discussed in the section on head-tail patterning, the vertical through-line of the spine found in the head-tail pattern allows the basic neurocellular patterns to now sequence from upper to lower or lower to upper and carry the body into space.

As movement grows more coordinated and sophisticated, the grounding possibilities related to yielding and pushing sequence from the lower to the upper body. When coordinated with a spatial reach and pull to move to another place, the connection between lower and upper will produce a weight shift, with the whole body finding a new base of support. Sequences of yield/push and reach/grasp/pull can move through the body from upper to lower, and lower to upper to bring coordinated and virtuosic phrasing to movement. Once established as a movement skill, each of the basic neurocellular patterns can be coordinated to initiate from anywhere in the body and can move throughout the body to make complex coordination possible.

The capacity to stabilize one end in order to mobilize the other end, and then to release the stable end to locomote the whole body into the world, is present in many children's activities (see figure 3.16). You can see a young child experience the thrill of mobilizing the body into the world using upper-lower coordination when he engages in scooting, the most basic infant pattern. As development progresses, the pattern manifests in activities like hopping on a pogo stick, playing leapfrog, swinging from monkey bars, playing hopscotch (you

Figure 3.16   Activities commonly performed with upper-lower patterning.
Illustrated by Sydney P. Celio.

can often see the hopscotcher "holding onto" the air with their hands while the lower body quickly scoots between triangles and squares), biking, and swinging.

For adults, too, pursuits that involve upper-lower patterning can offer challenge and satisfaction. Many vigorous and strengthening activities like push-ups, pull-ups, squats, and dead lifts involve the upper-lower pattern, as homologous movement and as examples of one end through to the other end. Think about executing a barbell squat: You yield through the feet and lower body to push into the ground, and then sequence your push to mobilize your body upward and into space, pushing against the weight on your back. The push activates and becomes satisfying and invigorating once it is completed.

Upper-lower movements like these require the mover to efficiently coordinate yield/push and reach/grasp/pull into effective phrases that sequence between the upper and lower body. Such movements can be challenging, the kind of activities you might put off because they seem uncomfortable. Yet they can be satisfying when completed, as though you are on the other side of a challenge and feeling activated and organized in your body from having moved through the challenge. Imagine the dread you might feel going into a series of burpees or rope climbs, and the visceral satisfaction of grounding once you get going and the task is complete (see figure 3.17).

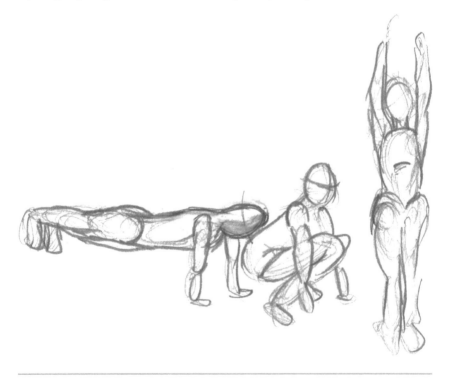

Figure 3.17   Adult activities highlighting the phrase of yield/push to reach/pull between upper and lower.

Illustrated by Sydney P. Celio.

For the adult, exploring the movement world of upper-lower patterning increases the connection and relationship between the upper and lower ends of the body and enhances efficient and easeful locomotion in the spatial world. Coordination and support at the middle of the body—that is, in the overall core and in the vertical core or spine—are central to the ability to connect and support movement between the upper and lower halves of the body. The earlier developmental patterns have taught the core about its ability to soften and respond to movements of the limbs, to allow impulses in one part to travel to another part, and to stabilize with supportive strength.

In upper-lower patterning, the core of the body is the channel through which messages between the two ends pass. When the core is able to stabilize, support, and sequence the neurocellular impulses between upper and lower ends, locomotion is coordinated and efficient.

A pathway important to the sense of connection between the upper and lower body is the one followed by the iliopsoas muscle (see figure 3.18). Primarily involved in hip flexion, the iliopsoas originates from the lowest thoracic

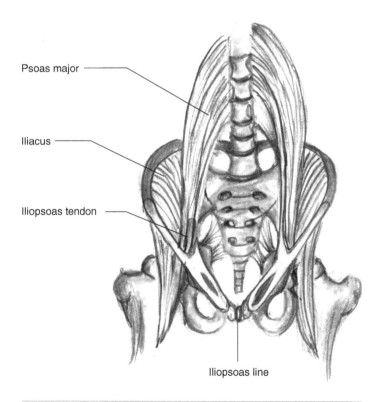

Psoas major

Iliacus

Iliopsoas tendon

Iliopsoas line

Figure 3.18   Iliopsoas line, a primary muscular pathway between upper and lower.

Illustrated by Sydney P. Celio.

and lumbar vertebrae, or the middle of the spine, runs through the organs along the spine, and reemerges to attach to the lesser trochanter of the femur, deep in the inner thigh. This pathway, which runs through the deep center of the body, provides a visual guide to the energetic and muscular connection between the front lower part of the body and the back upper torso, behind the heart and lung area. The iliopsoas connects both the front and back of the body and the upper and lower body.

Upper-Lower Activity

There are many possibilities for increasing your awareness of the through-lines of connection between the upper and lower body. One way is to visualize pathways traversing both over the skin and through the tissues underneath the skin. Imagine a pathway of connection traveling from the anterior, superior iliac spine—colloquially, your hip bones—to the acromion process of the scapula, roughly where the scapula meets the shoulder joint on the back of the shoulder. Visualize how the two places connect, and how the tissues linking them allow messages to travel between them, impacting both. You can also experiment with the connection from sternum to sacrum, thus giving you a pathway from front lower to back upper, and another from front upper to back lower.

Notice these locations on your body in your everyday sitting. The upper simultaneously rests and floats on top of the lower; making adjustments in the lower will affect the upper, and vice versa. For example, softening the chest or lengthening the neck upward will impact the grounding of the lower. Noticing how the messages pass between the two affords support and suppleness to sitting.

Upper-lower patterning may be less developed in adults than other patterns, thus it offers a rich opportunity for enhancing movement ease and skill. The potential for developing greater connectivity in upper-lower patterning is echoed in the movements Bartenieff designed (in conjunction with several students) known as the Basic Six. Several of them—including femoral flexion and extension (thigh lift), lateral pelvic shift, and sagittal pelvis shift (discussed in detail below)—directly address the importance of bringing attention to upper-lower patterning. The other movements in the Basic Six also address or reveal aspects of upper-lower patterning, though less directly.

When exploring upper-lower patterning, the "diaphragm" located at the lowest part of the pelvis—called the pelvic floor or the pelvic diaphragm or diamond—is a key to finding support and connection between the two halves. Bartenieff often referred to this area as the "dead seven inches" because of the tendency to bind up and lock off movement in the region. Try initiating movement from "way down there" (Hackney 2002, 120)—that is, from the lowest part of the pelvis. Learning to initiate movement here to propel you into space can free up messages to move between the upper and lower parts of the body, through a supportive core. It also increases ease and efficiency in movement, reducing the discomfort associated with gripping in the lower back, abdominals, or hip flexors.

Another idea helpful for finding throughness between the upper and lower parts of the body is to visualize the anatomical structures that some refer to as the five diaphragms of the body (see figure 3.19). Each of these horizontal layers of tissue provides an internal scaffolding that serves to support and connect what is above and below. They are: the arches of the feet, the pelvic floor, the diaphragm, the thoracic inlet, and the tentorium (the base of the brain). When working toward achieving buoyancy in the body, imagine the five diaphragms as metaphorical conversing trampolines; the body's internal organs buoyant in the support it receives from each horizontal layer and the internal structures sending messages between the horizontal layers.

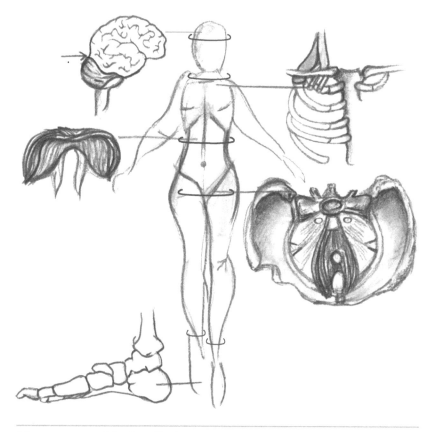

Figure 3.19 The five diaphragms.
Illustrated by Sydney P. Celio.

While certainly the upper body is more facile with expressive, refined movement, and the lower body more suited to locomotion and stability in the vertical plane, it is important that these patterns be developed in both ends to some extent. For example, ballet dancers reach with the moving leg in a tendu and then pull their weight forward from the supporting leg as they shift to execute a pas de basque. A cabinetmaker positioning a large cabinet to install it on a wall will need to push and stabilize a cabinet into the wall with the upper body in ways similar to the stability more commonly seen in the lower body.

For the adult, upper-lower patterning highlights both the distinction between the two ends and the ability of movement to sequence from one end to the other, an act of connecting the two. It also increases the potential for propulsion and locomotion into space. We often use upper-lower patterning to move in the sagittal plane (that is, mostly forward and back with some up and down): to do burpees across the floor in exercise class, to push stalled cars off the road, to be pulled by a boat as we skim the surface of the water on skis. We also sequence a push from the lower body into a pull with the upper body when rowing on a crew team, picking up grandchildren from the floor, or pulling weeds from flower beds. The rock climber feels supported by the grounded push in order to reach for a high crag; the chef reaches for a box of rice high on a shelf. The ability to yield, push, and ground in order to support a reach, grasp, and pull empowers us to move effectively through the world.

Upper-lower patterning is metaphorically meaningful. The yielding and grounding that phrases into a push brings a physical sense of knowing where you are, feeling present and connected to the surface you stand on. Reaching, grasping, and pulling relate to the physical experience of satisfaction when, supported by the ground and your core, you reach to achieve a goal. This sequencing of force through the body and into space feels satisfying.

KEY POINTS FOR THE UPPER-LOWER PATTERN

- Upper-lower patterning is about locomotion, propulsion, and weight shift that get you moving into the spatial world.
- In infant development, the upper-lower stage is about differentiating between what the upper body can do and what the lower body can do, and how each brings unique functional and expressive capacities.
- Homologous movement is the symmetrical movement of parts of the upper or lower body—for example, throwing both arms upward simultaneously.
- The basic neurocellular patterns of yielding, pushing, reaching, grasping, and pulling integrate and sequence through the body in the upper-lower pattern to produce efficient movement.

- Upper and lower halves of the body are connected by the torso, the core, and the vertical core to create supported through-lines and relationships between the two ends.

Body-Half Patterning

The next phase in motor development is known as body-half patterning (see figure 3.20). This pattern divides the body along the spine, or the vertical core, to distinguish the right and left sides from one another. The distinction between the two sides allows each to perform separate actions in relationship to one another. When the right side stabilizes, the left side can mobilize, and vice versa. Being familiar with the two sides and using them differently enables you to clarify relationships of stability and mobility, which is useful in producing efficient sequences of movement. In this context, stability is about grounding and rooting in one half of the body, while mobilizing is about activating free and easy movement in the other half.

In infant development, body-half patterning is made possible from the physical skills and support gained during the earlier stages of motor development. Learning about the soft and mobile spine in the head-tail pattern sets up the differentiation between left and right that is the basis of body-half patterning. Later, the movement into space made possible by the strong, bony spine provides the support needed for organizing the midline in the body-half stage of development.

Next, upper-lower patterning distinguishes the three limbs of the upper body from the three limbs of the lower body, providing the ability to locomote through space. Now, in the body-half stage, the whole right side or the whole left side, including the limbs, are able to participate in and organize movement, as to bring connection to the upper and lower through one side of the body. Also now possible is for movement to sequence from the lower on one side through to the upper on the same side, or from the upper through to the lower on the other side.

As babies continuously challenge their motor skills, developing from crawling and creeping to walking, they progress through body-half patterning at each stage. First, babies learn to roll from their backs to their fronts using body-half patterning as they reach with toes and fingers of the same side to rock, pulling themselves over their bottoms to land on their stomachs. Later, learning to creep on

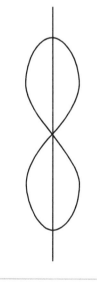

Figure 3.20   Body-half symbol.

Figure 3.21   Stable/mobile relationships vital to a lateral weight shift.
Illustrated by Sydney P. Celio.

their stomachs, they will ground and root through the big toe on one side to push along the inner leg, elongating that side of the body while contracting the other side, bringing the knee and elbow toward each other and the eyes around toward the flexed limbs to repeat on the other side (see figure 3.21). Later still, when learning to walk, a little one might first cruise along the edge of a sofa. This strategy affords stability to the half of the body in contact with the sofa, and mobility to the free side. Finding stability through body-half patterning is also seen in the elderly as they hold onto countertops or canes to ground through one side in order to mobilize the other side.

Through body-half patterning, the entire moving body gains access to the vertical plane of movement. Earlier, in the upper-lower pattern, movement was organized in the sagittal plane: The body scoots forward and backward following a push from the upper or lower body. Now, the movements in the body-half pattern are organized laterally around the spine, with a stable side offering support while the mobile side flexes inward or lengthens outward. Stabilizing one side to mobilize the other later translates into shifting weight laterally, from one leg to the other, as the side you are moving away from mobilizes to propel the body to the stability of the newly supporting side.

For adults, body-half patterning differentiates the right and left sides of the body around the spine. Experientially recognizing the two sides of the body helps clarify and organize movement by helping you recognize which side a movement initiates on or finishes on and how the other side supports these movements. The distinction between the right and left side of the body can also promote expressivity. You may notice variations in how you use the different sides of your body. Over time, this distinction begins to form unique identities likened to discrete inner characters or aspects of self. For example, the right side of the body may seem indifferent to contact and may prefer controlled movement, while the left side may feel sensitive to and desirous of touch and prefer more sensitive movement exploration. The unique qualities of the two sides are like two different aspects of the self.

Body-half patterning sets up lateral weight shifts, moving the body from one base of support to another, in this case the other leg (see figure 3.22), propelling the body to the new leg and then stabilizing it there. Shifting your weight laterally occurs in walking—the body weight moves from one leg to the other with every step. The yield, push, reach, pull phrase from earlier patterns are now organized laterally, one side yields and pushes while the other side reaches and pulls to move the weight laterally over a new base of support. When one side struggles to stabilize the body during a lateral weight shift, there can be pain and discomfort from compensations made on either the same side or the other side. Sacroiliac joint pain—pain around the upper gluteal muscles—might be soothed by finding greater stability through the painful side of the body.

Becoming informed about the symmetry and connections of the body's internal structures can help you find stability and grounding through one side

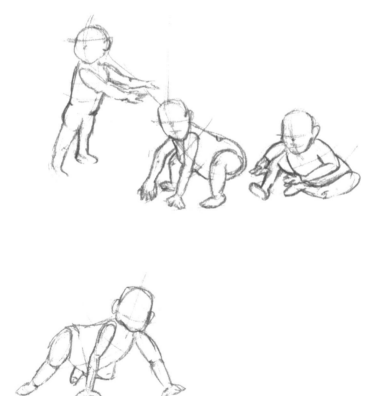

Figure 3.22   Progressing from Upper-Lower to creeping.
Illustrated by Sydney P. Celio.

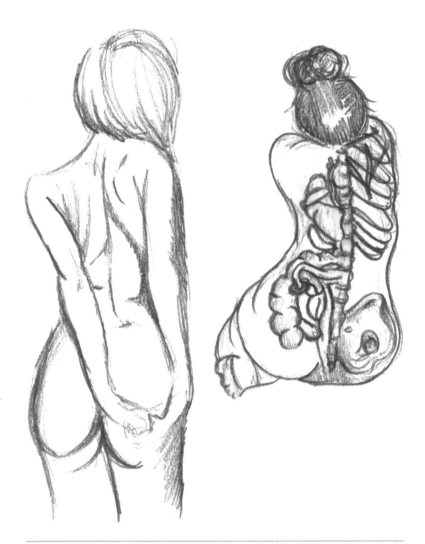

Figure 3.23   Internal imagery and symmetry relationships highlighted by body-half patterning.
Illustrated by Sydney P. Celio.

of the body. Imagine the internal relationships along one side of the body:
lung to ovary (or, for men, a corresponding location), ribs to pelvis, scapula
to pelvis, proximal joints of knee and elbow, hand to foot, eye to big toe (see
figure 3.23). These inner pairings highlight the up/down infrastructure and the
side/side imperfect symmetry of the inner body and provide more possibilities
for inner relationships and, from there, stability and mobility.

The ability to stabilize on one side in order to mobilize on the other side
eventually leads to more complex sequencing of movements throughout the

body. Like the infant who is learning to propel itself into its environment, adults, too, need the stability of grounding to be able to mobilize the whole body into space, grounding and propelling from one side of the body to the other, and then quickly steadying that momentum by stabilizing one side and suspending the other. This transferring and tossing around of your weight can feel like riding a roller coaster of power and mobility and then halting the ride with the smoothest of brakes.

Body-half patterning is important in several ways, especially in distinguishing between the two sides of the body to set up lateral weight shifts, and the stability/mobility relationships that lead to complex and dynamic movement. Body-half patterning is present in many movements, including everyday actions like walking up and down stairs while holding the handrail, extending a hand to another person to shake hands, or exiting a vehicle that is high off the ground (the side of the body inside the vehicle grounds itself to shift the weight toward the outside of the vehicle before extending toward the ground below).

Athletic training uses body-half patterning, in many instances sequencing through it, on the way to other Patterns of Total Body Connectivity. For example, athletes who play racquet sports, like squash and tennis, often use body-half patterning to propel their weight around the court and to stabilize their movements to generate power behind their swing. Boxers use body-half patterning by rooting the back foot to stabilize that side of the body and then mobilize the front side of the body to unleash a powerful jab from the arm of the mobilized side. Skateboarders and snowboarders use one side of their bodies to steer the other, more stable side.

Yoga asanas invoke body-half patterning in poses like triangle pose, half-moon pose, and reverse warrior. In these poses, lateral flexion of the spine curls one side of the body inward upon itself, while the other side lengthens the limbs, extending them into space. When doing these asanas, pay attention to how stability through one side of the body supports the movement and promotes stillness in the body that can make them much easier.

Dance training at the barre is also often organized in body-half patterning. One hand holds the barre while the same-side foot is grounded for stability, generating a base of support for the side of the body away from the barre, sometimes called the working side.

Sophisticated phrasing of stability and mobility makes virtuosic and complex movement appear clear and coordinated and efficient. Dancers prepare for and execute turns, basketball players make hook shots and layups, pitchers wind up and release, goalies dive for a puck, riders mount the backs of their horses. In these intricate movements, body-half patterning and cross-lateral patterning (see the next section) sequence in and out of one another.

Exploring the Body-Half Pattern

Tune into one side of your body. What does it feel like? What do you use it for? What does it like to do, and how does it like to move? Try moving it in its preferred way, and notice what associations come up. Imagine this side of your body as its own character. Who is this part of you? How is this character expressed in your life? Now try the other side. Who is this other side and what does it express? What needs does it have? Let each side play this out, and see what surfaces.

KEY POINTS FOR THE BODY-HALF PATTERN

- Stability and mobility come alive at the body-half developmental stage.
- Body-half patterning brings clarity between the two sides of the body. It can help organize complex sequences in the activities of many sports: the focused windup of a pitcher, the quick jab of a boxer, the takeoff and landing of a figure skater's triple axel.
- The two sides of the body can have unique functional and expressive natures; exploring these can reveal metaphors for different parts of the self.

Cross-Lateral Patterning

The cross-lateral stage (see figure 3.24) of motor development divides and connects the body along its diagonal, **cross quadrants**—for example, from the lower quadrant on one side through the torso to the upper quadrant of the other side. Cross-lateral patterning emphasizes three-dimensional motor capacities, including spiraling and rotation (see figure 3.25) that are supported by a deep diagonal connection running through the body. Its complexity is made possible by all that has been learned in the earlier developmental patterns.

Peggy Hackney chose the term *cross-lateral* because she believed it most accurately reflects the pathway of connection being described (Hackney 2002, 178). The common term for the organization of opposite quadrants and limbs of the body in human motor science and other movement-training systems is *contra-lateral*. But the prefix *contra-* implies antagonism or opposition instead of connection and support.

In earlier developmental phases, the basic neurocellular patterns yield/push initiate a sequence into reach/grasp/pull. In cross-lateral patterning, the reach/grasp/pull sequence initiates movement. The desire to "reach for" becomes part of how

Figure 3.24   Cross-lateral symbol.

Figure 3.25   Diagonal through-line and inner spirals running through the body and outward from it.

Illustrated by Sydney P. Celio.

the infant mobilizes into his world. He moves his limbs across the midline that was set up in the body-half pattern. A little leg or arm reaches across the vertical core of the body and the body is twisted into a three-dimensional spiral involving whole-body rotation. When this happens, the reach is supported by a diagonal through-line to the cross limb. When the left arm reaches across the body, the right leg supports and stabilizes. Next, a pull from the left arm activates a neuromuscular impulse in which the whole body spirals and rotates. The phrase of yield, push, to reach, grasp, pull is now organized from one quadrant of the body through the body to the diagonal quadrant.

Cross-lateral patterning gives the moving body greater access to the horizontal plane. Earlier developmental stages promoted access to the other planes of movement, and now the whole spatial world is fully available for the infant to move in and through. Head-tail patterning allowed the first experience of all three planes of movement; still, the body was not yet mobilized to move through the planes. Next, in upper-lower patterning the body was mobilized into the sagittal plane, moving forward and backward through space, from the three limbs of the upper body and the three limbs of the lower body. Later, body-half patterning allowed the body access to movement in the vertical plane, via lateral flexion, extension, and weight shifts. Now, finally, through cross-lateral patterning, the body moves more fully in the horizontal plane, spiraling, rotating, and reaching across its center.

For older children and adults, cross-lateral patterning facilitates whole-body rotation and support for complex movement. The diagonal relationship connecting the cross quadrants encourages spiraling and rotation. To get a sense of the ringlet nature of this pattern, you can imagine the deep inner spiral as a mobile corkscrew that allows you to condense and spread your central axis, rotating and spiraling around it. Or you can visualize the spiral of your central axis as a Slinky or as the double helix of DNA that can expand and contract through the whole body.

It is worth noting that cross-lateral patterning does not involve a twisting motion. Twisting is an action of pulling the body into an antagonistic relationship between quadrants without the support of a deep diagonal through-line. Because of the lack of deep support from the core for the whole body, twisting can strain parts of the body.

Cross-lateral patterning highlights the capacity for rotation at the joints and throughout the entire body. When Irmgard Bartenieff taught rotation, she emphasized fluid and gradually changing proportionate relationships. This means that rotation is not a flipping action, but one of gradual rotational change that happens over the whole course of the action. To visualize rotation in this way, imagine it as a process in which all cells participate in dynamic and three-dimensional proportionate change to facilitate spiraling throughout the whole body.

One way of facilitating rotation is through **distal steering,** which occurs when the part of a limb farthest from the center of the body initiates rotation throughout the whole limb. Try rotating your right arm one way and then the other by leading the movement with the pinky and thumb, imagining the arm spiraling around an axis that starts at the middle finger and runs through the arm. Now try this in the lower body, rotating the leg by leading with the pinky and big toe to create rotation all the way into the pelvis.

In many cross-lateral movements, one diagonal cross stabilizes so the other can fully mobilize. Take the example of a right leg and left arm as a **mobile cross**. The limbs cross the central vertical core of the body, moving toward one another, carrying with them the right knee and left elbow, right hip and left shoulder. Simultaneously the **stable cross**—that is, the left leg and right arm—actively stabilize the limbs through the deep diagonal core. When the mobile cross radiates outward, the stable cross continues to provide support (see figure 3.26). The mobile cross can reach and fold into itself or reach and extend outward. In both cases, cross-lateral patterning conveys the whole body into spiraling and rotation.

The core that has dynamic pliability supports full spiraling ability of the limbs. The cross-lateral spiral that moves through the body involves a deep diagonal support in the torso to connect and organize the body. This diagonal through-line is spatially organized to connect the body's innards complexly to the outer world (see figure 3.27). It runs three-dimensionally through the guts, front to back, side to side, and up and down. You can feel the right lung bulge from shape flow support backward into a right-back-high spatial pull, while the left ovary (or corresponding location) bulges forward toward a left-forward-low spatial pull. In Shape qualities terminology (see

Figure 3.26   Stable cross and mobile cross.
Illustrated by Sydney P. Celio.

chapter 5), the right lung area could spread, retreat, and rise, while the left ovary and lower digestive tract area could spread, advance, and sink, creating a spiral deep within the torso that supports full-bodied cross-laterality.

The cross-lateral pattern allows you to access rotation throughout the entire body. Many basic movement activities hint at cross-laterality, but few get you fully invested in it. Aging and sedentary activities can diminish access to rotation, so returning to it is especially important. Try the X-rolls described in the following sidebar. Cross-lateral patterns feel especially wonderful after long hours of being sedentary, when complex movement is both craved and so forgotten to the body. Spiraling movements offer relief from a lack of movement and can restore welcome sensation to the body. They are satisfying and mobilizing; you are simultaneously accomplished and youthful; you are whole, have accomplished something, and possess effervescent potential for movement. Ideally, even walking is supported by cross-laterality. With each step, the easeful spiraling and sequencing of the reach-pull of the legs moves through the torso in a supported rotating motion in the upper body as the opposite leg and arm move forward at the same time.

Figure 3.27   Deep diagonal and three-dimensional through-line.
Illustrated by Sydney P. Celio.

Cross-lateral patterning comes up often in the worlds of movement training and athletics. Think of spiral stretches and grapevine footwork, or weight training that involves stabilizing one diagonal cross while mobilizing the other. In dance classes, clarifying cross-lateral patterns helps dancers organize turns and spirals, and makes remembering sequences easier.

In disciplines involving complex movement, like dance and sports, you will see the cross-lateral pattern phrase quickly with the body-half pattern to set up sequences of stability and mobility, such as flying and falling through the environment. Think of a right-handed outfielder who reaches left, back, and high with his gloved hand, catches the ball, and then throws it to first base utilizing a right-back-high to left-forward-low windup and release pattern. First the player's reach for the ball involves a cross-lateral pattern. He then passes through a body-half pattern as he stabilizes and prepares to throw the ball to first, finishing the throw in cross-lateral. Whenever there is winding up to unleash power, as in soccer, the phrasing between body-half and cross-lateral patterns grants the mover access to her fullest dynamism and mobility as she winds up to fly or wildly spiral into stability.

X-Rolls

There are many variations on this movement. For this one, lie on your back on the floor. Float the left leg over the right leg, as though it is tracing a traffic cone lying on its side (see figure 3.28). This reach and pull with the left leg will sequence through the torso, eventually pulling your front body to the floor as the left arm comes around, tracing its own traffic cone. Now focus on leading with the arm to spread the upper body to return you to your back. Next, do the X-roll with the right leg. Repeat a few times.

KEY POINTS FOR THE CROSS-LATERAL PATTERN

- Developmentally, cross-lateral patterning emerges from the reach, grasp, and pull of a hand or a foot that initiates an instinctive response from the cross limb.
- Rotary function and capacities facilitate the full spiraling of the limbs.
- Three-dimensional spiraling through diagonal quadrants of the body integrates spatial intent with whole-body rotation.
- In complex movements such as those in dance and many athletic pursuits, body-half and cross-lateral patterning quickly phrase from one to another to produce the virtuosic flying and falling through the environment that is so exhilarating to do and to watch.

Figure 3.28 X-rolls.
Illustrated by Sydney P. Celio.

The six Patterns of Total Body Connectivity, which follow the progression of the basic neurological patterns present in human motor development, help people identify relationships within their bodies during movement and heighten the experience and understanding of specific movements. When applied to adult movement, the PTBCs support easeful and efficient functioning of the body. They also offer metaphoric and expressive interpretations of how the developmental motor progression relates to perceptions of the environment, such as the association between core-distal patterning and the understanding of the relationship between "me" and "world."

Prefundamentals and the Basic Six

This section discusses movement experiences, sometimes called exercises, that hone in on specific, fundamental movement skills. They represent the most simplified and isolated aspects of movement. The Patterns of Total Body Connectivity described in the preceding section are organizations of movement, and the movement experiences described in this section, known as the Prefundamentals and the Basic Six, are embedded within the PTBCs, and enhance body connectivity. For example, femoral flexion and extension can be used to enhance the through-connection between upper and lower body.

The Prefundamentals

The Prefundamentals, or prefundies, were inspired by Irmgard Bartenieff's go-to ways of working with sensation and movement to foster connections within the body and to mobilize the body in preparation for propulsive, into-the-world movement. Like the PTBCs, the prefundies are a more recent way of organizing Bartenieff's work; in other words, she did not call them the Prefundamentals. They developed from her preparatory experiences with which her students have deliberately integrated the principles of developmental movement. The prefundies are based on exercises that Bartenieff would guide her students through to have them seek sensation and "get into" their bodies before moving into more complex experiences. They were about "dropping into" the body and "coming into self." The Prefundamentals are embedded within and support the first three Patterns of Total Body Connectivity—breath, core-distal patterning, and head-tail patterning—and offer ways to explore more possibilities for enlivening and connecting the body. Try using them as templates whose basic ideas you can riff off of to explore what the PTBCs, Basic Six offer. You may notice the Prefundamentals make new movements possible too.

Opening and Closing from Breath

The first Prefundamental, opening and closing from breath, is about letting the breath both guide change in the body and invigorate movement. It is about fostering internal vitality, inviting your breath to move through your body's tissues, growing and shrinking the body, opening and closing it. Like the gurgling infant, you can "sing the breath song," so to speak, giving audible sound to the flow of the breath. It can be an amorphous opening and closing of the body in which the body expands and contracts, without specific goals toward what it looks like, except for being guided by the breath.

Besides amorphous opening and closing, Bartenieff also taught two versions of this exercise that entail specific movement sequences. In one version, the whole body opens or closes at once, to facilitate the experience of coming into and out of the core of yourself. The other version involves successive phrasing, in which the upper body initiates the opening or closing and the lower body follows, or vice versa (see figure 3.29). In any variation, the breath remains the guide.

Figure 3.29   Successive openings and closings initiated from the upper body and lower body.

Illustrated by Sydney P. Celio.

Rocking Along Kinetic Chains

This experience encourages you to use sensation to develop your understanding of the connections between parts of your body and explore how impulses and movements in one area can move through you to affect other areas. To rock along a kinetic chain, yield and push in a pulsation pattern from one part into a surface, like the floor. Allow the yield and push to send a message from that part of your body to another part of your body. As this becomes more familiar, experiment with sending the message through your body and out into space.

The version Bartenieff taught is known as heel rock. Lie on your back on the floor with your legs extended. "Rock" from the heels by using the pressure of your heels on the floor in concert with flexion and extension of your ankle or tarsus joint. Allow the message of rocking to travel through your body and out your head (see figure 3.30). Bartenieff used this experience to help her students develop the sensation of connection from feet to head. She also used it as a diagnostic tool to see where movement was restrained and where the message was successfully traveling through. Although Irmgard Bartenieff only worked with heel rocks, you can explore rocking along other kinetic chains. Another example of pathways you can rock along begins by lying on your back or lying on your front surface with the forearms and hands supported by the floor and head lengthened gently forward and up. From here, yield and push from your hands and forearms sending the rock along the arms, through area of the lungs and the line of the latissimus dorsi to your tail (coccyx and sacrum).

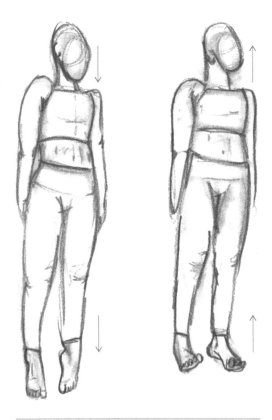

There are several important things to keep in mind as you rock. First is where the rocking starts, then where it moves to, and of course how it moves through the body. Having a clear sense of the place of initiation and where the message ends is vital to its pathway. Peggy Hackney and Janice Meaden have often said "give it a place to go," meaning that the rocking is not amorphous, but has a clear spatial pathway and intention that clarifies how it moves through the body and out to the space beyond.

Figure 3.30   Heel rocks with implied initiation and movement through the body that goes under the heart and out the head.
Illustrated by Sydney P. Celio.

There are many pathways available to experiment with, and as you discover areas of the body that crave an enlivened connection

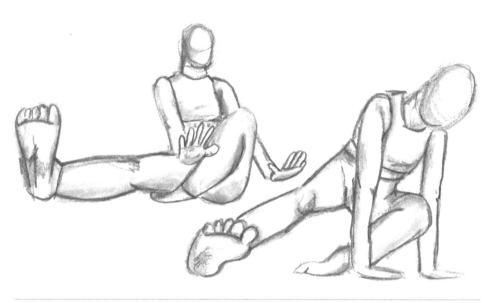

Figure 3.31   Rocking from hands to tail.
Illustrated by Sydney P. Celio.

to the whole, find ways to rock to foster sensation and connections. Rocking can be an effective part of any movement-based warm-up. Babies do it to get going. You will often see them "revving their engines" as they get to know and activate their kinetic chains in preparation for bigger movement. It is also useful as a way of mobilizing and preparing adults for activity (see figure 3.31). Think about the pathways you will use in whatever activity you're warming up for. For a basketball player, the pathway of feet to hands is important in a jump shot; perhaps find a way to rock along this entire pathway. For a hockey player, the ability to propel the weight from one leg to another is important; try sitting on a Swiss ball and rocking from one foot to the other through the pelvic floor to help facilitate the rhythms of explosive power and rooted stability needed for that sport.

Tracking with the Eyes and Tail

This movement experience mobilizes both ends of the spine and changes the whole head-tail pathway through stimulation from the external world. Eye tracking, which occurs when the eyes follow visual stimulation, is part of the developmental progression. As the infant gains awareness of her surroundings, her attention and seeking of information through the senses of the head end leads her into the world, establishing early inklings of a reaching pattern. The tail can also attend to the environment, causing the infant to lead, seek, reach, and follow stimuli. Bartenieff had students track with their eyes, stimulating the curiosity that was generated from the head to activate

L/BMA in Your World: Rocking in Jazz Dance

Jeffrey Peterson, CLMA, Associate Professor of Dance, Muhlenberg College

Rocking along kinetic chains is a primary physical training in my jazz-dance technique class. I approach rocking as a manifestation of overlapping, active yield-push phrasing and more passive but directed reach-pull phrasing. My students and I find that this mind-set regarding rocking supports our grounded, easy, rhythmic, whole selves in jazz dance. In designing my classes, I intersperse rocking in various forms across and within the duration of a class. This continuously reminds the body to relate to the earth in order to manifest its rhythm, while encouraging the spine to relax into a "groove." We rock lying down both supine and prone, at midlevel on all fours, and while standing. I coach these rocking sessions to bring out the overlapping phrasing of yield-push and reach-pull, directing the activated and grounded energy from each yield-push to travel freely through and out the body in head-tail, upper-lower, body-half, and cross-lateral ways. I find that this approach provides the foundation that my students and I need to integrate ease, groove, and rhythm in highly complex jazz dancing. The rocking serves to release unnecessary tension, and shakes loose any physical or psychological misperceptions regarding the efficiency possible in jazz dance.

and mobilize the whole body. You can also experiment with tracking from the tail, though you will have to imagine eyes down there. Tracking, leading, and reaching from each end of the spine can awaken supple movement through the whole spine. As the eyes and the tail end engage in their environment, the whole supple, open pathway between head and tail also fully participates, assisting you in "swimming through the spine" (figure 3.32).

Irmgard Bartenieff's Basic Six

Content in this section is adapted from *Notes from a Course in Correctives* by Irmgard Bartenieff, *Body Movement: Coping with the Environment* by Irmgard Bartenieff and Dori Lewis, and *Making Connections: Total Body Integration Through Bartenieff Fundamentals* by Peggy Hackney.

The movement experiences now known as the Basic Six were developed by Irmgard Bartenieff, with several of her students, at the nudging of her community to create written material and movements salient to her work. She organized

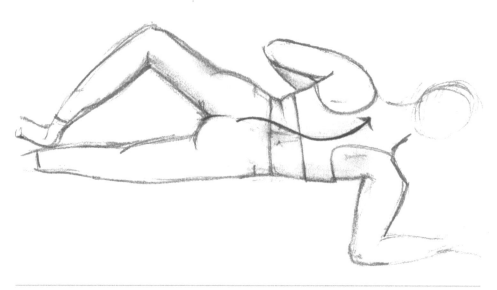

Figure 3.32   Example of spinal response to tracking with the eyes as if the head had just turned upward and the spine followed.
Illustrated by Sydney P. Celio.

the exercises for *Notes from a Course in Correctives*. The term *correctives* was later changed to *fundamentals* to avoid the implication of fixing the body; instead, the movements are intended to focus on opening new pathways of connection and finding new possibilities for movement.

The Basic Six are fundamental elements of movement. They are prototypes whose goal is to get to the simplest version of what all human movement requires (Groff 1990). As specific movement experiences, they are pared-down and isolated versions of movement, but embedded within other, more complex movements. They are embedded within the Patterns of Total Body Connectivity and are an opportunity to look at where movement patterning could be improved. As you develop skill with the Basic Six, the basic movements can be expanded to progress toward increasingly challenging movement experiences, including changing a movement's relationship to gravity, or increasing stability and mobility challenges.

When working with a fundamental, Bartenieff often suggested "challenging it in relationship to gravity"—meaning finding new approaches to explore the movement other than lying down, such as in seated, standing, or off-vertical orientations. You are encouraged to explore in this way with the Basic Six. As you find new possibilities within your neuromuscular system, try moving a pattern to new levels and in new relationships to gravity. This gem from Bartenieff offers another way to conceive of organizing simple and complex phrasing in movement training. If, for example, you are finding the propulsion of the pelvis to a new base of support in a lateral pelvic shift, try it standing up. If you are finding the interplay between stability and mobility in a body-half flexion, try standing and stabilizing one side to mobilize another. This can also go in the other direction; if a movement pattern feels complex or disconnected at the standing level, try it at another, possibly lower level, where gravity offers new information and you can hone in on what is needed with a different approach.

Note: I was taught to explore different qualities of effort, imagery, shape, and spatial intent to help me find new pathways of connection and expressive potential in each of the Basic Six. I will include some notes on my experiences in the following descriptions.

Femoral Flexion and Extension

Femoral flexion and extension, originally called "thigh lift" by Irmgard Bartenieff and renamed by Peggy Hackney, is the action of flexing the femur in the hip joint toward the torso. While the action itself sounds simple, the goal of the exercise is to activate only what is needed to allow the coordinated flexion of the head of the femur in the acetabulum, also known as the socket of the hip joint. The flexion of the leg toward the torso is followed by an easeful lengthening of the femur as the hip joint moves into extension. This action is meant to be performed with a supportive, though not rigid, core, which keeps the pelvis from rocking "like a boat in a storm."

Femoral Flexion and Extension Movement

Description

Begin on your back with your feet in "stand"—that is, flat on the floor. One foot, arch and big toe, will root into the ground while the knee on the other side flexes toward your nose (see figure 3.33). Then allow the leg to move back to where it began.

Variation

To explore heel slides: Begin again in "stand" and let one heel slide along the floor away from the body until the leg reaches its full length (see figure 3.33). Then slide it back along the floor, returning to the "stand" you began in.

Imagery Ideas

- Imagine an inner line of connection between the inner border of the stable foot and the lesser trochanter on that same side that then runs through the pelvis and torso and out the head that helps ground and stabilize the body through the stable side, or the side where the foot remains grounded.

- As a preparation of the inner channel that grounds one side for stability, imagine a marble sliding from your sternum along the line of the iliopsoas then along the inner thigh and through the arch of the foot and big toe and the pouring into the ground.

- To find the pathway and line of the iliopsoas, imagine little bungy cords running between the back of the heart/thoracic area and the lesser trochanter/inner

Figure 3.33   Basic version of femoral flexion and extension with added heel slide option.

Illustrated by Sydney P. Celio.

thigh. The cords have a buoyant and springy nature and can easefully float the knee into hip flexion or feel supported as the leg lengthens into hip extension.

- To find the connection between heel and sitz bone, imagine sliding or dragging the heel through sand and leaving an imprint of its pathway. Notice how the extension of the femur in the hip joint feels juicy, massaged, and deep.

- Explore changing the Effort by bringing in free Flow, quick Time, and strong Weight. Perhaps imagine you are having a temper tantrum and kicking and sliding your toys away from you. This expressive image can help you find the rushing power of your lower half and keep you from getting bogged down by details that could be binding the action.

- Imagine riding spatial pulls, the infinite guy wires of space, as you lengthen the femur away from the torso and into extension, helping the center feel supported and organized while the limbs move into the environment.

Sagittal Pelvic Shift

Sagittal pelvis shift, called "pelvic forward shift" in Bartenieff's Basic Six, describes the action of the pelvis sliding forward along a spatial pull in the sagittal dimension. The important aspects of this movement include the engagement of the hamstrings to move the pelvis forward without excessively using the gluteal muscles. If this happens the pelvis will be high off the ground. In this basic version, the shift of the pelvis forward over the feet happens while lying on your back. This is congruent with hamstring action while standing in vertical and when walking to pull the pelvis forward over the new base of support.

Sagittal Pelvic Shift Movement

Description

Begin by lying on your back in the stand position. Root down into the floor with your feet to lift the pelvis slightly off the ground, about an inch (see figure 3.34); feel the remnants of the femoral flexion as the pelvis hovers. Engage your feet into the ground, visualize the heel to sitz bone connection and pull the pelvis forward and slightly upward so the weight of the pelvis will feel like it has been taken over by the feet. Lower the pelvis by "slicing" straight downward through the femoral crease, returning the sacrum to the floor.

Imagery Ideas

- Imagine the pelvis as a hanging basket, dangling from the knee, tibia, and fibula, and whose weight helps the pelvis shift and cut through femoral flexion.

Figure 3.34   Basic 'stand' in which the back is supported by the floor, the knees are bent, and bottoms of the feet are grounded. Notice the soft crease in the front of the hip joint.

Illustrated by Sydney P. Celio.

- Trace the line of pull from big toe to arch to heels along the back of the leg and to the sitz bone. Imagine it with the flexible and springy tensile nature of a spiderweb, that is both strong enough to pull with force and delicate enough to release its hold.

- Imagine the feet like those of a frog, with suction cups, or like wide, sticky bath mats; their ability to root into the earth allows the pull of the pelvis over them to be strong and grounded.

- The pelvis actually rides on a shallow diametral pull—two unequal spatial pulls—from back and low to forward and a little high. Clear intent in space can facilitate the shift. You could imagine that your pelvis is about to water ski and be pulled out of the water as the boat's motor fires up.

Lateral Pelvic Shift

Lateral pelvic shift, called "pelvic lateral shift" in Bartenieff's Basic Six, describes the action of the pelvis sliding laterally or to one side or the other. The lateral pelvis shift builds in complexity from the prior two exercises of the Basic Six, and its important aspects include the ability to shift your weight from the lowest part of the pelvis, the yield/push traveling from the feet to reach/pull through the lesser trochanter on the side you are moving toward to shift the pelvis over a base of support, involving rotation of one femur internally while the other rotates externally.

Lateral Pelvic Shift Movement

Description

Begin by lying on your back in the stand position. Again, press down into the floor with your feet to lift the pelvis slightly off the ground, about an inch; feel the remnants of the femoral flexion as the pelvis hovers. Slide your pelvis to one side with a yield and push from one foot, and let it phrase into a reach and pull through the lesser trochanter you are moving toward. Notice the independent rotation of each leg (see figure 3.35). Lower the pelvis as though it is dropping straight downward through the femoral crease, returning the sacrum to the floor. The curve in the lumbar spine is still present and supported through the front of the torso and lower abdomen.

Imagery Ideas

- The classic image is that of a typewriter carriage sliding back and forth for each new line.

- To add the grounding of the sacrum between each slide, imagine the pelvis sliding along a pathway shaped like new unstapled, staples so that the pelvis moves laterally across the top of the staple and then slices downward along the vertical leg.

(continued)

Lateral Pelvic Shift Movement (continued)

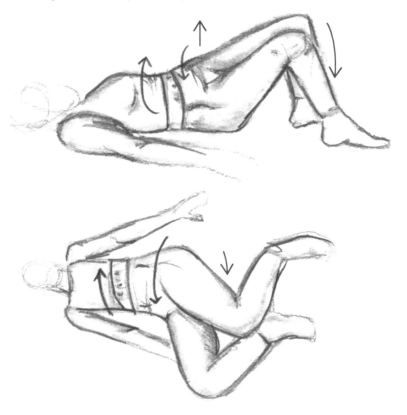

Figure 3.35   Lateral pelvic shift that allows independent rotation of each femur.
Illustrated by Sydney P. Celio.

- Imagine sliding your pelvis to the forward corner of the horizontal plane. As in the sagittal pelvic shift, this intent into space patterns the neuromuscular system.
- Imagining my feet in thick, warm mud helps me allow the change to happen throughout my whole body.
- Making sounds like "HA" and "sssssssss" and "ssshhhhhh" may help you find subtle Effort shifts. Directing the sound to specific parts of your body helps you enliven areas less present with the exercise.

Body Half

Body half exercises as part of the Basic Six are different from, though connected to, body-half patterning in the Patterns of Total Body Connectivity. Body half as part of the Basic Six is about laterally flexing one side of the body and extending the other, which laterally flexes the spine.

Body Half Movement

Description

Begin by lying on your back with your legs extended and not too far apart, so that the hip flexors are relaxed and the pelvis is neutral (see figure 3.36). Slide the elbow and knee on one side of your body toward each other along the horizontal plane such that the only movement upward and downward is to accommodate your anatomy. Allow the very topmost and bottommost parts of the head and torso to come along, bringing the spine into lateral flexion. The nonflexing side will further elongate.

Variation

Once you have found this with ease and a supple core, experiment with adding asymmetric tonic neck reflex (ATNR). As you flex to one side, the eyes and neck rotate the head to look at the extended side of the body (see figure 3.37). Next, let your eyes initiate the movement to switch to the other side. Repeat this several more times. Leading the side change with your eyes is a neurological foundation for hand-eye coordination.

Figure 3.36 Basic body half movement from the Basic Six.

Illustrated by Sydney P. Celio.

Figure 3.37 Asymmetric tonic neck reflex variation on the body-half movement.

Illustrated by Sydney P. Celio.

(continued)

Body Half Movement *(continued)*

Imagery Ideas

- Imagine that the head and tail are little feathery brooms sweeping across the floor, or the spine is a flowing reed shifting back and forth, blown by a breeze on one side. The side you imagine the breeze on will create different initiations and experiences of this movement.

- As preparation imagine stabilizing support through the one side—what will be your elongating side—through the deepest part of your center that radiates outward and connects lower and upper on that side. Then, from this support, allow the other side to fold inward.

- Imagine something you want in one hand or dangling just beyond it. Let your desire to see and grasp this object be the impetus for the switch to the other side.

- Try this with free Flow and sustained Time as if you were lying on a beach and could pour your cells into the sand as you lingered and indulged in switching sides. Perhaps the impetus you desire is a cool, moist, sweet treat that directs your attention to the other side.

Arm Circle

The Basic Six exercise called arm circle highlights rotary function in the upper body that is supported by the lower body. Rotary function is important in body connectivity because it encourages muscular engagement from a greater range of muscles around a joint instead of overusing a few that fall along shared, planar lines of pull. Investing in rotary function in the arms can help develop a greater range of motion in the upper body and release extra tension around the shoulders, neck, and back. Sometimes referred to specifically in the upper body as scapula humeral rhythm, it means giving full expression to the rounded, ball-like shaped head of the humerus as it sits in the glenohumeral joint.

Instrumental to the scapula-humeral rhythm in this experience is grounding and anchoring the lower scapula toward the tail. This is not a freezing of the scapula downward, but a mobile grounding that facilitates fully realizing rotary function of the humerus.

Arm Circle Movement

Description

Begin by lying on your back. You can decide if you prefer the legs extended or in stand. Or, as we will discuss later, you can integrate the diagonal knee reach with the arm circle for a full-body experience of rotary function. To initiate the movement, one arm travels along the floor to the top of the circle, over your head, then across to the other side of the body, downward, across the pelvis, and back to where the circle

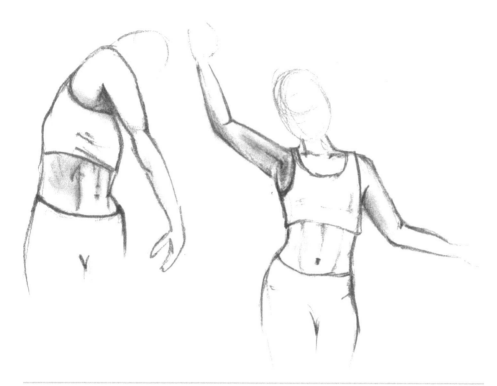

Figure 3.38 Pathway of the arm in an arm circle.
Illustrated by Sydney P. Celio.

began (see figure 3.38). Now that you understand the basic action, notice that the scapula can root downward toward the tail to initiate the movement. Check that the elbow and wrist remain soft and supple, let the sternum and chest also be soft and accommodating to the action as the eyes follow the hand, and allow the movement to travel into the lowest part of the pelvis.

Variations

- Once you have found this with ease and a supple, accommodating torso, try reversing the direction of the circle.
- Irmgard Bartenieff had several versions of the arm circle, one that included internally rotating the forearm, the radius, and ulna as they came across the torso. She used this variation to set up body patterning for the Space harmony scales. This version can feel great and gives clear information on how to avoid collapsing the humerus into the chest as it comes across the body.

Imagery Ideas

- Explore letting the humerus rotate around its big rounded head to get a sense of how much mobility and rotary potential is present at that joint. Imagine that it has the sheen of a pebble polished by years in the water.

(continued)

Arm Circle Movement *(continued)*

- Imagine the opening and closing of the spine of a book to allow the sternum to soften and hollow as the arm comes across, and to widen and expand as it opens the body.

- Explore initiating the circle from different parts of your body: pinky, thumb, medial epicondyle, etc. See what each initiation brings that might be useful for you.

- Consider the ever-changing Shape qualities of this exercise: As the arm travels along its pathway the body processes through spreading, rising, advancing, enclosing, sinking, and retreating.

- Hold a marker or chalk in your hand, and imagine drawing the pathway of the circle. Also try holding a ball, and use its roundness to give you information about the roundness of the head of the femur.

- Imagine you are wearing the most luxurious dolman sleeve and that its width and drape carry the torso and pelvis along in the spiraling and rotation.

- Try grounding the ovary location on the cross side of the arm that is moving; this is especially important if you do the variation with the diagonal knee reach discussed in detail below. You could ask a friend to touch you there with a pressure that helps you feel the area anchoring and hollowing into the ground.

Diagonal Knee Reach

The diagonal knee reach, also called "knee drop," involves complex rotary coordination. It highlights rotary function in the acetabulofemoral joint (hip joint) that is different between the two legs. Because each leg has its own pathway, one will internally rotate while the other externally rotates. This is different from the common spinal twist found in many stretching programs, and means the rotation is not twisting and stressing the lower spine, instead it occurs at the hip joint, whose design is compatible with a greater range of rotation. Try both versions to experience how they are different from one another. When I experience a diagonal knee reach and I am reminded of how much rotary mobility I have, I feel refreshed, walking is easier, and my torso and lower back feel stronger and more centered. The diagonal knee reach is often combined with the arm circle for a whole-body experience of rotation and spiraling along the diagonal.

Diagonal Knee Reach Movement

Description

Begin by lying on your back with your feet in stand. Let your knees lower toward the ground in a right, forward, and low spatial pull, and allow the torso to spiral and soften away from the reach on the diagonal (see figure 3.39). Hollow and yield through the torso to bring your body back to center. Try it on the other side. Notice how the rotation is happening between the femur and the hollows of your hips, not at your spine, though there may be a small amount of rotation at the spine depending on how far you lower your knees.

Variation

As mentioned above, integrate the arm circle with the diagonal knee reach (see figure 3.40). Begin with the arms extended out to your sides, palms down and, as Peggy Hackney instructs, with your middle finger in line with the base (inferior angle) of your scapula. As your knees initiate the movement to the right forward low diagonal, let the left hand rotate gradually to a left, back, high diagonal. Feel the deep spiral through your torso that radiates into your limbs, and begin the sweeping arm circle overhead, along the side, across the torso, and back to where it began. As with the variations discussed above, you can also circle the arm in the other direction or with gradated internal rotation of the circling forearm.

Imagery Ideas

- Notice the distinction between the two legs. Now, try initiating the movement by rooting down through the inner arch of one foot and the outer edge of the other. Continue to invest in this rooting as the knees move to the diagonal pull.

- Try placing a ball against the wall or a piece of furniture to keep it in place. When you perform the knee reach, let your knees lower only until they rest on the ball. This can help keep the pelvis and sacrum rooted, facilitating a restful release of the muscles around the pelvis and femurs.

- As you initiate the spiral, imagine your inner vertical core spiraling like a barber-shop pole or a classic red-and-white straw.

- Feel the powerful rooting downward of the ovary location on the same side of your body as the knees are lowering.

Figure 3.39   Diagonal knee reach with spatial intent through the knees and three-dimensional spiraling through the torso.
Illustrated by Sydney P. Celio.

Figure 3.40   Diagonal knee reach with arm circle.
Illustrated by Sydney P. Celio.

Touch to Facilitate Body Connectivity

Touch can facilitate greater connectivity, ease, and awareness in movement by increasing sensation in ways that will foster new possibilities for movement.

Touch is a vulnerable and powerful experience. In the Laban/Bartenieff work, touch is not a given or an expectation. It is important to learn that you can say yes and no to touch from another person. Saying no to touch can be an empowering reminder of your ownership of and agency over your body. When working with others, ask permission to touch that includes where on their body the touch will be and what kinds of touch you will deliver. If someone decides not to be touched they can use their own hands, or you can assist them in finding other ways to experience the purpose of the touch.

The following are basic ideas for incorporating touch that are easy to learn and particularly useful for enhancing body connectivity. The types of touch discussed below are part of a larger body of work developed by Peggy Hackney and Janice Meaden with Ed Groff and Pam Schick as part of Integrated Movement Studies' "Touch for Repatterning" curriculum. Each brought other training perspectives including Body-Mind Centering, Irene Dowd's kinesthetic anatomy and neuromuscular re-education, and massage therapy to the curriculum. This is part of a much larger body of work, but this will get you started.

Being with Touch

Use this method to become present with the connection between your body and your partner's. Being with touch asks the toucher to be present with and listen to what is underneath their hands. It does not seek to do anything or ask that the person being touched do anything besides be present with what is there. Try this type of touch on the torso. As the toucher, you may want to check in with the person you are touching, asking questions like, "What are you noticing?" Or, "Is this pressure okay? Would you like more or less?" Keep the dialogue going to demonstrate that conversation about what is happening is part of the experience.

Locating Touch

Use locating touch to help your partner get a sense of where different parts of the body are sited and how they relate to other parts. Locating touch can go to one body part or slide along a pathway. It is like using your hands to say, "Focus your attention right here." Try this type of touch to locate the hip joint or the lesser trochanter or the base of the scapula. After locating an area or part of the body, cue your partner to notice how that area relates to another area.

Sliding Touch

Locating touch can phrase into a sliding touch, where the toucher uses her hand to slide along or trace a line or connection on the body as if to bring awareness to the connection between one area and another.

Sending Touch and Receiving Touch

Use these techniques to find a connection or pathway through the body. Sending touch has directionality that give an energetic quality of sending information through the body's tissues. Receiving touch gathers or receives the sending touch somewhere else in the body. For example, try placing a hand on the sternum, and imagine you can send a message through the sternum. Place another hand on the sacrum, and imagine this hand can receive the message being sent by the top hand. The directionality in this kind of touch is clarified by the receiving touch. In this example, the hand on the sternum is sending a message in a down and back direction. Explore this type of touch with multiple pathways through the body.

Summary

The Body category is a complex and multilayered look at movement that encompasses where movement initiates in the body, how it sequences through the body, how it is organized in the body, and the most basic elements of movement that are important to full physical functioning. Irmgard Bartenieff's work addressed "what is fundamental" in movement and is the foundation of this category. The aspect of the Body category known as the Basic Six directly comes from Bartenieff's perspective on movement. Her perspective has been further developed by her students and those in her lineage. The Bartenieff fundamentals are based on the developmental motor patterns and include breath, core-distal, head-tail, upper-lower, body-half, and cross-lateral patterns. Working with the Body category is useful for increasing your functional and expressive skills.

CHAPTER

4

Effort

"It is impossible, of course, to describe the essence of the movements. But sometimes one can experience the same sort of tremendous impulse to move, for example, in a fight, in danger, in ecstasy and in passion . . ."

(Laban 1975 *Life*, 51)

*A*ll movement contains within it an energetic or dynamic nature. This dynamic nature gives movement its color, or feeling tone, and suggests the drive of the inner attitudes from which the energetic coloring manifests. The Effort category in Laban/Bartenieff Movement Analysis is about the energetic aspect of human movement—some say it is like the spice that gives movement flavor. The Effort category was originally inspired by the term *antrieb,* meaning *drive* in German; it "represents the organism's urge to make itself known" (Bartenieff and Lewis 2002, 51). *Effort* was called *Eukinetics* by Rudolf von Laban.

Effort is present in all areas of your moving life and is in constant fluctuation. As you read this, notice the energetic life of your body, and let it change. That shift in energy is a fluctuation in your effort expression. Just as you perceived effort in yourself, you will also observe it in others. You have probably observed another person and noticed the impression of feeling tones driving their movement. You also likely noticed how the feeling of the movement was not constant; instead it changed over time. Perhaps you were recently at a sporting event where the athletes' fluid, supple, and powerful movement shifted toward a rushing, quick, snapping energy as the event came to an end. The Effort category in L/BMA gives the ability to address these observable changes in energy.

The Effort category is about the quality of your energetic investment as it is revealed through movement. Effort highlights the vast range of energetic movement possibilities. When learning Effort through the Laban/Bartenieff framework, track your associations, preferences, and discomforts with certain efforts. You will notice that some aspects will feel familiar to you, while others are new and challenging. These insights reveal your effort signature, the energetic preferences you perform regularly and return to. For example, you may learn that you gravitate toward movement with power and force, or perhaps you prefer a delicate, airy quality to your movement. The preferences and associations that you become aware of through the L/BMA lens of Effort offer insights into your effort signature and values you hold around movement.

Expanding your effort associations is a generative process that grows the range of effortful dynamics you can manifest in movement. A limited effort palette is tiresome and flat. Having access to the full range of Effort qualities enhances your moving life. As you begin to pay attention to your effort preferences, you may notice that some associations hinder your willingness to manifest an effort physically. Explore these associations by asking yourself to notice them in your life—they are most certainly there—and what they bring you. This will help you develop a richer understanding of effort and to manifest it more consciously and completely.

Effort Factors and Elements

There are four **effort factors**, sometimes called motion factors: Flow, Weight, Time, and Space.

Within each effort factor are two effort elements, which are polarities of each other and lie on opposite ends of a spectrum (see the list that follows). Each one reveals a different quality of energetic expression. Take the example of the Time factor: your movement could be urgent and hasty on one end (quick), or on the opposite end it could be lingering and indulgent (sustained).

Flow: free or bound

Weight: light or strong

Time: sustained or quick

Space: indirect or direct

Figure 4.1 shows a graph, or grid, representing each effort factor and its associated elements. The single slash line running from right high to left

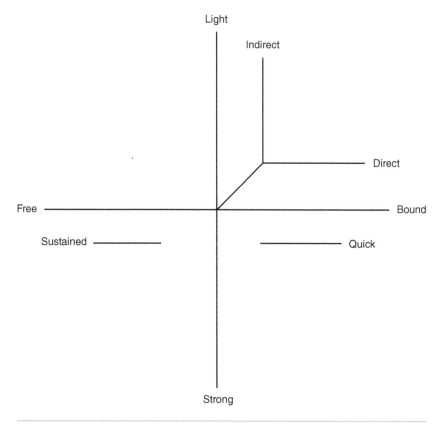

Figure 4.1   Effort factors and their elements.

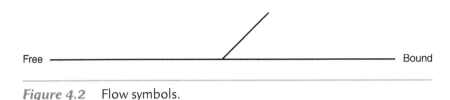

Figure 4.2   Flow symbols.

low is the effort stroke. The effort stroke is present in all effort symbols, signifying the category of Effort as opposed to the category of Shape or Space. The effort stroke can be present with one effort symbol or multiple effort symbols can share the same effort stroke. When multiple effort symbols share the same effort stroke, it means these effort elements have occurred simultaneously in an effort cluster or constellation. (More on that later in the chapter.)

Imagine a line extending from the effort stroke in figure 4.1. This imaginary line can be used to divide the polarities of each spectrum. The effort elements on the high left corner are considered expansive types of expression in that they reflect a quality of expanding and indulging; the elements in the lower right corner are considered condensing and fighting in terms of their expression because they are thought to reflect a compressive nature.

Flow

Flow effort, the baseline of movement, is about the quality of investment in your continuity as it is manifested in movement. It is the inner attitude toward ongoingness. It can be free, a.k.a. outpouring, easeful, and expansive, or bound, a.k.a. withheld, controlled, and contained (see figure 4.2).

Explore Your Continuity

Notice your current sense of your baseline of flow. Are you hardening the edges of your container or body wall, as if to keep the insides in and the outside out? Or are you letting your tissues be porous, as though the inside and outside are having an easy dialogue? Try fluctuating between these two energetic qualities. Imagine that your body's tissues could open and soften, allowing your body to become porous and easeful. Then try hardening and containing your body, endeavoring to keep it all together. Now let yourself oscillate between these possibilities and notice what it feels like to fluctuate your Flow.

L/BMA in Your World: Free Flow Effort and Empathy

Marin Leggat Roper

Free Flow effort touches on my capacity to be receptive and open to my environment—to give and to receive. This ability is crucial in group processes where different opinions, perspectives, or cultural frameworks make consensus difficult.

From personal relationships to professional settings or politics, I feel an argument brewing, first through the sensation of bound Flow creeping into my chest. My breath becomes shallow, and I feel my torso becoming more held, more rigid, like chain-link armor bolting around my chest. Indeed, bound Flow in this situation is about self-preservation.

Yet, if my intention is to understand someone who is different from me, or to be able to hold another's perspective in the spirit of cooperation and consensus building, I need to "stay open." Staying open isn't just a state of mind; it is a physical intention that begins by my freeing my Flow. I do this by sensing, then deepening, my breath. I intentionally engage subtle shape Flow in my torso to encourage the easing of my ribs and lungs, the opening of my joints, the literal softening of my heart. Besides the subtle, almost imperceptible movements happening in my torso, I also tap into my Weight sensing to allow Flow to move between my lower and upper body.

From this state of free Flow, I seek to sense the breath of that person standing across from me. How is she moving? What is she sensing? (If I could, I'd reach out and place my hand on her sternum and take a minute to just breathe together.) Observing and engaging from a place of free Flow opens channels for empathy that can neutralize potentially toxic environments by "giving and receiving" at the most basic levels of our physiology.

Weight

Weight effort is about the quality of how you use your mass and invest it in relationship to gravity, and how this is manifested in movement. It is about an inner attitude toward one's mass, not the quantity of one's mass. Weight can

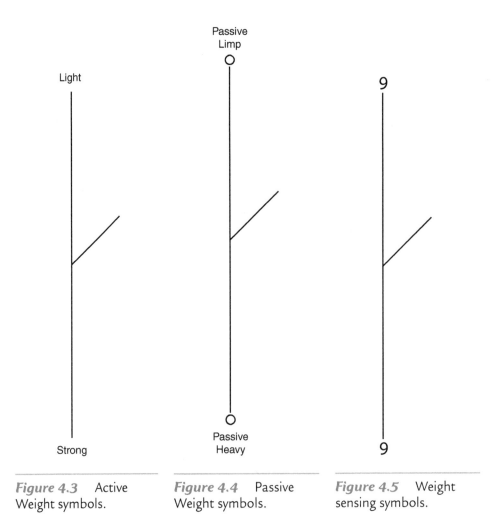

Figure 4.3   Active Weight symbols.

Figure 4.4   Passive Weight symbols.

Figure 4.5   Weight sensing symbols.

be rarified and delicate, or condensed and powerful. Weight effort is unique to the Effort category because it consists of three options for expression: active, passive, and sensing (see figure 4.3).

Active Weight effort in Laban/Bartenieff Movement Analysis is described as an active investment in the mass of your body in relation to gravity. Weight can fall on the light end of the continuum (rarified, delicate, feathery, overcoming gravity) or on the strong end (condensed, powerful, roaring, working with or into gravity).

Passive Weight effort is described as a passive investment in the mass of your body in relation to gravity, as though the energy is being drained out. Passive Weight can be limp on the light end or heavy on the strong end (see figure 4.4).

Weight sensing is described as a fluctuation between active and passive Weight, as if you are sensing the mass of your body in your tissues (see figure 4.5).

Figure 4.6   Time symbols.

Time

Time in L/BMA is about the quality of how you use your instincts and impulses regarding time and how they are manifested in movement behavior. It is the inner attitude displayed outwardly toward the passing of time or how much time one has. It can be sustained, a.k.a. lingering, prolonged, and gradual, or quick, a.k.a. urgent, sudden, and hasty (see figure 4.6).

Space

Space is about the quality of how you perceive and pay attention to the environment, and how this is manifested in movement behavior. It is about the inner attitude manifested outwardly toward the focus of your attention. It can be indirect, a.k.a. multi-focused, all-encompassing, taking it all in, or direct, a.k.a. pin-pointed, laser-like, channeled (see figure 4.7). Often Space effort is linked to vision and the eyes, however your attention can manifest throughout your body; you can attend to the world through a hand or the back of your neck.

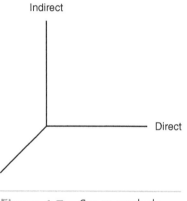

Figure 4.7   Space symbols.

Effort Qualities and Psychological Associations

The effort qualities have been associated with psychosomatic experience including Carl Jung's four functions of consciousness (see table 4.1) (Laban 81 *Mastery*) (Moore, 156-158). These associations are useful in practice for finding the efforts in movement; they can lead to meaningful reflections on where and how effort is present in our lives. However, these are associations, not truths, and are not substantive for observation and interpretation. Using these associations for decoding the movements of others can lead to inaccurate interpretations.

TABLE 4.1   Effort Factors and Psychological Associations

EFFORT FACTOR →	PSYCHOLOGICAL PROCESS →	JUNG'S FUNCTION
Flow	Precision	Feeling
Weight	Intention	Sensing
Time	Decision	Intuiting
Space	Attention	Thinking

These psychological associations bring out the emotional tones in effort and are useful to explorations of how effort manifests functionally and expressively in our lives. The following sections give examples of how effort manifests in daily life connected to the psychological and Jungian associations.

Explorations of Flow

Flow is about how you approach continuity and goings-on; it is about your feelings and how you relate to your doings. You can control and bind your actions, such as when you restrict your energy in a tense conversation to keep yourself from letting it all out, or when you need controlled precision to thread a needle. You can also free up your approach to your activities, such as when your see a long-lost friend and run toward her with unbridled excitement, or devour your dinner with wild abandon.

Explorations of Weight

Being about your intention and your mass, Weight affords the sensation of your tissues having density and kinetic potential. You can forcefully press your foot on the shovel and into the dirt, and you can put your weight behind a commitment. On the expansive side, you can sense your viscera untethered from earth and floating into the ether, or you can delicately brush the snowflakes from your dog's head.

In the passive aspect of Weight you reveal your exhaustion, wilting from the heat and the exertion as if there were nothing left within you to hike another step, or heavily dropping onto the couch, resigned to something you heard in the news.

In a moment of Weight sensing you vacillate between actively engaging your mass and settling into passivity, not quite sure where you stand on the issue and if you want to speak up. You are feeling what your guts and your body's mass tell you.

*L/BMA in Your World: Weight Effort
and Animation*

Leslie Bishko, Associate Professor, Animation and Dynamic Media

People say that animators "breathe life" into characters. Animation creates a continuous experience in time via a sequence of images that create the illusion of movement. The illusion generates a perception of living, intentional beings, even in the absence of physical bodies or minds. What animators do is in stark contrast to the phenomenological notion of lived experience.

Animators strive to create the sense of weight moving in relationship to gravity, because weight makes characters believable. Ironically, the only term we have for this in animation is *weight*. L/BMA gives us a deep understanding of the role of weight in animation.

When we observe people moving, we see both their physical form and the movement that their intention manifests through their physical being. As mentioned, animation constructs the *illusion* of the physical being; there is no physical form. Movement in animation creates the *illusion* of the materiality of the plastic form: the character's physical substance.

In animation, how body parts are sequenced contributes to the illusion of the materiality of the plastic form. Sequencing gives a sense of the weightiness and materiality of body parts. Successive sequencing in animation helps to augment a sense of connectivity to and through the core, and underscores initiation of movement that sequences through the body and communicates clear intent.

In animation, weight shifts generate the illusion of the functioning structural relationships of the body, in relationship to gravity and the vertical. Effective illusions of weight shift are the most fundamental component of functional believability in animation. Getting it right, then finessing it to serve expression, takes skill and practice.

Explorations of Time

You intuit the possibilities of the moment, making decisions as you process what is happening now and how you want to address what happens next. As you hurry from one errand to the next, waiting at the checkout counter to buy eggs, for instance, you abruptly decide to add a candy bar to your purchases. Or, eager to be home and intuiting the best route to take, you make a quick left as you notice traffic thickening ahead. On a hike, having reached the top of the mountain and had lunch, you linger, indulging in the moment and letting go of all that needs to be done. You let yourself rest and feel the cool air and bright sunshine before making the trek back down. When considering a car purchase, you take your time, drawing out the decision.

Explorations of Space

You consider how your attention and thinking are organized. When considering what to have for dinner, you expand your thinking to include new options and scan all the shelves in the pasta aisle. You take an expansive perspective when thinking about where you want to go on vacation next year. Shifting from indirect to direct, you scan your memories for times when you have used indirect effort in Space to spread your attention, and you select a specific moment to think about. It is important for you to channel your focus when you are plucking the A string on your violin, or you could miss it and hit the E string by accident. You usually pinpoint your thinking and talking points on an issue before you bring it to your colleagues for their consideration.

KEY POINTS

- Effort is about the quality of the energetic investment present in human movement. As you move throughout your day, these are in constant fluctuation as the energetic expression of your movement shifts and morphs from moment to moment.

- There are four main effort factors: Flow, Weight, Time, and Space. Each factor has two elements that are opposites of each other. Flow can be free or bound; Weight can be strong or light (both of which further consist of three options for expression: active, passive, and sensing); Time can be quick or sustained; Space can be direct or indirect.

Effort Intensity and Combinations

Because you are a living, moving human being, the four effort factors are always present in some way—time is always passing, you always exist in space, you always have mass, and flow continuously happens. What determines Effort in the L/BMA sense is how it is revealed in *movement* at any given moment—for example, you would describe an urgent, hasty movement with the quality of compressing time as having quick Time effort, but you may not speak to Weight because it was not highlighted by the movement. In short, in the Laban/Bartenieff framework, you say an effort is present if it is actively revealed in movement. This means that not all efforts are present in a given movement or series of movements; rather they fluctuate and change as the energetic dynamic of the movement burbles along.

One way the fluctuation in effort happens is through changes in the intensity of effort. Effort intensity can range from barely perceptible to highly amplified. The image of a volume knob on a stereo is helpful for understanding this concept. When you turn up the volume, the sound is louder; turn it way down and it becomes barely perceptible. Like sound, effort varies in intensity. It can be highly intense, loud, and fully invested, or low in intensity, diminished, muted, and barely there. Notice your energetic intensity right now as you read this. At what volume is it present?

Another way energy fluctuates in movement is by loading and unloading the various effort factors. *Loading* and *unloading* are terms used to describe the addition or removal of an effort factor. As the energetic tones of movement change, individual effort factors combine to create multifactor effort clusters. Continuing with the music metaphor, the loading and unloading of efforts is like a song that starts with the guitar, then the violins enter, and finally the piano is added; each new instrument "loads" the music. As the violins fade out, the sound is less full, or in effort terms, it is less loaded. Time effort could be loaded with Space effort when you focus laser-like attention on a nearby bee; using quick Time effort, you urgently direct your attention to its buzzing by impulsively pointing your finger directly at it.

Effort expression is ever changing, continually shifting in intensity and load. In the description of human movement, when certain effort factors combine with other factors, the combinations are given specific names.

When two effort factors are present it is called a state.

When three effort factors are present it is called a drive.

When all four effort factors are present it is called full effort.

States

States describe the coming together of two effort factors. There are six states—remote, rhythm, stable, mobile, awake, and dream. Each state has four possible configurations of effort factors: two present, and two missing. The states are less loaded than the drives, and can be harder to feel in movement.

The states are listed in table 4.2 with their associated effort factors; each is paired with the state whose effort factors are opposite. The italicized statements reference the combination of the Jungian associations with the effort factors.

TABLE 4.2 States and Their Effort Factors

REMOTE	RHYTHM (NEAR)
Space and Flow *I attend to my feelings*	Weight and Time *My mass decides*
STABLE	**MOBILE**
Weight and Space *My thinking intention*	Time and Flow *I intuit my feelings*
AWAKE	**DREAM**
Time and Space *I attend to making decisions*	Flow and Weight *I sense my feelings*

Drives

Effort drives describe when three effort factors come together. There are four drives—vision, spell, passion, action—each with eight possible configurations. When studying the drives, notice both the effort factor that is present as well as what is missing. The missing effort factor is important to the feeling tone or "coloring" of the movement. The three drives with Flow are known as the "transformation drives," as if to suggest that the presence of Flow in the drive makes the experience marked by the potential for a dramatic shift.

Vision Drive

Space (thinking), Time (intuition), and Flow (continuity) merge together untethered to the material world. You drop out of Weight effort, which is associated with sensation and mass (see figure 4.8).

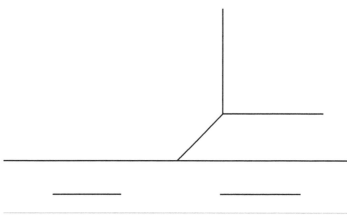

Figure 4.8   Vision drive symbol.

Evocative Description

> Normally you feel the burden of gravity; you grapple and push against its downward pull, weighted down by its relentless pressure, or you effervescently delight as you rebound buoyantly into it. Weight grounds you and brings you in touch with the sensate world. However, at times, you neutralize gravity, as if the intensity of your mental processing has stripped you of dealing with it. Free from gravity's grasp, in Vision Drive you are in a weightless landscape of thought, intuition, and continuity. You are deliberately planning, outlining, indulging in having an out-of-body experience, or freely soaring on the wings of instinct. Or holding a vision for the future or a memory of the past that is not about the self, but about what could be, after all it is not really about you.

Spell Drive

Space (thinking), Weight (sensation and mass), and Flow (continuity) are concocted into an enchanted trance. You drop out of Time effort, which is associated with intuition and decision making (see figure 4.9).

Evocative Description

> Generally, you are aware of the passing of time, measured in consistent metrics of seconds, minutes, and hours. Yet your lived experience of time is not of a metered consistency; it expands and contracts. When your awareness of the passing of time disappears, you may feel otherworldly or magical, as if in a trance or called to experience life out of the ordinary. As your awareness of time slips away in spell drive you may find an uncanny sense of being drawn in, mesmerized. Good storytelling,

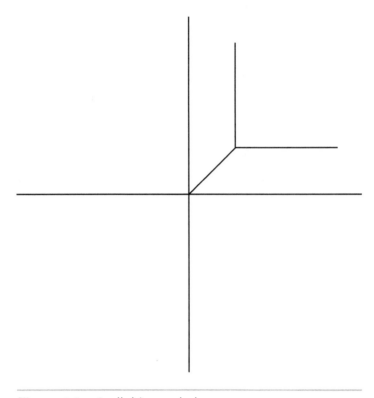

Figure 4.9   Spell drive symbol.

religious ceremonies, and trances pull you into their web through the configurations of this drive.

Passion Drive

Time (intuition), Weight (sensation), and Flow (continuity) swirl together into emotional absorption. The Space effort, associated with attention and thinking, drops away (see figure 4.10).

Evocative Description

You are an attentive being, spending much of your life tuned in to your environment and consciously behaving according to the cultivated social mores. In these times your attention is either directed toward a single point of interest, or you are indirectly taking in all that is around you. But sometimes this attention drops out, and you get lost in a rush of feelings: delirious with anger, giddy with joy, sunk in sorrow, indulgent in delight. Absorbed by the grip of emotion, you are passionately overtaken by a surge of feeling, captivated by your inner senses you indulge to feel them, dancing wildly in the fantastical world inside of you.

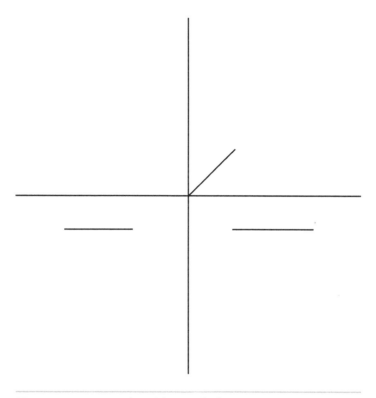

Figure 4.10   Passion drive symbol.

Action Drive

Time (intuition), Weight (sensation), and Space (thinking) pop together and then disappear, leaving no lingering feelings. The Flow effort, associated with feeling and continuity, is missing. Because Flow is absent, action moments happen, and then they are over; when they go on and on, Flow inevitably returns (see figure 4.11).

Evocative Description

It happens in a moment, elongated or instantaneous, and then it is over, leaving no residue of feeling. Because of the absence of Flow, there is a sense that the moment came out of nowhere and disappeared just as it appeared leaving no trace in the movement of having happened, an experience of weighted thinking and deciding all at once. You can punch your "power there now," or float your "delicacy lingering every-where." You can slash with instantaneous, all-encompassing force, as the ogre emerging from under the bridge, or flick your fairy sparkles everywhere with a quick, effervescent gesture, sending them throughout the forest. In action drive, mass, time, and attention come together

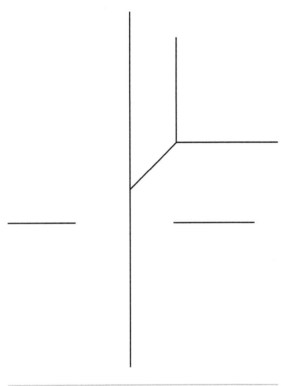

Figure 4.11   Action drive symbol.

and disperse, the movement travels on to what is next.

Every possible configuration within action drive has been named and studied. The evocative language in table 4.3 (in italics) presents each configuration of action with examples of adding everyday words to evoke effortful movement. Play around to create new associations for yourself.

The eight configurations of action drive can be combined with their affinities in Shape qualities and Space to form Laban's Action Drive Scale.

Exploring the Drives

Evocative language and sounding is helpful when learning and teaching drives. Because the effort language can feel dry, it often will fail to elicit a kinesthetic response that brings out the desired effort. Finding language, images, soundings, and experiences that reference and bring effort to life in movement is helpful. The above evocative descriptions are there to inspire you. Try building evocative sentences (similar to those started in tables 4.2 and 4.3) by combining word associations from the effort elements into phrases that layer information. For example, *you linger as you spread your delicate attention* (sustained, indirect, and light), or *you channel your power quickly* (direct, strong, quick), or *your rage swirls and surges inside of you* (bound, strong, quick). As you move them, notice what it feels like to move and inhabit the energies you describe. Identify places in your life where this effort configuration is present.

When working with people who are not versed in the Laban material yet who want specific movement dynamics, the more you can work from what they already know in terms of movement and images, the more likely they will find the dynamics they are looking for. Having a large "pocket" or "bank" of images and words and experiences to help them get there will make you more successful.

The loading of three effort factors and the absence of one makes the Drives an effective tool for learning effort. As you move in accordance with a particular drive, notice what it feels like when an effort factor is absent; this will help you get to know what it feels like when it is present. Also, in any drive

TABLE 4.3   **Action Drive—Examples of Evocative Language**

FLOAT	PUNCH
Light, Indirect, Sustained *My delicacy is present lingering everywhere*	Strong, Direct, Quick *My power is there now*
GLIDE	**SLASH**
Light, Direct, Sustained *I linger in channeled delicacy*	Strong, Indirect, Quick *My urgency explodes everywhere*
DAB	**WRING**
Light, Direct, Quick *I focus my gentle, urgent, pinpointed attention*	Strong, Indirect, Sustained *I scan in prolonged might*
FLICK	**PRESS**
Light, Indirect, Quick *I move with airy, all-encompassing briskness*	Strong, Direct, Sustained *I linger with honed-in force*

moment, effort intensities vary, meaning, for example, one factor may feel most prominent, with the other two present but at lower intensity.

You will likely notice that certain effort elements like to come with other elements, perhaps quick Time and strong Weight like to come together and are hard for you to tease apart. This challenge with learning the drives asks the mover to separate the effort elements that often come together in their personal movement preferences. Separating and clarifying efforts that are similar is a physical skill drill that brings greater clarity to your capacities as a mover and observer of movement.

KEY POINTS

- As effort fluctuates from moment to moment, it varies in intensity. It also loads and unloads—that is, gains or loses—effort factors.
- When various aspects of effort come together, it is called an effort constellation. When there are four efforts present it is called full effort. When there are three efforts present it is called a drive. When there are two efforts present it is called a state.
- There are four drives: vision, spell, passion and action.
- There are six states: remote, rhythm, stable, mobile, awake, and dream.
- Each of the drives and states have many possible configurations of individual effort factors.

Effort in Life

Effort is present in all movement, from day-to-day mundane tasks, to the celebrations and sorrows of heightened emotion, to the displays of virtuosic movement present in dance and athletics. Watch children play an imaginary game or on a playground. Their effort is lived out to the maximum. Their little bodies will giggle, fly, command, tag, hide—all with great energetic intensity. The explorative effortful lives are important to their development, providing them with a range of ways to experience themselves and their world.

In adult life, effort manifests in day-to-day activities. You can hurriedly scan the intersection before turning, in an indirect and quick awake state. Or you can use your controlled and channeled strength to press the can opener into the can with a strong, direct, and bound spell drive. Effort is rich with expression, leaving an impression about a mover's inner state: The hurried driver enters the intersection with an urgent turn of the wheel. The sleepy chef dismissively drops vegetables into the pan with a free, passive limp, indirect gesture.

The study of effort makes evident how vast and diverse the options for energetic investment in movement are. Effort is always in flux, changing from moment to moment. Within this flux there are preferences and personal signatures that are unique to an individual; they give impressions like "she has a lot of free Flow," or " he has a preference for quick Time." Or the statements may be more evocative in tone, such as, "he is easy going," or "she is always in a hurry."

Despite your preferences, you have access to the full range of effort expression. As you explore this category, expand your choices by deliberately manifesting a wide range of effort possibilities. This can be exhilarating and uncomfortable, both physically and mentally because associations with certain efforts can be loaded with prior knowledge and assumptions. Perhaps you believe that you don't have the option to linger in sustained time, or strong weight is not ladylike. These prejudices can foster limitations in your movement and influence how you interpret the movement of others.

Activity: *Your Personal Effort Signature*

Learn more about your personal effort signature—the types of effort you return to over and over. Questions to ask to get to know your Effort signature: Which Effort elements do you like? Which do you gravitate toward and feel comfortable in? Which, if any, feel so familiar that they are like a home to you?

After you identify your preferences, consider what these Efforts bring you. How does it feel to live them out?

As you learn about your preferences, you will also learn about the types of effort that you may shy away from. It is satisfying to grow your effort range to include those that you are less familiar with. Which Effort elements do you feel challenged by? What associations and ideas do you have with that effort? Perhaps it reminds you of something unpleasant. Explore where in your life that effort is already present. Consider what it offers and how it might be valuable and what it could bring you. And consider how you can manifest it more fully. Sounding, singing, and speaking are very effective ways to enliven a fuller range of effort. Try a light, elongated, and delicate coo-ing, or let a powerful, pouring roar emerge; perhaps a quick, bouncy song or a tired, giving-up sigh. Let these sounds and many others permeate you moving body and inspire your dynamic life.

Effort in Dance

Dance is full of the dynamism of ever-changing effort. Each style of dance and many choreographers have effort preferences specific to their form. Although individual dancers have unique styles, the forms they dance generally preference specific efforts. Dancers who want to develop skill in a specific style will want to physically understand the effort preferences of that form. Hip-hop often fluctuates intensely between bound and free Flow. Ballet generally prefers light Weight, while many African diasporic forms prefer strong Weight; in both forms, however, there are many examples in which the opposite effort polarity is present and important.

Thinking in terms of effort is useful for developing dance technique. As dancers develop range and clarity with effort choices, their ability to use effort to assist their skills increases. Learning a pirouette with a phrasing of bound to free Flow may help a beginning dancer prepare with control and then unleash that control for a generous turn. Or the "right there" nature of direct Space Effort could help dancers dial in the precision of a jazz arm or landing a jump or turn.

Choreographically, effort is exciting; it brings dynamic thrill and subtlety to dance performance. Choreographers can develop a "world" based on a specific effort expression, or draw the audience's attention to a movement by making distinctive effort choices. Effort gives meaning and flavor to a gesture or character and creates dynamic contrast within a work. When a composition feels creatively stuck or energetically monotonous, exploring new effort choices can allow new possibilities to surprise you.

Effort in Athletics

Athletic performance also benefits from the study of effort. Like dance styles, most sports have effort preferences. Although individual athletes have personal styles within their sport, there are certain effort skills that commonly show up in their sport. A boxer may flutter like a quick, light, bound hummingbird's heart before executing a strong, quick, and direct jab at an opponent. A tennis player may discover that increasing the amount of free Flow she uses makes it easier for her to get around the court. Being able to shift quickly on the effort continuum is important to success in many sports. Athletes and coaches can study the effort preferences of a sport and the style of an individual athlete and develop warm-ups and exercises that foster efforts relevant to success, and cool-downs that offer recuperation from the effort demands of their sport.

Effort in Theater

A character's effort signature is an important part of character development and how that character is perceived by the audience. How a character uses effort is expressive of who they are and what motives them. A character's Flow baseline, for example, will register in the audience as a perception of who this character is and what they value. Do they bind their Flow to keep things together, or approach life with the ease of free Flow? The complexity and nuance of a character's effort choices influence who they are perceived to be and how they interact with the other characters and the narrative.

L/BMA in Your World: Self-Defense

Michelle Gay

I teach a unique self-defense seminar that utilizes Effort as a way of empowering people to recognize how they can be both dominated and dominating in everyday situations. Through the context of self-defense, we use effort to empower people to assess and avoid the potential for violence. The efforts that we focus on are direct/indirect Space effort and quick/sustained Time effort. We begin with Space effort exercises to distinguish the different approaches of attending or paying attention to our environment. Participants also discover that how they pay attention is observable to others and is a potential factor in whether or not they are targeted. Participants complete the seminar with the ability to demonstrate clearly the "doing" of being and looking alert. We also do movement exercises that distinguish between quick and sustained Time effort and how the two can be used to dominate in our interactions with one another—for example, when a predator hurries the victim to a second location or slows the victim to keep them vulnerable to attack. Bringing awareness to these dynamics allows participants to better assess their own interactions overall and reveals ways that others may attempt to dominate them. Participants leave with an embodied awareness of Time and Space effort and how they can be used in multiple contexts.

Summary

The Effort category highlights the quality of the dynamic and energetic life of all movement. Effort is described using four factors—Flow, Space, Time, and Weight—each of which is divided into polarity spectrums with each end called effort elements. Effort is expressive in that it gives color to the emotional and energetic nature of movement. It is also functional because it is intrinsic to the accomplishment of the many movement tasks of life, from opening a jar to turning a pirouette to making a tackle. In order to "make it real," find lively and meaningful ways to engage with the energetic dynamics in movement such as: work with evocative language and imagery to describe and evoke a kinesthetic response, use sounding to manifest what is less known to you, and mine your life for effort already present in order to call it forth in desired contexts.

CHAPTER 5

Shape

"*Forms are closely connected with movement. Each movement has its form, and forms are simultaneously created with and through movement.*"

(Laban 1974, 3)

T he body itself has a visible shape. Think of the skin, the edges and curves of the body, and how they morph. As the body moves, its three-dimensional and changing form shifts in response to desire and the need to express one-self. The body adjusts and readjusts its form—spreading and enclosing, growing and shrinking, moving toward and away—in ways meaningful and significant.

Right now, as you read this, notice the form of your body. How does it feel to be in this form? What is it conveying to you? How does it function for what you are doing? Now let it morph and change. Notice the choices you made. Perhaps the form of your body opened or closed. Perhaps the form grew or perhaps it shrank.

The form and forming processes of the body is the focus of the category known as Shape in Laban/Bartenieff Movement Analysis. Because of its focus on form, this category clarifies the appearance and structure of the body's movements and is useful in any context where the physical form is important.

As you will notice, the Shape category provides information about move-ment that is different from that provided by the categories of Body, Effort, and Space. Through Shape you are addressing the body's appearance, structure, and silhouette, and how it is morphing and articulating in movement.

The Shape category is a more recently developed aspect of Laban/Barte-nieff Movement Analysis. Although Laban talked about the shape of the body occasionally, the contents of the Shape category were developed mainly by Warren Lamb and Judith Kestenberg through their applications of it in business and in infant development, respectively. Their contributions have since been defined and organized by the larger Laban/Bartenieff community, especially Peggy Hackney and her colleagues at Integrated Movement Studies, into what is presented in this chapter.

As it currently exists, there are five aspects of the Shape category, each of which highlights a specific element of shape. Each aspect asks unique questions about form and form change, for example: How is the form change supported by the inner "guts" of the body? Toward where is the form changing? How is the body changing shape in relationship to itself and its environment? What is the basic, archetypal form the body is making?

The five aspects of the Shape category are the following:

1. Opening and closing
2. Shape flow support
3. Shape qualities
4. Modes of shape change
5. Shape forms

Figure 5.1   Shape stroke symbol.

All symbols in the Shape category have two parallel lines running from right high to left low. This is called the **shape stroke** and signifies that the associated symbol is a member of the Shape category (see figure 5.1).

Opening and Closing

Opening and closing are the most basic ways to look at shape change (see figure 5.2). Is the form of the body opening outward, or is it closing inward toward itself? Notice that we're using the *-ing* forms of these words. They are process oriented and thus tune the observer's eye to track changes in the body's process of forming, not a static form.

Although these are very basic terms, giving words to what is simple can be profound and clarifying. You can open yourself to something, or close yourself off from it; you can close around something to engulf it, or open to move away from it. Tracking the simplest aspect of form change sheds light on how the form-ing process remains in constant flux throughout the day—you open and close, open and close, open and close. This aspect of movement passes through your body as undercurrents to every interaction and task you pursue.

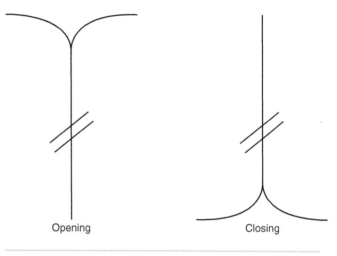

Figure 5.2   Opening and closing symbols.

Shape Flow Support

Shape flow support, the innermost aspect of the Shape category, describes the internal support for form change. In biology, the term *motility* means the ability of an organism or substance to move. As an adjective, motile also describes one who has the ability to move spontaneously. It can be used to describe a person whose prevailing mental imagery takes the form of inner feelings of action. Taken together, these definitions speak to shape flow support as the inner motility of the body's form change. It encompasses postural support for movement emerging from deep within the body.

The concept of shape flow support was developed from Judith Kestenberg's research on infant development and has since been added to the Shape category. As Ellen Goldman said of the process of refining this concept with Kestenberg, "We wanted to differentiate content from form" (Goldman 1990, 132).

The most basic way to describe shape flow support is in terms of growing and shrinking (see figure 5.3). It is often linked to the growing of the torso during inhalation and the shrinking of the torso during exhalation; however, it can be present without being linked to the breath's inhalation and exhalation.

Within the general categories of growing and shrinking, shape flow support can be further delineated into smaller units (see figure 5.4). These include

- Lengthening/shortening in the vertical dimension
- Widening/narrowing in the horizontal dimension
- Bulging/hollowing in the sagittal dimension

Widening, lengthening, and bulging exemplify the growing side of shape flow support. Narrowing, shortening, and hollowing represent the shrinking side.

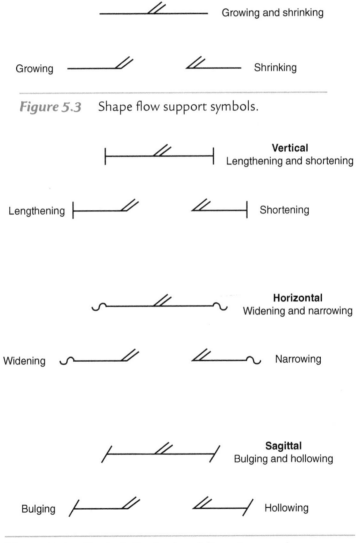

Figure 5.3   Shape flow support symbols.

Figure 5.4   Symbols for further delineating growing and shrinking.

Shape flow support can happen as either bipolar or unipolar organization. In bipolar variations, both ends move in a growing or shrinking manner. In unipolar variations, only one end of the body is specifically investing in shape flow support—for example, the core is hollowing backward, or the head is lengthening upward, but the other end is not affected.

This aspect of Shape enlivens the torso and creates the internal support for form change. By promoting inner motility, it provides the sense that movement can go anywhere in the body—the body is invigorated by its underlying potential and moved by its internal support. When shape flow support is encouraged in a movement practice, form change throughout the whole body feels supported, is enlivened by inner vitality, and is capable of fulfilling the movement demands it confronts. At times, the internal support for form change is consciously guided, as in the hollowing of a core-distal body pattern; at other times it is unconscious to the mover, as when a baby bulges its back to suckle and take in food, or when a virtuosic running back narrows his body, maneuvering to avoid a potential tackle.

Shape flow support is useful in dance and athletics by providing a sense that the whole body is mobilized by internal support. When a dancer appears stiff and rigid, as if the body lacks support for the movement and the desire is to find more, investing more deeply in this aspect could be helpful. However, totally diminishing shape flow support is also a valid choice and could be useful to movers in many ways, for example, say a choreographic statement.

Activity: Touch for Flow Support

Touch is helpful in developing shape flow support. You can experiment with a growing and shrinking touch on the torso, in which the toucher's hands mirror and increase the sensation of growing and shrinking that naturally occurs in the body of the person being touched. This is especially noticeable as the person breathes, for example. Said another way, the hands match and echo the shape flow support already present. To experience this, ask a partner where on their torso they would like to be touched. Let your hands notice and follow and highlight their torso's rhythmic growing and shrinking. If you want to get more specific, you can use your hands to highlight the presence of each aspect of shape flow support: lengthening, shortening, widening, narrowing, bulging, and hollowing.

KEY POINTS

- Shape flow support is the internal postural support for form change.
- On its simplest level, shape flow support is the growing and shrinking of the body, usually the torso, and can be experienced in relationship to breath.

- Shape flow support can be further delineated into lengthening and shortening, widening and narrowing, bulging and hollowing. It is the inner motility that enlivens movement.

Shape Qualities

The aspect of the Shape category known as shape qualities addresses the question of toward where a form is moving. Shape qualities evoke the sense of the body morphing toward something. As with *opening* and *closing*, the *-ing* construction of the words used to describe this aspect honors the fact that they are a process-oriented aspect of Shape; the form is doing something; the shape of the body is changing and now you can be more specific about where in the environment it is morphing toward.

The six shape qualities are shown in figure 5.5.

1. Rising—moving toward up-ness
2. Sinking—moving toward down-ness

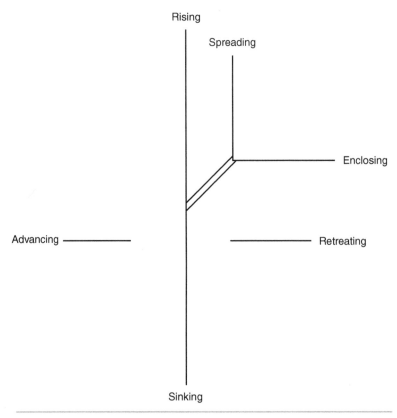

Figure 5.5 Shape quality symbols.

3. Spreading—moving toward and opening to side-ness
4. Enclosing—moving toward and closing to side-ness
5. Advancing—moving toward forward-ness
6. Retreating—moving toward back-ness

The shape qualities are linked to the **spatial matrix**, but they are not *about* Space or arriving to reveal a spatial pull; they are about the process of form change. The spatial matrix is the mapping of the space around the body into cardinal directions (discussed further in chapter 6). Rising and sinking are linked to the vertical dimension, spreading and enclosing the horizontal dimension, and advancing and retreating the sagittal dimension. Shape qualities encourage the mover to feel how the form change expands and contracts in relation to the spatial environment.

The shape qualities are useful in many aspects of movement, including increasing virtuosity and skill by clarifying where a form change moves to. They also hold meaningful associations that can be explored metaphorically and physically.

Shape qualities can be integrated with the Body category to improve body connectivity because they clarify the process of form change to support understandings of how the body itself molds and moves through an action. You would likely find them useful if you were coaching sprinters as they crossed the finish line to continue advancing into the finish, or a squash player to experience full enclosing as preparation for a backhand. You would also likely find spreading useful as you stood on a ladder, reaching to paint the eaves of your house, or sinking as you peered under the car to see if there was a branch stuck in its underside.

In chapter 3, "Body," shape qualities are used to describe the Basic Six exercise called arm circles. When doing an arm circle from Irmgard Bartenieff's perspective, the body will move through a cycle of rising, enclosing, sinking, and spreading. Integrating the knowledge of shape qualities into the arm circle clarifies what the form of the body is doing and invites greater participation through the whole body and greater support through the torso for the rotation of the arm.

Another example of when to use shape qualities knowledge to enliven body connectivity is during a lateral (side-to-side) weight shift. Instead of thinking about propelling from one base of support to another, try thinking about spreading and enclosing at the base of the pelvis. Or, if you wanted to propel your weight forward into space, you would explore advancing at the base of the pelvis.

In the Laban system, shape qualities are connected to Effort. **Affinity,** a term used to denote a natural pairing of different aspects of the Laban/Bartenieff system, describes the relationship between shape qualities and effort elements. The links are as follows and, you will notice, are congruent with the graphs for each (see figure 5.6):

Rising—Light Weight

Sinking—Strong Weight

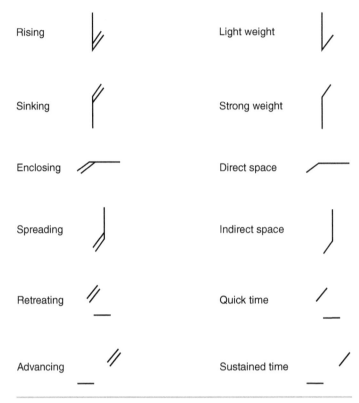

Figure 5.6   Shape and Effort graph symbols.

Enclosing—Direct Space

Spreading—Indirect Space

Retreating—Quick Time

Advancing—Sustained Time

These affinities emerged early in Laban's observations of commonly occurring movement in his world, though latter models developed by Laban sought far more complex relationships and patterns (Laban 1974 and Moore 2009). He perceived that these qualities of movement often occurred congruently, like retreating to back-ness with quickness to get away from danger, or sinking with strength to hammer a nail. (He saw them spatially, not in terms of shape, because he did not have a Shape category or shape qualities at the time.) As a practice of training the body, the couplings of Effort, Shape, and Space that Laban conceptualized are often combined. It is also fun to pull them apart and play with dis-affinities or incongruities—for example, rising with a powerful roar (strong Weight effort) if cheering for a favorite team, or sinking with delicacy (light Weight effort) to transplant a fragile flower.

Activity: Shape Qualities

The words and movements associated with shape qualities have a metaphoric nature that encourage personal meaning-making. You might rise to power or sink in despair; you could enclose to safety or spread love; you can retreat to the comfort of your home or advance your career. Develop your own associations for the various shape qualities. Next, develop a movement that uses those shape qualities and expresses your associations as if to reveal your metaphors through movement. Notice how your "effort life" gets involves and supports your expressivity.

KEY POINTS

- The shape qualities are about how the form of the body changes toward something in its environment.
- The six shape qualities are rising, sinking, spreading, enclosing, advancing, and retreating.
- Shape qualities are useful in many situations where clarity of form change matters.

Modes of Shape Change

The modes of shape change provide a lens for considering how the form of the body changes in relationship to self and environment.

The modes of shape change were in part developed from observations of babies moving as they seek to meet their needs and express themselves in relationship toward themselves, or in order to connect with their world, and eventually to create and mold their environment (Peggy Hackney, conversation with author, March 3, 2018). The movement of very young infants initially occurs in relationship to the self; they squirm, wiggle, and adjust as they seek comfort. Movement in this mode is self-referential and comes from the infant accommodating its needs. As the infant's awareness of the world grows, so does its desire to bridge to it—to bring something into the self, to move something away, or to indicate (point to) something. The young mover also develops an awareness of her ability to create and mold her world, in effect changing her form in a three-dimensional relationship with the environment.

While the inspiration from developmental movement may seem clear in infants, it is likely not as clear with the complex possibilities and motivations of adult movement. Further, reading someone else's intention in movement, as the developmental lens does, will be influenced by the observer's interpretation of intention. In order to help you learn and tease-out the distinctions between each mode of shape change, the definitions below are written to include the developmental perspective with a form-oriented definition.

The modes of shape change and their associated symbols (see figure 5.7) are:

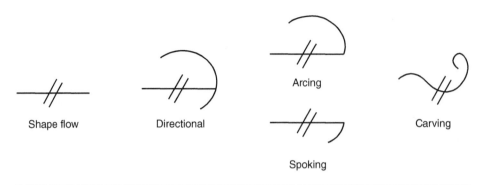

Figure 5.7 Modes of shape change symbols.

- **Shape-flow mode:** These describe change that is associated with self-to-self relationships—for example, seeking comfort, adjusting, and settling. In a sense, this mode is "all about me"; it is a response to personal needs. The action in space may appear less structured, or to the observer amorphous, but this does not make it less valuable.

- **Directional mode:** These are about connecting with the environment. They are location-oriented and are associated with making bridges between the body and its surroundings; specifically, the body actively connects to or indicates something in its environment. These modes can be further delineated into **arcing** and **spoking.** Arc-like modes follow sweeping pathways (like tracing the inside of a bicycle wheel), while spoke-like modes trace linear pathways (like the spokes of a wheel). Arc-like modes often involve movement at one joint of the body, whereas spoke-like modes often involve movement at two or more joints.

- **Carving mode:** These modes actively engage with and alter the environment. They involve three-dimensional movements that form, contour, sculpt, shape, adapt to, and accommodate one's surroundings. They often reveal curvilinear trace-forms in the ether.

These modes clarify the process of form change in many movement pursuits. Different athletic and physical activities reveal a preference for certain modes of shape change and a lack of investment in others. For example, ballet preferences directional and some carving modes, especially in the dexterity of the feet. Other movement practices accentuate directional movement, including yoga and general strength training. Movement practices that emphasize carving include white-water kayaking, which requires the kayaker to constantly form, accommodate, and carve both paddle and water to maneuver the boat through eddies and tongues and to surf waves. Shape-flow mode appears in all styles of movement, though they are rarely spoken of, as the mover adjusts to his or her own needs. For example, before a power-lifter performs a clean and press, you will often see her execute movements with shape flow as a mode of shape change as part of getting settled and preparing for the lift.

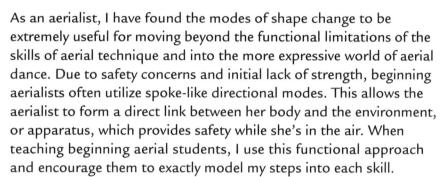

L/BMA in Your World: Aerial Dancing

Elizabeth Stitch

As an aerialist, I have found the modes of shape change to be extremely useful for moving beyond the functional limitations of the skills of aerial technique and into the more expressive world of aerial dance. Due to safety concerns and initial lack of strength, beginning aerialists often utilize spoke-like directional modes. This allows the aerialist to form a direct link between her body and the environment, or apparatus, which provides safety while she's in the air. When teaching beginning aerial students, I use this functional approach and encourage them to exactly model my steps into each skill.

Over time, I have noticed that it is difficult to break this initial pattern and begin to explore other options for changing the form of the body and connecting with the apparatus. In analyzing my personal aerial performance, I was surprised to observe my own strong preference for the directional mode, particularly the Arc-like form. While this mode can lend a more graceful feeling to a movement, it is essentially similar to the spoke-like mode in terms of the expressive statement it makes in connecting to the apparatus. In this context, both directional modes of shape change are straightforward and utilitarian, which is by no means negative, but they are expressively limited and not what I always want to convey.

One of the things I love most about Laban theory is that it gives me a map into lesser-known places in my movement signature. Following this map into the co-creative realm of carving has offered me not only a different relationship with my apparatus, but also new possibilities for movement invention. It has also guided me as a performer into the vulnerability of sharing my inner life with the audience through specific moments of shape-flow mode of shape change. With this full palette of expressive possibilities, my movement experience feels more satisfying, which keeps me coming back to my apparatus for further exploration in the air!

Day-to-day activities offer insight into various modes of shape change. Shifting to seek comfort while reading is an example of shape flow as a mode of shape change; it can provide a sense of settling into oneself. Shopping for and cutting vegetables both preference the directional mode. Knitting and crocheting are examples of the carving mode being used in the process of giving form to or creating something.

The modes of shape change can also be a template for making contact with another body. You might be adjusting for your own comfort and accidently bump into another person. You might directionally bridge to someone for a formal handshake or a celebratory high five. You could use a carving motion to massage and knead the shoulders of a loved one who has had a long day.

The modes of shape change ask the observer to interpret the mover's intention. This can cause confusion, but it is worth exploring and teasing out. Sometimes the mode an observer sees is different from what it feels like as a mover. For example, to the observer of a violinist, creating a vibrato may appear as occurring in the directional mode: The finger is placed on the string and begins moving quickly side to side. From the perspective of a trained violinist, however, vibrato may be experienced as a carving mode: she is actively vibrating and sculpting the string in three dimensions to give shape to the sound that emerges from the instrument. Despite the potential differences between what an outsider notices and what a participant notices, as you gain insider experience you will want to supplement your observations with nuanced and felt knowledge to support and enhance your ability to describe and coach the activity.

Activity: Modes of Shape Change

Because the modes of shape change are developmentally based, they hold metaphors for a learning or creative process.

First, think about activities you enjoy; what modes do they preference? How do these preferences reflect your needs and values?

Next, think of an activity in which you have a high level of creativity and proficiency. Remember how your journey with it began. As a beginner, you were not formed and refined. Your learning was probably an unstructured process of gaining familiarity, followed by bridging to the activity, defining it, making sense of it, and, finally, acquiring the ability to express complexity and make something new.

KEY POINTS

- The modes of shape change describe how the body changes form in relationship to the self and the environment.
- The three modes are shape-flow, directional, and carving.
- This aspect of the Shape category is useful because it clarifies the mover's intention and relationship to their environment.
- It can be used functionally in athletics and physical training to improve a player's technical skill, and expressively in performance and communication to create an impression of how you approach your world. Modes of shape change are also useful for creating warm-up and recuperation rituals.

Shape Forms

Shape forms, sometimes called still forms, are archetypes of common sil-houettes. They provide a basic look at how the body's form is organized or designed in ways that resemble well-known shapes. Fully realized shape forms are not common in everyday moving life, yet when they do appear they can be interesting and expressive.

The symbols for the five shape forms are shown in figure 5.8.

1. Pin: linear and elongated. Think of a diver sliding hands first into the water.
2. Wall: planar, wide, and flat. Think of a soccer goalie outstretched to make a save.
3. Ball: rounded and spherical. Think of the tight form of a gymnast in the tuck position dismounting from the uneven parallel bars.
4. Screw: spiral-like and twisted. Think of the lacrosse offender keeping the ball and stick away from a defender.
5. Tetrahedron: pyramidal, angular, four sided. Think of a defensive line waiting for the hike of the football.

As basic descriptions of the silhouette of the body, the shape forms are useful for getting a group of movers to look coherent. For example, in cheerleading, routines frequently incorporate pin-like, wall-like, and ball-like shapes when the flyers are soaring in the air. The clarity of these shapes gives the appearance of uniformity of movement, even when individual nuance is present in other aspects of the movement. When teaching beginning dancers, shape forms can anchor a complex movement phrase by giving dancers a clear objective for landing before moving again into the next complex sequence of actions. And although yoga doesn't use the specific language of Laban/Bartenieff Movement Analysis, the asanas and much of the cuing has a Shape-related emphasis.

The shape forms are often used to guide movers through Bartenieff-based movement phrases. For example, a core-distal opening-closing pattern might

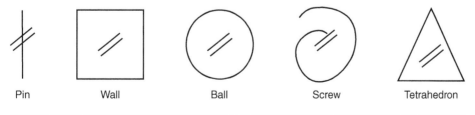

| Pin | Wall | Ball | Screw | Tetrahedron |

Figure 5.8   Shape form symbols.

be described as, "Be a wall on your back, close to a ball on your side, open to a wall on your side." Using the shape forms to instruct and guide movement gives movers a clear sense of the design and structure of the body.

Activity: Shape Forms

Each shape form contains the seeds of many possible associations. Form your body into one of the five shape forms, then live into it and let it speak to you by noticing associations that emerge from it. Bring this association to life in movement. For example, a pin-like shape could hold an association with a persnickety, tea-drinking grandmother. Or a wall-like shape could inspire the image of a bouncer at the door of a dance club, setting a boundary with his body.

KEY POINTS

- The shape forms describe basic archetypal silhouettes.
- The five shape forms are pin-like, wall-like, ball-like, screw-like, and tetrahedron-like.

Summary

The lens of the Shape category focuses on the form of the moving body by clarifying how its three-dimensional silhouettes morph and change. The five unique aspects of the Shape category are: opening and closing, shape flow support, shape qualities, modes of shape change, and shape forms. These allow you to answer questions about form and form change, for example: How is the form change supported from the inner "guts" of the body? Toward where is the form changing? How is the body changing shape? What are basic, archetypal forms? Study of the Shape category is useful to many movement pursuits, especially those interested in how the body looks or in accomplishing specific tasks, like throwing a ball. The Shape category is expressive and can highlight meaningful information on human relationships and perceptions of movement.

CHAPTER 6

Space

"Movement is, so to speak, living architecture—living in the sense of changing emplacements as well as changing cohesion."

(Laban 1974, 5)

A s you move through life, traveling from place to place during your day, your movement changes based on where you go. Notice where you are as you read these words. How is the spatial environment organized? Where are you in this space? How do you move through this space? How does it feel to be in this environment? The Space category is about how the body moves through its surroundings and how that movement "speaks"—how it is meaningful.

The following discussion of the Space category is organized from the general to the specific. The chapter begins with a look at the ways the body interacts with space and how it uses space to create rhythms of mobility and stability in movement. Next, the aspects of the chapter address the environment where movement happens and the space taken up by the body in that environment. Getting more specific, a discussion of the kinesphere addresses the movement sphere immediately surrounding the body and how the body moves through that imagined sphere. The chapter concludes with a brief look at Laban's space harmony pursuits.

Engaging with the Space Around You

Space is not empty; it is an alive partner, a collaborator in movement. Space stabilizes and mobilizes your body. You can engage with space in constant rhythms of inner and outer, and fluctuations of stability and mobility. As a partner in movement, the guy wires of space can hold you up and support your balance. You can also give up on a spatial investment and collapse into space. You can reveal space, indicating it, stirring it up, or pressing into it. Space can magnetize you and pull you into it. You move through space, traveling and locomoting to new places while riding and holding onto the invisible lines that run through it.

Just imagine: as the young being moves from the womb into the world, the space around the little body changes. The baby moves from a liquid and compressive environment to an airy environment of open space. The environment in this new world is different than it had been before. There are new potentials created by the surfaces on which the body rests and the gravity which keeps it on those surfaces. Gravity impels this little body downward. There is definitely up-ness and down-ness, and soon other directions too.

This sensitive, new body has three-dimensional inner space. As it experiences its inner space, it also experiences the space "out there" beyond its edges. This is a two-way tensegrity conversation, as the outer space also helps the little body feel its center and the spatial pulls inside of it. Now, there are new things to engage with, and the space keeps changing to new environments: a seat, a body, a nipple, a different body, a surface, a new surface. As the developing infant's awareness of their environment grows, they will be attracted to the environment—touching it, reaching or pressing into it, intending for objects in it, *and* will have aversions to it and feel the need to get away from smells, touch, temperature, and sounds that do not feel good. Even now the space is a vibrant and dynamic partner in movement.

The adult body, too, is activated by the spatial world around it. In space, Laban saw rhythms of exertion and recuperation, stabilization and mobilization as many moving bodies dealt with bipedal verticality, addressed the tasks of life, and expressed their inner workings. Watching adults move you will notice that the adult body is constantly moving in relationship to its environment, constantly engaging the space around it. Clearly, the adult body is affected by space, riding its lines of energy, and intending into space to meet its needs and satisfy its goals. It shifts slightly to alleviate the pressure from gravity, it changes level, it reaches out to something, it recoils away.

The following concepts were used by Laban to express relationships between the moving body and its spatial world. In each of these concepts, you can imagine that the inner body and outer space entwine. Imaginary lines of energy move through space, then through the body, and back out to space. Space attracts and magnetizes the body, pulling at and changing the spatial environment inside the body. The body moves into space, and the space moves in and through the body.

Spatial Pull

Spatial pulls are the infinite and invisible guy wires of space that guide movement, like lines of inherent potential energy running through space that are revealed by the moving body (Hackney 2002, 242). You can imagine spatial pulls as lines cording through the environment, penetrating the body and emerging on the other side (see figure 6.1). The body can invest in spatial tensions and ride these spatial pulls as one might ride a roller coaster, propelled into movement by the attracting or magnetizing forces on the body, or held stable and balanced by an equal investment in countertensions.

Spatial Tensions and Countertensions

"Spatial tensions are the springboards for mobility" (Bartenieff and Lewis 2002, 103). **Spatial tensions** are the investments the body makes in space. A **countertension** is an investment in space in an opposite direction. Movement is a continuous, gradual shifting of spatial tensions. You invest in and release spatial tensions to experience the stabilizing and mobilizing quality of space that "guarantees upright stability as well as continuous readiness to

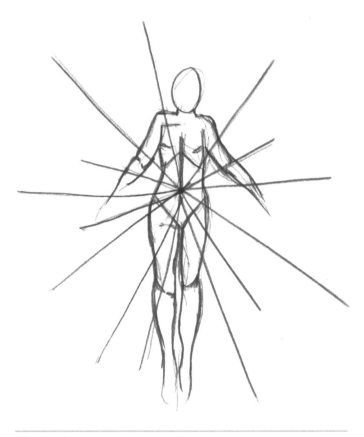

Figure 6.1   Body with spatial pulls.
Illustrated by Sydney P. Celio.

move in space" (Bartenieff and Lewis 2002, 103). Try investing in a spatial tension and then finding a countertension that brings you into stability. Then fully release one of them. Notice the mobility that comes as a result.

Spatial Intent

Spatial intent is aiming or intending to go toward space. It is about the mover's drive into the spatial world. The mover's intention in space clarifies the action.

In human motor development, spatial intent emerges from the desire to get something—to "go for it." Spatial intent organizes the infant's developing body around what it wants. As was discussed in chapter 3, desire organizes the neuromuscular system around the goal and leads to realizing new movement patterns and techniques. In older children and adults, spatial intent typically emerges from the desire to go somewhere or reach something.

Spatial intent can result in unconscious movement, or it can be executed deliberately to increase movement efficiency and balance and to develop the sophisticated fluctuations of stability and mobility common in virtuosic movement. One example of this in dance is an arabesque. Sending the limbs into space with clear spatial intent imparts the sense that space is holding the body up. Releasing or further investing in spatial intent in one area will create movement. Try it out! You will also see athletes whose fully committed intent into space to catch a ball enables them to ride into space with controlled, thrilling mobility. Had they invested in the spatial intent in a counter pull they would have stayed much more anchored to stability.

Spatial intent clarifies the pathway of movement in space and improves efficient functioning. To perform a squat in basic strength training, imagine spatial intent in the sitz bones: On the descent, the right sitz bone moves with intention toward right back low, and the left to left back low. For the ascent, the spatial intent toward forward high through the pelvic floor returns the body to stand.

Trace Forms

The ethereal nature of movement leaves behind invisible remnants. Trace forms are the invisible lines that remain from the pathway of the movement—like the condensation trails left by aircraft exhaust. Trace forms are made visible when people play with sparklers on holidays and in slow-shutter photography that captures the trails left behind by moving objects.

Laban saw trace forms as the intersection of Body, Space, and Shape. He wrote that the architecture of movement "is created by human movements and is made up of pathways tracing shapes in space" (Laban 1974, 5). Trace forms leave evidence of the shape and pathway of the body in the ether (see figure 6.2).

Figure 6.2   Body with trace forms.
Illustrated by Sydney P. Celio.

Key Points

- Space mobilizes and stabilizes the human body. You can deliberately engage with Space to support your movement.
- Spatial pulls are the invisible guy wires that you can metaphorically "ride" to mobilize movement.
- Spatial intent is the desire or intention to move a certain way that patterns and organizes your movement.

- Trace forms are like the contrails of movement left behind in Space.
- The options for interacting and engaging with Space can pattern and organize your movement, increasing the potential for stability and mobility.

General Space and Personal Space

Movement happens within an environment. The environment influences the movement that occurs and people's perceptions of it. The term **general space** describes the place in which a movement event occurs. Said another way, when you look at a general space you are addressing the spatial context in which the movement happens—for example, a dance studio, a crowded city street, an unmarked path in a national forest, an office, or a construction site. Each of these environments suggests certain movements that are encouraged and others that are discouraged.

Personal space is defined as the space the body occupies. As you read this passage, your body is taking up space; the area it fills is your personal space. With just the information offered from a consideration of general space and personal space, you gain a sense of the body in a place, including scale, proportion, and location.

Imagine you are sightseeing. You walk into the entrance of a grand building. You notice that it is defined by specific spatial characteristics, including structural and design elements. You also notice how you feel in it, how you move through it, and what it reminds you of. As you tune your perceptions to this place, you notice that the general space seems to organize people's personal space, including how the bodies move through the space and how they engage with the environment immediately around them.

The Kinesphere

Laban developed a word for describing personal space: **kinesphere** (Laban 1974, 10). The kinesphere can be thought of as the movement bubble, or spherical space, that the body occupies without taking a step (see figures 6.3 and 6.4). It is "that part of space which can be reached with the extremities" (Laban 1974, 29). Laban often compared it to an aura, and like an aura, the kinesphere is always with you. If you take a step, your kinesphere goes with you (Laban 1974, 10). As you move, the space your body takes up changes, and your kinesphere grows, shrinks, morphs, and adjusts with these changes.

Figure 6.3   Kinesphere symbol.

The concept of kinesphere comes to life as you move through the different spaces of your world, your kinesphere traveling with you to each new place. Paying attention to kinesphere brings insight into the general movement patterns of an environment. Kinesphere reveals personal and cultural preferences, and makes it easier to understand and adapt to different situations.

Although the kinesphere is the most general way to talk about the sphere of movement around the body, there are further distinctions within the concept that can lend insight to movement, including size of the kinesphere, various locations within the kinesphere, and how the body moves through and reveals its kinesphere.

Psychological Kinesphere

The **psychological kinesphere** is the space a person pays attention to or identifies as their own, and that they fill with their energy (Peggy Hackney, conversation with author, March 3, 2018). Like the physical kinesphere, the psychological kinesphere grows and shrinks based on how much of the space a person recognizes and claims as theirs (figure 6.5). Psychological kinesphere lends itself to interpretation, and thus is less concrete than other aspects of the Space category; however, it can be useful for coaching performers and describing your perceptions of a psychological attitude.

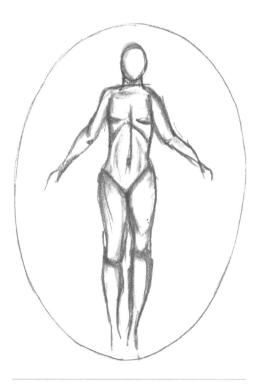

Figure 6.4   The kinesphere.
Illustrated by Sydney P. Celio.

To connect to the experience of a large psychological kinesphere, imagine you are camping alone. You are in your tent and hear an unusual noise outside that is likely a squirrel but could be something else! You begin paying attention to every sound made in what seems like the entire woods, as if you could hear and sense everything that was happening all around you for miles. It is as if you have expanded your sense of the sphere around you to psychologically encompass a very large range. In the case of a small psychological kinesphere, now imagine you are on an airplane and want to keep to yourself and eventually doze off. In order to let the neighbors in the nearby seats know you are not there for conversation, you draw your sense of what is yours to be very small and inwards toward yourself, as if to say "this is my space, and only this. I am not interested in what is beyond my thoughts and sensations."

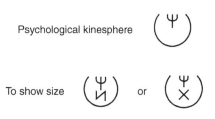

Figure 6.5   Psychological kinesphere.

Shared Kinesphere

Each individual has his or her own kinesphere; however, you can share your kinesphere with another. Sharing a kinesphere happens when the movement space of one person's kinesphere entwines with one or more others' kinespheres. Shared kinespheres are common in dance, for example in contact improvisations, or with close and intimate companions.

Reflect on where and with whom you share your kinesphere. What does it feel like to do so? When have you felt that someone shared or tried to share your kinesphere when you had not invited them to do so?

Reach Space, or Size of the Kinesphere

One aspect of kinesphere to consider is its size. If you pull your limbs in close to your body, you most likely have decreased your reach space; you could say you made your kinesphere smaller. If you then extended your limbs out away from the torso, you have increased your reach space and made your kinesphere larger. Organized like nesting Matryoshka dolls or concentric spheres, the size of the kinesphere reflects the extent of reach space the movement occurs in immediately around the body. The size of the kinesphere ranges from close to the body's center to as far out as the limbs can possibly extend.

The sphere of movement can be very small, small, medium, large, and very large—also known traditionally as very near, near, middle, far, and very far reach space (see figure 6.6; Hackney 2002, 223).

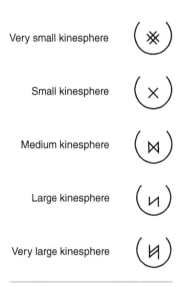

Very small: defined by the concentric sphere located at and just beyond the skin

Small: defined as the concentric sphere at the distance of the proximal joints

Medium: defined as the concentric sphere at the distance of mid-limb (elbows and knees)

Large: defined as the concentric sphere at the distance of the distal limbs when outstretched

Very large: defined as the concentric sphere at the farthest edge of one's reach space

Imagine how the bodies in an environment like a crowded city subway may have to occupy

Figure 6.6   Reach space symbols.

a near (small) reach space to accommodate the cramped quarters and the other bodies sharing the train. It may be very different from that of someone who is alone on a mountain summit, whose far (large) reach space would include taking in the expansive view with outstretched arms and legs. Also notice when movement is incongruent with these community norms. Are there times when a large kinesphere would be appropriate on a crowded subway?

Levels, Zones, and Super Zones of the Kinesphere

There are ways in Laban/Bartenieff Movement Analysis to specifically map where in the kinesphere movement occurs. These include the use of levels, zones, and super zones.

Levels

The kinesphere is divisible by level or altitude: high, middle, and low (see figures 6.7 and 6.8; Laban 1974, 12-13).

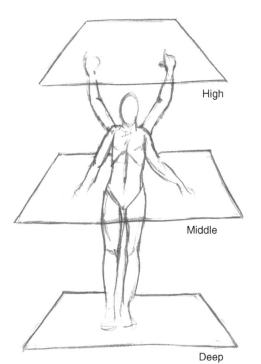

High is associated with the area from the sternum up.

Middle is associated with the level of the belly button.

Low (sometimes referred to as deep) is associated with the area below the pelvis.

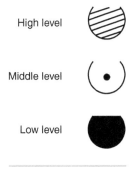

High level

Middle level

Low level

Figure 6.7   Body with kinesphere and levels.
Illustrated by Sydney P. Celio.

Figure 6.8   Level symbols.

L/BMA in Your World: Teaching L/BMA in Japan
Yuko Hashimoto, CMA, PhD

I teach L/BMA to students training to be physical education teachers in Japan. Through the teaching experience and from students' feedback, I am convinced of the importance of sharing the Laban/Bartenieff perspective to this population. Many students who want to become P.E. teachers think that movement equals sports, and that learning is done by mimicking the teacher. The students know about the movements in their favorite sports, but they do not know how to talk about movement. As students learn to regard movement through the Laban/Bartenieff lens, I notice that their movement choices change, especially how they look at and understand movement. What they consider and can identify in movement expands. Their understanding becomes much wider to include movement in human life. Students also gain confidence in their own movement beyond their favorite sports; they get better at observing movement and are able to teach others about it with a more useful vocabulary.

Zones

Zones are the regions of the kinesphere easily accessed by the corresponding limbs. "The zones of the kinesphere become apparent and are felt at the moment when they are touched by the moving body" (Laban 1974, 29). For example, the zone of the right leg when standing would include the regions of right, low-to-middle, and front and back (Moore 2014, 102). The zones are defined by up/down (sometimes referred to as high, middle, and low), right/left, and forward/back.

The zones provide information about places within the kinesphere that are frequently visited, and those that are less visited. Consider the zones you visit. For example, if you are a sous chef at a restaurant, and chopping vegetables is part of your preparation, you likely spend a lot of time with your hands in the forward middle zone. Move to this place. What does it feel like to have your hands here? What comes to mind in this zone? What other activities could take you there? Typing. Feeding your infant. How do you organize your guts to feel supported in this familiar place? Now go to an unfamiliar zone within your kinesphere. What associations emerge here?

What does it feel like to be here? How do you organize your guts to feel supported in this unfamiliar place? Try moving between the familiar and unfamiliar zones.

Super Zones

The super zones describe an area like a zone, except less frequently visited. Super zones happen when a limb goes beyond its "normal" or anatomical range. For example, a downward dog in a yoga class gives the right leg access to the high level when it reaches toward the ceiling (a super zone for the leg) (Groff 1990).

Spatial Matrix

The **spatial matrix** is the symbol system used to clarify where in the kinesphere movement happens and how it moves through the kinesphere. It is like a symbolic map of the kinesphere that illustrates specific areas that have been studied and explored within the Laban/Bartenieff community. The components of the spatial matrix allow you to get specific about how movement happens in the sphere around the body.

Direction Symbols

These symbols demarcate where movement occurs in relation to the center of the kinesphere. They indicate the direction of the movement. Each of these symbols emerges from "place," a central point demarcated by the rectangle (see figure 6.9).

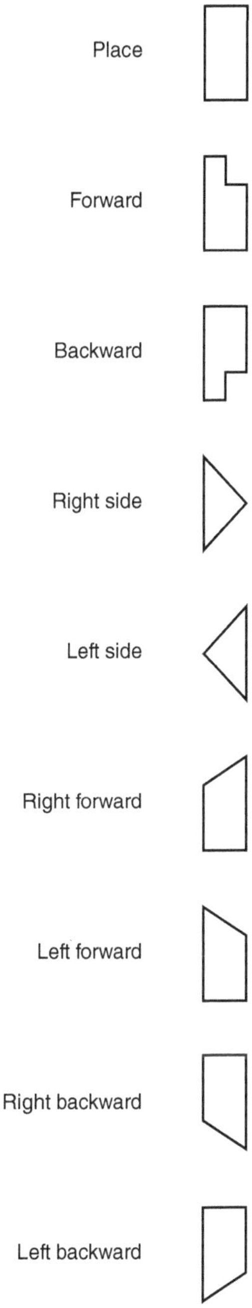

Level Symbols

Each direction symbol can be shaded in to provide information about a movement's altitude or level (see figure 6.10).

　　Low: indicated by solid shading

　　Middle: indicated by a dot, or "belly button"

　　High: indicated by slash marks

Place

Forward

Backward

Right side

Left side

Right forward

Left forward

Right backward

Left backward

Figure 6.9   Direction symbols.

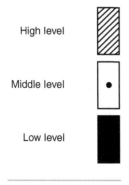

High level

Middle level

Low level

Figure 6.10   Level symbols.

The details from above come together to form the whole spatial matrix which features 27 symbols for specific points and corresponding spatial pulls of the kinesphere (see figure 6.11). You will notice the symbols contain information on right/left, forward/back, and level. These 27 points are the basis for further space information including dimensions, planes, and diagonals, and the crystalline forms Laban was interested in that formed the architecture of his movement scales.

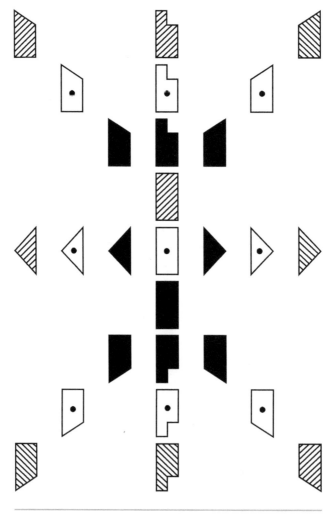

Figure 6.11   Sample of whole directional matrix.

Activity: Learning Spatial Matrix Symbols

To learn the spatial matrix, draw the symbols on a large piece of paper such as a sheet of blank newsprint. Make them large enough to accommodate your body. Stand on the symbol for place to locate yourself in the center of this kinesphere. Then add the symbols for forward and back, side and side, and right forward, right back, left back, and left forward. Again, stand on the symbol for place, then move in the different directions you have drawn, and visualize the connections. Next, add altitude information to your drawing. Again, stand in the middle. This time run through part of a favorite activity, and notice what symbols would "light up" as you pass through them. Throughout the exploration keep your hips (anterior superior iliac spines) aligned with place and facing forward. If you turn your hips, you have turned your front and will be moving to a new front.

L/BMA in Your World: Dancing and Choreography

Susan Barnard

I am a dancer and choreographer. Since studying the L/BMA material and becoming a Certified Movement Analyst, I have grown acutely aware of my own and others' physical and psychological kinesphere. It reveals so much about a person's feeling state as well as about how one likes to express him- or herself.

As a dancer and choreographer, I know that varying the physical kinesphere changes the intent in the piece. If a movement encompasses more space through a far reach kinesphere, both locomotor and nonlocomotor, it may appear more intense, more fully stated, more "in your face." Likewise, varying the psychological space could imply more introversion or extroversion. Does the dancer want to be seen or not? Just change the psychological kinesphere.

Recently I choreographed a piece, *Mortared with Love,* that used American Sign Language as a base. Throughout the piece, we built three walls that moved back and forth upstage. We used a large physical and psychological kinesphere combined with direct Space effort. In contrast, the three sections that lay between the walls employed a softer and varied-size approach. These were purposeful choices regarding kinesphere, and they show how spatial intent and kinesphere size can significantly impact the emotional tone of a piece.

Approaches to Kinesphere

Approaches to kinesphere, sometimes used synonymously with the term *spatial tensions*, describe the pathway of a movement through the kinesphere (see figure 6.12; Bartenieff and Lewis 2002, 107).

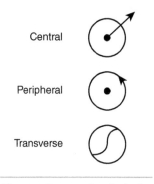

Central

Peripheral

Transverse

Central: Like a radiating line of energy, in a central approach, movement radiates or penetrates between the center and the edge.

Peripheral: As though creating an edge, in a peripheral approach, movement travels along a consistent distance from the center of the body.

Transverse: Similar to "stirring the pot," in a transverse approach, movement cuts between the center of the body and the edge of the kinesphere.

Figure 6.12   Symbols for approaches to kinesphere.

Approaches to kinesphere are useful for coaching athletes and dancers to clarify how a movement progresses through the space around the body. For example, you want to help your cheerleading team clarify the pathway of the arms, and you want them to clearly reveal the edge of the space around their bodies, so you may ask them to use a peripheral approach to their kinesphere, yet they also are specific into themselves.

Activity: Exploring Your Kinesphere

Use approaches to kinesphere as a metaphor to think about how you engage with aspects of your life. What does it feel like to be on the periphery of an event? What does it feel like to pierce through the center of an issue? What does it feel like to "stir the pot" or traverse through a forest?

Exploring the Kinesphere

You can get a sense of how movement speaks by exploring the associations and metaphors of your kinesphere. For example, the high zone can be associated with celebration, worship, achievement, and power. Language suggests this with phrases like "He ascended to power," or "She is going up in the standings," or "Rise up in praise." Similarly, the low zone can indicate depression, loss, and weakness with phrases like "The poll numbers are getting low," or "She is down in the dumps," or "I am at the bottom of the pecking order."

The right and left sides of the kinesphere are often used to indicate political alignment and values. On a personal level, consider what you do on the right side of your kinesphere that is different from what you do on your left. As a right-handed tennis player, you may prefer a forehand to a backhand, but you target your opponent in a way that forces them to hit a backhand.

The forward and back zones of the kinesphere can be associated with the passing of time. For example, the forward zone is generally understood as the future, while the backward zone is the past—if one moves from the past into the future they are said to travel forward. This association is present in language through phrases like "Back when we were kids," or "The past is behind me," or "Looking ahead to tomorrow's forecast."

Metaphorical associations are made visible in our everyday conversations with gestures that reference spatial connotations and suggest patterns of thought. As you did in the earlier exercise in which you mapped the kinesphere while performing a familiar activity, you could also map the kinesphere during a conversation and gain insight into how use of the kinesphere leaves subtle impressions about someone's values and emotions and influences the mood of the interaction. For example, imagine you are talking to a co-worker who continually gestures toward place high when they speak about your shared boss; you may start to realize that this person has linked place high with power. Other aspects of their movement, like effort choices that come together with the place high gesture, may give you the impression that this person holds resentment and ill-feelings toward people in power.

Kinesphere can illuminate the expectations of the social world around you. Different social settings have unique assumptions about what is appropriate and what is out of place. Knowing about kinesphere will guide your understanding of what a situation expects of you. Kinesphere may be useful in observing a character who seems out of place or who is acting differently than would be expected; the size or approach to kinesphere may be part of what seems unusual. Observing a peripheral approach to kinesphere may leave you feeling as though your colleague is setting a boundary, or waiving a boundary normally adhered to.

Certain activities carry preferences and styles for moving in and through the kinesphere. Bring to mind a favorite activity: squash, hip-hop, basketball, gardening, rock climbing. Imagine yourself engaging in this activity and your kinesphere lighting up in the various zones as your body moves through them. What zones light up regularly during the activity? What zones stay relatively dark? Are there super zones? What approaches to kinesphere are present?

Finally, connecting to your kinesphere can give you options for your rhythms of exertion and recuperation; nothing feels better after hours of sitting in a plane, occupying a small kinesphere, than stretching and enlarging your personal movement bubble, your kinesphere, as much as possible!

- Space is expressive!
- Movement is influenced by the spatial environment in which it happens.
- The kinesphere is a term Laban developed to describe the sphere of movement around the body that one can occupy without taking a step. It is one's movement bubble.
- You can get specific about kinesphere, including describing its size, where in the kinesphere movement is happening, and how the body reveals the kinesphere and moves through it.
- The spatial matrix maps specific points in the kinesphere.

The Body in Space

Laban drew from many disciplines, including mathematics and architecture, to develop his perspectives on human movement. He saw Space as an imaginary architecture that stabilizes and mobilizes the body. As the body moves through space, stability and mobility are in constant fluctuation. Laban noticed that specific spatial pulls evoked feelings and potentials for mobility and stability, and that it was possible to organize movement by deliberately riding spatial pulls.

Directions, Dimensions, and More

Laban was specifically interested in mapping how the body uses and moves through the Space around itself. A significant portion of his inquiry into Space involved applying principles of geometry to the moving body. Thus, he aligned the center of the human body with the center of the cross of axis—his term for the point at which the three cardinal dimensions intersect. He then sought pathways and patterns of movement from this perspective. This section defines these aspects of the Space category.

Cross of Axis

The **cross of axis** is the intersection of the three cardinal dimensions.

Directions and Dimensions

A **direction** is a line in space that is one end of a dimension, like up, or right. A **dimension** (see figure 6.13) is a line in space with one spatial pull in two directions, like on an X, Y, or Z axis.

The vertical dimension is up/down. The sagittal dimension is forward/back. The horizontal dimension is side/side. The dimensions form the internal

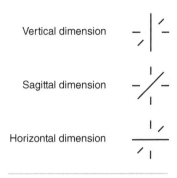

Vertical dimension

Sagittal dimension

Horizontal dimension

Figure 6.13   Dimension symbols.

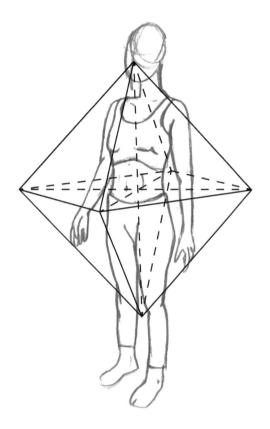

infrastructure of the octahedron, and when applied to a human body highlight the three-dimensional nature of the body and human movement (see figure 6.14).

Planes

A **plane** is a flat surface containing two unequal spatial pulls (cardinal planes). The vertical plane is mostly up/down with some side/side. The sagittal plane is mostly

Figure 6.14   Dimensions applied to the human body and connected to one another to form an octahedron.

forward/back with some up/down. The horizontal plane is mostly side/side with some forward/back (see figure 6.15). Laban believed the planes corresponded with the generic shape of the human body (see figure 6.16). A **diameter** is a line in space connecting the opposite corners of a plane with two unequal spatial pulls (also see figure 6.16).

The planes form the internal infrastructure of another crystalline form. If you connect the corners of each the result will be the form known as an icosahedron (see figure 6.17).

Diagonal

A **diagonal** is a line in space with three equal spatial pulls. There are four diagonals that form the internal infrastructure of the cube (see figure 6.18).

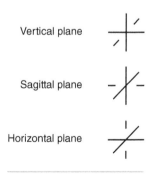

Vertical plane

Sagittal plane

Horizontal plane

Figure 6.15   Plane symbols.

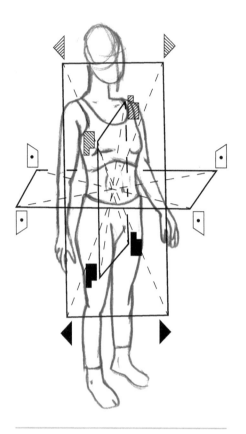

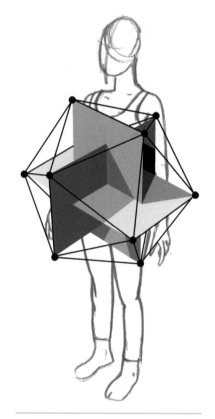

Figure 6.16   Body with planes and diameters.

Figure 6.17   Body with the corners of the planes linked to form an icosahedron. This, like other crystalline forms, can grow and shrink. In this image it is smaller, but it could be larger encompassing the whole body and the farthest reach space.

Spiral

A **spiral** is a line in space with three spatial pulls that change unequally.

The perspective of dimensions, planes, diagonals, etc., clarifies where in the body's immediate surroundings movement is happening. In this aspect of the Space category, the term *spatial pull* describes the number of spatial tensions acting on the lines in space based on principles of geometry. Laban believed that the number of spatial pulls present in a movement affected the rhythms of stability and mobility. He observed that as the number of spatial pulls increases, so does the body's mobility and potential mobility.

You can explore stability and mobility in relationship to dimensions, planes, diagonals, etc., by imagining the center of your body as the center of the cross of axis. Explore moving through the dimensions in any order (Laban had specific ordering and sequences he was interested in). See what moving through the dimensions feels like in your body. Consider where you enact them in your life, what they offer to you as a mover. You can do the same for the planes: cycle along the flat surface of a plane, or move from the corner of one plane to the corner of another. Where are these present in your life? A left hook in boxing skims the horizontal plane. A jumping jack cycles the vertical plane. Finally, try moving along a diagonal pull, as though you are standing in a cube and are moving from one corner

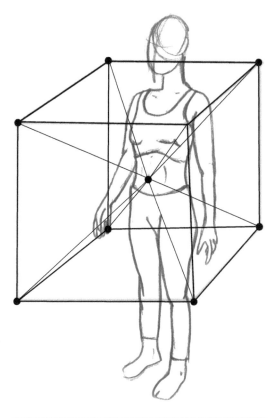

Figure 6.18   Body with diagonals; forming internal infrastructure of cube.

diagonally, along three equally changing spatial pulls, to the opposite corner. Notice how the rhythms of stability and mobility feel different to you as you ride the different rhythms of the spatial pulls. Perhaps they elicit a specific feeling or physical memory.

The Dynamosphere

Moving through the spatial world is a dynamic and energetic experience. Laban described the effortful energetic movement through the kinesphere as the **dynamosphere**. "The study of movement deals with the spatial order of the paths which the limbs make in the kinesphere, and also with the connection between outer movement and the mover's inner attitude. This attitude is not only shown in the choice of a certain path or the employment of a certain limb, but is also characterized by the choice of dynamic stresses" (Laban 1974, 27). For example, a boxer punches to left, side, middle crystalizing into an action drive moment or strong, quick, and direct effort. A poet scans the distance, moving through the horizontal plane as she traces where sea meets sky with her fingers, using light, direct, and bound attention passing through spell drive.

Laban perceived that Space and Effort frequently came together, and that the coming together yielded recurring associations, or affinities, between some regions of the kinesphere and certain types of Effort. He understood that there were no rules, and that different efforts could manifest anywhere in the kinesphere, yet he saw these specific correlations between Space and Effort as harmonic movement.

The dimensions, planes, and diagonals form the "bones" or internal infrastructure of the platonic solids that Laban studied in space harmony theory. He also prescriptively layered Effort into his scale investigations of space. Many fabulous resources for further investigation into this aspect of Laban's research are listed below.

Space Harmony

Laban's study of **space harmony** emerged in part from his interest in the natural sequences of movement in everyday life. He observed themes and patterns of movement in space in different movement disciplines and aspects of human life including sport, work, and performance. As part of this study he developed prescriptive sequences of movement, some that echoed common phrases he saw in movement and others that challenged common phrases and brought new possibilities to the moving body. This prescriptive ordering of movements was informed by putting the moving body inside platonic solids and moving through them in specific ways, sometimes with specific efforts. These are known as **scales**, like scales that a musician would practice. Each scale has specific sequences for placement of the body and for pathways to those placements. The sequences and use of space create unique experiences and associations. This material has been well documented by many others. It is beyond the scope and focus of this text, but it is highly suggested that you review the following resources for more information.

Bartenieff, Irmgard, with Dori Lewis. *Body Movement: Coping with the Environment*. New York: Routledge, 1980.

Laban, Rudolf von. *Choreutics*. Annotated and edited by Lisa Ullman. London: Macdonald and Evans, 1966.

Laban, Rudolf von. Ed. Lisa Ullmann. *The Language of Movement: A Guidebook to Choreutics*. Boston: Plays Inc., 1971.

Laban, Rudolf von, with Lisa Ullmann. *The Mastery of Movement*. 3rd ed. Boston: Macdonald and Evans, 1971.

Moore, Carol-Lynne. *The Harmonic Structure of Movement, Music, and Dance According to Rudolf Laban: An Examination of His Unpublished Writings and Drawings.* Lewiston NY: Edwin Mellen Press, 2009.

Preston-Dunlop, Valerie. *Point of Departure: A Dancer's Space.* 2nd ed. London UK: Dance Books, 2008.

Space in Everyday Life

The needs of everyday life pattern the body in specific spatially motivated ways: Typing at a computer is typically done in forward middle, and retrieving fruit from the bottom drawer of the refrigerator would mean reaching to forward low. Based on what you understand about movement in space you may want to reimagine how you design and create the spaces in which you live to consider your movement preferences and desires. Perhaps you want your space to offer options for movement, or you want your space to focus your attention. Perhaps you place a standing desk near a window to watch the street, or perhaps you have a horizontal surface to rest on in the middle of your space. Or perhaps you divide items that you frequently reach for between low and high shelves to encourage you to move to different levels throughout your day.

Space clarifies and organizes movement. Space-related cues are common ways to communicate movement. Think of instructions for movement like "bring your arm up," "chest forward," or "shoulders down." Directions like these orient your body in the spatial world. You can also track where you tend to move frequently, and places you access less often. Visiting the lesser-known places in your kinesphere can challenge and enliven your movement. Try moving to back low with the left arm. As you do this, keep the arm soft and supple, hollow the core for support, and let the tail reach to shift your weight. Notice how it feels to organize your body around a spatial position that is less familiar. If you play sports or dance, many of the technical skills associated with different movement disciplines include specific ways of moving through the space around the body often connected with approaches to kinesphere. Clarifying the pathways through space used in your specific interests can be very important to skill development and technique.

You can actively use space to support you. If you struggle with balance you can imagine space holding you up, or holding on to space as an extra support. You can also imagine sending parts of your body into space as a way of mobilizing the body and organizing your movement. For example, in order to move easily from sitting to standing, imagine your pubic bone riding a forward high spatial pull, while your feet root into the earth and your heels pull your pelvis forward and up. Irmgard Bartenieff worked brilliantly with this concept to mobilize her patients into movement they did not know they could do.

Trained dancers and athletes often have remarkable attunement to space. As you watch them you may feel as though you can see them riding and playing in space to create movement. Although their dynamic use of space may be unconscious to them, it makes them pliable, stable, and dynamic as space moves around and through them, and they around and through it.

Summary

The body moves through and reveals the space around it. To consider Space in general terms, you can describe where movement occurs and the Space occupied by the body. The kinesphere is the sphere of movement immediately surrounding the body. The concept of kinesphere allows you to map where movement happens in that sphere and the pathway it takes. You can also engage with space in specific ways, including riding spatial pulls and using spatial intent to mobilize and stabilize your movement.

CHAPTER

Phrasing

"The interplay between movement elements and sequence is the foundation of the tension and excitement of phrasing. Movement phrasing is a classic example of the whole being more than the sum of the parts."

(Levine 1986, 3)

You may have had the experience of witnessing two people doing the same sequence of movements, yet the two movers looked very different from one another. This was likely because of their unique ways of phrasing the movement. Phrasing, a less-developed part of the Laban/Bartenieff framework, allows you to see patterns and relationships in movement as they emerge and unfold over time. It also accounts for what is individually unique about movers performing the same sequence of actions.

This chapter will briefly introduce several aspects of phrasing relevant to the L/BMA lens, including defining what a phrase is, how a movement sequences within the body, how one thing becomes another in movement—that is, how the elements of BESS progress through a sequence, and where and how emphasis is placed within a phrase.

Phrase

Phrases are "perceivable units of movement that are in some sense meaningful" (Hackney 2000, 1). Phrases have a beginning, a middle, and an end. They also contain a through-line, like units of movement that are strung together. The beginning and end of a phrase are considered its boundaries or edges. Notice that within a phrase there is a sequence of actions—the sequence refers to the order in which the elements of movement occur.

Examining how phrases are described in other expressive disciplines can offer insight into how phrasing manifests in movement. In a written musical score, phrases are notated with a curved line over or under a series of notes, indicating that they are strung together. A phrase in writing would be a sentence or a clause in which a series of words is strung together to create meaning. A phrase in movement is much like these; it is a series of movements that is strung together and delivers an expressive and functional impression.

In Laban/Bartenieff Movement Analysis one option for writing a phrase is through a phrase bow (see figure 7.1). A phrase bow allows you to show that the elements inside of it are linked together as a meaningful unit of movement. The phrase bow is often used as a shorthand reminder of linkage and sequence as if to say *these things are linked together and happen in this sequence.*

Figure 7.1   Phrase bow.

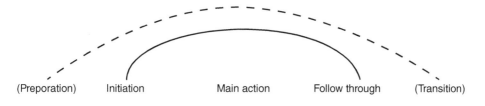

Figure 7.2   Phrase diagram.

Phases of a Phrase

Peggy Hackney has developed a model to outline the phases of a phrase (see figure 7.2). Before a phrase even begins, there is a moment of inner preparation in which thought processes organize around the action. The next phase is initiation—when the action begins, including where and how in the body it starts. Initiation takes the mover into the main action—the primary "what happens" of a movement phrase. The final phase is the follow-through, characterized by the phrase coming to an end. The transition is the pause or rest between one phrase and the next. This can also include the rebound or upbeat into the next phrase.

Activity: Practicing Phrase Boundaries

To practice recognizing phrases in movement, watch a movement event for what seems like it is coming together in a unified through-line. You may begin by saying "now" or "begin" and "end" every time a phrase begins or ends. You can also try sounding or singing phrases.

Phrase Length

Phrases have a duration of time, referred to as **phrase length**. Some phrases are relatively long, while others are short. You may notice someone's preferences around phrase length in movement; perhaps they have a propensity toward long or short phrases, or to form a repeated rhythm of a long phrase followed by a short phrase.

Phrase Patterning

Consecutive phrasing, when one phrase ends and another begins, is the clearest type of Phrasing to observe. Sometimes more than one phrase is happening at any given time. Or a new phrase begins before the prior one comes to its final end. This is called an **overlapping phrase**. Another phrase patterning option is **simultaneous phrasing** when different phrases happen at the same time within the same body—for example, when the right hand is executing one phrase while the lower body performs another (Maletic 1983).

Phrase length and phrase patterning are part of one's personal style and are essential to a comprehensive look at movement. Consider, for example, how an individual basketball player prepares for, shoots, and finishes a free throw. Clear phrasing, including clear beginnings and endings, organizes movement for full efficiency and dynamism. It patterns the neuromuscular system to fulfill its intent.

Effort Phrasing

Effort Phrases are a specific area of study within L/BMA that includes examining how efforts load, intensify, and change. Effort is in constant fluctuation, thus seeing and performing Effort phrasing takes practice. Like all phrases, effort phrases have boundaries and can be organized into beginning, middle, and end. You can look more specifically at effort phrasing by considering the sequencing of efforts within a phrase.

As described in chapter 4, loading and unloading happen when effort factors are added to or subtracted from an effort phrase. When an effort factor is added, the effort is said to be loading. When an effort factor is dropped, the effort is unloading. Loading and unloading involve shifts in a movement phrase's energetic statement, resulting in the presence of more or less energetic investment.

You will also experience a shift in energetic tone when efforts intensify within a phrase. This is like turning up or turning down the volume. Effort intensity can shift in all the efforts present in a movement, or it can happen in just one of the efforts. For example, a strong, free, quick passion drive could be amplified by adding intensity to all the efforts, or by adding intensity only to the strong Weight aspect of the effort. Accents can be imparted to effort phrases through the addition of Time and Weight, which gives the phrase emphasis.

Phrase Emphasis

This aspect of Phrasing is specific to effort and deals with where and how a phrase is energetically loaded. As discussed in chapter 4 (and reiterated above), Effort loads or unloads and intensifies or decreases in intensity. Looking at how Effort creates emphasis within a phrase allows you to get increasingly specific about how the energetic tones in movement crystallize or punctuate the statement. A thorough investigation of this aspect of Phrasing is beyond the scope of this text; however, it is worth briefly addressing.

Within a phrase of movement, the loading and intensifying of Efforts create emphasis. In phrase emphasis, you are dealing with *where* within a phrase emphasis is placed. A phrase could have no emphasis, it could have a consistent emphasis, or it could have an emphasis in the beginning, the middle, or the end. For example:

- In an **even-emphasis phrase**, an energetic shift may occur, but it repeats in a way that marks the whole phrase as having a consistent level of energy.
- In a **beginning-emphasis phrase**, the beginning of the phrase is energetically the most loaded.
- In a **middle-emphasis phrase**, the middle of the phrase is energetically the most loaded.
- In an **end-emphasis phrase**, the end of the phrase is energetically the most loaded.
- In a **multi-emphatic phrase**, emphasis happens in multiple places throughout the phrase.

KEY POINTS

- Phrases are a unit of movement with a through-line. They usually have a beginning, middle, and end.
- Movement phrases often happen one after another, though multiple phrases can be present within the same body at the same time. Phrases have varying lengths.
- Within a phrase, emphasis may be placed at the beginning, middle, or end, or be even. Each of these possibilities colors the expressive and functional nature of the movement. The study of effort phrases specifically addresses how the energetic tones in a phrase shift throughout the phrase.

Sequences of BESS Elements

Phrasing also addresses how specific elements of Body, Effort, Shape, and Space come together and dissolve. Making a list of all the BESS elements within a movement event may provide a sense of what is happening in that event, but a list is limited to a series of moment-to-moment stills and thus does not allude to how the moments are linked. Understanding the sequencing of BESS within a phrase allows you to look at how elements of movement appear and disappear, and come together in meaningful statements.

Within a phrase of movement containing a beginning, a middle, and an end, the aspects of BESS change throughout the course of the movement. The framework of BESS provides the elements of movement. The sequencing is how those elements come together and dissolve in ways that give a phrase its expressive and functional life. Phrasing involves "keeping both elements and sequence in continual relation to each other" (Levine 1986, 1).

Imagine that your colleague has a preference for long phrases—in both speech and movement. In a recent budget meeting, one of his shorter phrases catches your attention for its length and the specific sequence of BESS information contained within it. The phrase begins with retreating and spreading using direct, free, and sustained vision drive, and then moves into a direct, strong, stable state with spoking as he places his finger in a forward middle position on the updated budget. It ends as he looks at you with a direct, sustained, and bound-flow vision drive as he advances in his torso. This phrase and sequence of movements within it feels especially important to you, as though he is saying he has seen the big picture and made his decision, and wants you to know that the vision is set and it is not about either one of you.

Phrasing is related to pattern recognition. As you look at the sequencing of BESS within phrases you will not be able to pick up on everything that is happening. Movement is simply too complex. You will, however, begin to recognize patterns within phrases. Important phrase patterns repeat and reveal themselves over time. Perhaps one person ends her phrases with passive, heavy Weight Effort, while another person begins his by hollowing and retreating with indirect Space Effort.

How BESS progresses within the boundaries of a phrase will influence the evocative and expressive nature of the movement, and may impact its functional outcomes. A baseball pitcher may need to shift his sequence of BESS in order to throw a faster curve ball. A trial attorney may notice that her points are lost when she ends her phrases with indirect sustainment and underlying shape flow as a mode of shape change; as the phrase ends, she drops her gaze towards place low.

Sequences of Movement Within the Body

The sequencing of movement through the body is another lens of Phrasing. This aspect of Phrasing was important to Irmgard Bartenieff, who believed that bodily strength arose from the phrasing of muscular actions more than from muscular hypertrophy (Hackney 2002, 48). Working with sequences of movement within and through the body has been addressed in earlier chapters more fully, but it is important to revisit here.

L/BMA in Your World: Reflections
Peggy Hackney

As a young dance student who knew L/BMA, I felt empowered to really perceive the movement in my own body as I was being taught a dance sequence. I was what was called a "quick study." I could easily follow along with the movement of the teacher or another student, and then I could repeat it. Or I could play with it improvisationally. I could make it mine. I could do this because I was not simply look-ing at the outward form or Shape of the movement. I knew the basic elements that made up the combination: how it could be organized in terms of sequencing in body connectivity, or dynamic phrasing of effort, rhythm, or spatial pulls. This in turn let me create material on the spot. L/BMA was like a magic tool for instant choreographic play!

Simultaneous, Successive, and Sequential

Within a larger phrase, movement initiates and moves through the body in observable and patterned ways. This aspect of phrasing was covered in chapter 3 as simultaneous, successive, and sequential body-part phrasing. It addresses questions such as: Where in the body does movement initiate? How does it move through the body?

Yield and Push, Reach and Pull

The phrase of yield and push, and reach, grasp, and pull (now called basic neurocellular patterns by Bonnie Bainbridge Cohen) represent other phrases important in L/BMA (figure 7.3). The ability for the body to set up and follow through in sequences of yielding to pushing to reaching to pulling establishes patterns of movement throughout the body and in relationship to the world around it. These patterns, in turn, produce mobility and locomotion into space (see chapter 3 for more information).

Summary

Phrasing is a relatively new and still-developing territory for Laban/Bartenieff Movement Studies, though its importance to the perception of movement cannot be overstated. Phrasing organizes what is happening in movement

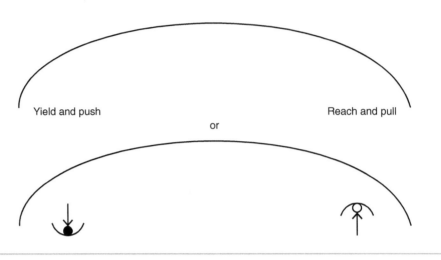

Figure 7.3   Yield and push, reach and pull phrasing.

through time. A phrase, a unit of movement that has a through-line, and a beginning, middle, and end, contains duration, change, and relationships between aspects of BESS. The specific approaches to looking at phrases include examining their length, patterning, and emphasis. Effort phrases are a specific study within Phrasing that address how Efforts change within a phrase to give it energetic shifts, including loading, unloading, and intensity. Finally, Phrasing also includes the sequencing of Body, Effort, Shape, and Space over time; the different elements of BESS come together in specific ways to create movement and the sequencing of movement through the body. The ability to look at change through the lens of Phrasing allows you to address the complex and constantly morphing nature of human movement.

PART III

INTEGRATING AND APPLYING BESS

While reading in part II about basic bodily actions and the categories of Body, Effort, Shape, Space, and Phrasing, you likely noticed that although the focus of each chapter was on a single aspect of movement, the other categories are also present in any movement event. So far in this book you've been encouraged to keep the categories separate from one another, but now that you have a sense of each individual category, you can begin to integrate them to gain a more comprehensive understanding of human movement.

In this phase of your learning, when you look at, describe, or perform movement you will weave together what you see from one category with what you see from another—for example, you might use a statement such as "She was rising with lightness and quickness." By doing so, you obtain more information about what is happening in the moving body.

In movement, different aspects of BESS constantly come together and dissolve. Human movement can be described through ever-changing and sequencing constellations of BESS. How BESS layers and phrases from one moment to the next gives movement its unique and nuanced coloring. And how you uniquely organize and phrase BESS provides the distinctive movement preferences that make your movement specifically yours. In some cases, these constellations may form a body attitude, the repeating patterns and clusters of BESS that seem like a habitual attitude of your body. In other cases, you will experience surprising and unconventional constellations of BESS. Either way, you have the tools and skills to explore it all.

Integrating BESS allows for a greater understanding of the personal aspects of movement. Two people could fold their arms across their chest or bend over to tie their shoes; however, that simple explanation of the action does not give a complete or even detailed picture of what was happening in terms of movement. Having more information—about, for example, the Effort life, the modes of Shape change, and the body-part phrasing involved—could yield a very different interpretation that is both personal and context-specific to the same general action.

As you set out to integrate Body, Effort, Shape, Space, and Phrasing there are several things to keep in mind:

1. **Go back to the movement.** Movement is complex and constantly changing. Integrating BESS can get murky and confusing, but sticking with it leads to greater clarity and understanding. When you are unsure, go back to the movement. Do it, notice what you think is there, and then clarify your definitions in relationship to the movement. Ask yourself if what you think was there really was there. Use the movement itself to help you understand what is important in the movement and what is not. Talk yourself through it. Sing the phrasing and the emphasis of what you are doing.

2. **Make choices about what is important and what is not.** As you weave together information from BESS, you will notice that each of the categories is always present in some way. You are always in a Body. There is always form and a change in form that comes from Shape. You are always in Space and engaging with Space in some way, and there is always an energetic investment or Effort, even if it is very muted. When you observe and describe movement through an L/BMA lens, you will not be able to address every category at one time. Instead, decide on what is important. Some things will be more important than others, not everything that occurs will be important, and some things that are not happening will be important to note. The choices you make about what is important may differ from someone else's choices. As you gain skill with integrating BESS, you will want to develop consistency with your community so that you can agree upon accuracy. At the same time, you will want to contribute your unique perspective on how movement is meaningful.

3. **Clarify how each category is unique and what it brings.** Integration and layering are possible when the elements coming together are understood as distinct from each other. Early in the learning process you were urged to dive into each category and learn it for itself, without confusing it with the contents of another category. You likely noticed that there were likenesses between categories: An aspect of one category could evoke a movement experience that was similar to an aspect of another category, or an aspect of one category frequently shows up with an aspect of another category. Despite similarities among some aspects of BESS, each category focuses on a distinct facet of movement. Going to movement to tease out the differences between the categories and their aspects will help you recognize what each category covers and what it does not.

4. **Consider the Guiding Concepts and Organizing Themes.** Chapter 2 discussed basic Organizing Themes and Guiding Concepts of Laban/Bartenieff Movement Studies. As you weave all of BESS together, patterns will emerge that connect to these bigger-picture ideas. Use them to organize your perceptions and foster new understandings of movement.

5. **Reconnect to the Context.** Movement happens in a context. Without a context, or situation, the meaning and importance does not have grounding in the world. Continually bringing your awareness back to the context in which movement happens allows you to see it from a larger perspective and to weave the *what* and *how* with *where*, to anchor the movement in lived experience.

In the following chapters, you will be introduced to ways to use this material in your life, and you will learn about how others apply L/BMA in their work and lives. The ability to integrate and layer Body, Effort, Shape, and Space is fundamental to discovering the richness possible from the application of L/BMA to one's life.

Using Laban/ Bartenieff Movement Analysis in Your Life

"It is not enough to know what the goals are. One must understand the options from which to choose . . . and the strengths and weaknesses of those options. The deeper the understanding, the more power we have over our own movement and relationship to the world in which we move."

(Bartenieff 1979)

*A*s you gain new ways of seeing and making sense of movement, you will likely use Laban/Bartenieff Movement Studies to shed new light on areas already of interest to you. This chapter addresses things to consider as you focus the Laban/Bartenieff lens on what is important to you.

Organize Your Perspective

The Guiding Concepts and Organizing Themes discussed in chapter 2 provide ways to think about and frame your use of L/BMA to shed new light on your interests. Look through the list below of Organizing Themes. Which ones do you already utilize? Which ones stand out as worth investigating further? Perhaps you are very clear about function, but the expressive nature of your activities is less developed.

Function-Expression

Inner-Outer

Part-Whole

Stability-Mobility

Exertion-Recuperation

Example: Let's imagine that your area of interest is fitness and weight training. You have a hunch that the highly anatomical and functional way of thinking about movement that is common in fitness training could benefit from an exploration of the larger perspective of function-expression. This theme suggests that you look at the imagistic and expressive possibilities in strength training.

To make this even more concrete, let's narrow the focus to the exercise known as a deadlift. A conventional deadlift begins in a standing, bent-forward pose with deep femoral flexion and some knee flexion. The back is long, and the arms extend downward with the hands wrapped around a weighted bar that rests on the floor in front of the body. The action occurs as the feet push down into the floor to move the hips and knees into extension. As the hips extend, they move the bar upward to the level of the pelvis. This completes the lift, and the action is then reversed as the head arcs forward, the hips and knees flex, and the tail retreats, and the weight returns to the floor.

This exercise is often described as a way to strengthen the posterior chain, to work the glutes and hamstrings, to develop power, and build core strength. Trainers may tell clients that doing this exercise will help them learn to safely pick things up by using their legs. The deadlift is often cued through language like "back flat," "chin up," and "press." A well taught deadlift would likely include cues like, "Start tight. Think of doing a leg press off the floor. Push your body away from the floor. As the bar reaches your knees drive your hips forward into the bar" (Paul Torcello, conversation with the author, July 13, 2018). Phrases like these get at important functional aspects of the deadlift and clarify safe execution, but the expressive nature is more or less ignored. Expression likely seems unimportant, but let's consider: What are the potential expressive inroads to a deadlift, and what could be gained from approaching it expressively?

Possible expressive perspectives on the deadlift include asserting your power into the earth to pull something into yourself, or imagining letting your tail feathers fan back and up and your sitz bones smile as you lower the weight, or your head tracing the arc of the purple stripe of a rainbow as you pull the weight to extend upward. Or you could imagine that your pelvic floor is like an airplane taking off for flight. These images provide spatial and energetic information about the action to pattern your intention.

These expressive cues highlight different aspects of the movement than the functional cues do and bring other understandings of the movement to the forefront. If you were to execute or teach a deadlift from an expressive perspective, you might notice that the expressive influences the functional in surprising ways—the right cue can make what was previously challenging or impossible suddenly seem like no big deal. It can pattern the body to perform the movement without overwhelming the nervous system with technical details.

Other Organizing Themes can bring different insights to the deadlift: stability-mobility would highlight how these two principles are set up in the body and phrased during a deadlift. Subtle-simple-complex would explore the subtle sensations of the action and would tease apart the elements involved before putting them together into the complexity of the full deadlift action. Each of these varied perspectives can offer unique and valuable perspectives to what is happening in movement and how the L/BMA lens can bring new knowledge to your interests.

Observing the World Around You

In daily life, observing and interpreting movement is a routine practice. You notice your friends' energy changing throughout a conversation. You notice what you perceive to be tension between a couple sitting near you at a restaurant. You enter a meeting and interpret through movement cues that one person seems deflated and down, while another is visibly excited. By learning to observe movement through the lens of L/BMA, you get better at interpreting movement based on what is actually occurring.

L/BMA teaches you to work with what is present and important in movement. Thus, L/BMA emphasizes being clear about what is happening in movement and how this movement is meaningful in its context. This means that the observer has an active and central role in making meaning. As an observer and analyzer of movement, you can frame and support how you perceive movement to be meaningful. You cannot say what the truth of another person is or what a movement means to them. Your interpretation of any movement event is just that: an interpretation and not the truth of that event or that mover.

Interpretations of movement are shaped by the observer's values and understandings. Movement observation is a complex weaving together of what is happening and the context in which it is happening, with the lens of the observer actively filtering and shaping an interpretation. The nuanced, detailed information gathered through the L/BMA lens allows you to support your interpretations based on what you see, yet as an observer you are at the center of your interpretation. You can claim how you experience and make meaning of movement based on what you see and the context it happens in, but you cannot claim to read a mind or know a truth of the person you are observing.

The terms *meaning-making* and *interpretation* are often used interchangeably, yet it is worth reflecting on how they are similar and different. *Meaning-making* is a more recent term. The "maker" tag suggests that the meaning-maker, you, is at the center of your impressions and of the meaning you infer. It also suggests the importance of zooming the perspective in and then gradually zooming it back out. This asks that you be conscious of the role your perceptions play in shaping meaning. The word *interpretation* suggests a less consciously active process of making meaning from movement. Interpretation is like skipping from what happened to what it means with less attention paid to the role of your associations and perceptions.

This perspective may be different from the way movement interpretation is handled in other contexts. Pop-culture ideas about body language provide endless examples of linking a movement to a prescribed meaning. For example, crossing your arms means you are being resistant or a large, open posture means you feel powerful (West Side Toastmasters, n.d.). The challenge with these versions of decoding nonverbal messages is discussed in depth later in this chapter.

As an observer of movement your goals and needs will influence how you observe movement and what you observe it for. If you were a track coach and were watching a pole-vaulter on your team, you would observe their movement with the intention of finding ways to improve technique and thus increase the height of the jump. If you were a juror, you would observe the movement of a witness providing testimony for cues about credibility and congruency; however, this would be informed by what you perceive credibility and congruency to look like. If you were supporting a friend in need, you would be a sympathetic witness, taking in information and being present with your friend without needing to affect them. Each of these positions brings a different goal and thus a different frame to the observation of movement.

Informal movement observation happens continuously as you progress through your day. While simply being around and interacting with others, you make instantaneous interpretations of their movements without giving it much reflection. These events occur often, either in person or onscreen.

You can also engage in a formal observation process in which you actively and systematically witness and make meaning from movement. This kind of observation often involves video because it can be replayed for detailed analysis. Muting the audio can help to clarify aspects of movement by limiting the influence of sound on your perceptions. If you want to formally observe in real time, you will be observing mostly for themes and patterns, because you will not have the opportunity to repeat; yet when talking about observing live action, Bartenieff would say, "If you miss it the first time, do not worry, they will do it again" (Peggy Hackney, conversation with author, March 3, 2018).

The following section outlines the formal observation process.

The Observation Process

The observation process weaves *what* is happening in any movement event and the context in which it happens with *how* it is happening to provide an understanding of how movement is uniquely meaningful or "speaking" in that moment.

Check in With Your Sensory and Perceptive Processes

Begin the observation process by focusing inward and attending to your inner experiences and bodily sensations. Attuning to yourself first is a way of clearing the baggage of your perceptual filters and preparing to receive as fully as possible what you are going to be observing. As you drop inward and sense what is present within your sensory and perceptual systems, you may want to warm up by physically moving. Once you have prepared yourself to observe by attending to your inner sensations and honoring your needs, you are ready to begin attending outwardly.

Watch the First Time

The goal for the first time you observe is to attune with what you are seeing without the pressure of getting specific. You want to "get a feel" for the movement event. There are several ways of doing this, and each affords a unique sense of what is happening. For example:

- sounding or singing the phrases of the movement
- moving along with it
- saying "now" every time something happens that seems important

Gather First Impressions

After the first look, you can begin getting specific by gathering first impressions. Watch this round of the movement event by imagining that what you are seeing is landing on your eyes and filling you with its unique world view.

As you watch, track any memories, thoughts, associations, and feelings that strike you based on what you are seeing. Ask yourself: "What strikes me about what I am seeing?" Record your answers using evocative and descriptive words, images, symbols, or any other way of summarizing the impressions.

When you watch for first impressions, you may want to use a format from Authentic Movement that is useful for separating what is happening from your feelings about it. Try using phrases like:

"I see _____ doing _____ and I feel _____."

"When I see _____ I am reminded of _____."

"When I see you _____, I experience _____ in myself."

Some examples:

"I see Charlie doing jubilant cartwheels, and I feel elated and excited."

"When I see Aleja throwing her arm to the side, I am reminded of the time I jumped off the swing set into the pool."

"I see Olga punching the air, while wearing a stunning black dress, and I am reminded of the woman who lives next door yelling at the mailman."

Silently repeating phrases like these lets you track your experience of seeing what you are seeing and the interpretations that accompany it. It also separates your interpretations from the movement event itself. In other words, you know that the event and your experience of it are not the same thing, and when they are clearly distinct you can claim your experience and associations as an observer with a clarity that does not haphazardly project your interpretations onto the event.

Get Information About the Narrative Story

Once you have your first impressions written down, watch the movement event again, this time looking for the narrative story: What is happening, the context of the event, who is involved, and any other details you may want to include to give a more complete picture of the event. Now write down the narrative.

With the information from first impressions and the narrative story, write a sentence or series of sentences that captures the feeling tone and essence of the movement event. Use images, metaphors, and poetic and descriptive language to express the atmosphere and content of the event. As the observation gets more complex, this sentence or series of sentences will help ground your observation in what is happening and why it is important. If you are going to be writing a paper on your observations, keep this sentence at the top of your written document, and refer to it as a way of staying focused on what the observation is about.

Develop an Organizing Question

The next step in the observation process is to develop a question that can be answered by looking at the movement. This last part—*that can be answered by looking at the movement*—is often tricky. Questions that ask you to interpret what someone is thinking or what it means when an arm goes up (unless it is a referee at, say, a hockey game) or why something is happening are often not questions you can answer by looking at the movement. Questions you *can* answer include ones about how movement speaks to you, how it colors the event, or gives an impression. Here are some sample questions:

- How does this movie represent femininity in movement? What does this movement say about how womanhood is portrayed or should look?
- What are the choreographers saying about what power is?
- How does form change (Shape) speak in this video clip?
- Why am I getting the impression of childishness from this person?

Questions like these allow you to organize your observations and writings around how movement is meaningful—how it is "speaking" or coloring an event. They allow for nuanced and layered explorations of meaning that place you, the observer and interpreter, at the center of the meaning-making. They don't assume that you have some superpower that enables you to know the mover's inner, secret intentions. Developing questions that can be answered in this way takes practice. You may work on a question and realize, midprocess, that it cannot be answered merely by looking at the movement. If this happens, rework the question.

Gather Data for the Analytic Description

This is where your skills in Laban/Bartenieff Movement Analysis spring into action. The analytic description involves gathering data on the movement specifics through the lens of L/BMA. The information gathered during this phase of the observation process focuses on what is happening in the movement and how it is happening.

There are several general ways to work through the analytic description. The first time you watch for the analytic details, look at what stands out, record what feels important from the Body, Effort, Shape, and Space categories as well as information about the Phrasing, and notice if any category feels most important to the statement or feeling tone of the movement event. Next, based on what you saw, decide which method of gathering seems most useful for this event. The following options offer ways to gather information.

Look at Each Category of Body, Effort, Shape, and Space

Pick a category that feels important to this movement statement, and watch specifically for it. Notice what stands out and what is absent. Notice patterns— does something occur often and seem to have a specific purpose? Consider the relevance to the overall statement of what is present in the movement. Work through each category this way to bring to light how each is uniquely relevant to the statement.

Look for Clusters of Body, Effort, Shape, and Space

This method asks you to bring together information from all the categories of BESS to see how the event contains simultaneous layers from each category to form a unique and complex movement statement. To form clusters, draw (or imagine) four circles, one for each category, within which you can group your observations. When you see a moment that feels important to the statement, jot down (or think about) all that is happening in terms of each category within its respective circle to suggest the coming together of all the elements at once.

Look at Phrasing of BESS

To look at movement phrases, try singing or sounding them, and consider what from BESS seems connected or linked. Also consider how things are strung together in the movement to give color and tone to the expressive statement. This way of organizing your observations can enhance a blow-by-blow or moment-to-moment description by bringing in information about how movement is organized into meaningful units, sequenced, and loaded.

Make Meaning

Now that you have gathered analytic data through the lens of L/BMA, you can weave this information with your first impressions and your narrative story to address your organizing question. Fill in the big picture with detail. Compiling all of this information is complex and exciting. New understandings are revealed, and previously held assumptions are challenged. Go back to your first impressions, and consider how the data you collected and the questions you raised relate to them. Often there are gems of wisdom in your first impressions that make the analytical data you gathered relevant.

The meaning-making part of the observation process often takes the form of a paper or presentation, but it can also take form in a movement work in which the new understandings are used to create new choreography or to develop new cues to coach movement. You may find other ways observation is useful in your life, and you may learn to communicate your findings in meaningful ways—for example, in interactions where you desire a specific outcome, or in helping to get to know another person better.

If your interest lies in the realm of coaching, therapy, or teaching, observing movement using the approach outlined above is probably less common. More common for you is observing movement in real time, in live action, and working from what you see in the moment. You will probably not move through a procedural deep look at movement, but you may want to record on video moments that are particularly important and employ a version of the observation process when viewing them. Very often details and nuances that went unnoticed in the live-action moment but were observed through video can afford new information. And the skills developed by methodically working through the observation process can improve your in-the-moment observation skills.

Interpreting Meaning in Movement

Interpreting meaning from movement is complicated—like a tangled ball of yarn whose threads disappear in the knotted morass, intertwining with other threads and emerging in unknown locations to create unseen connections that are challenging to tease apart. That does not mean it is not worth a try; after all, humans unconsciously interpret movement all of the time. Recall a moment when you described someone's personality with subtle references to how they moved, or when you felt hurt by a quick, direct response from a colleague. Movement and how it is executed color our impressions of one another. Through Laban/Bartenieff Movement Analysis, you develop more tools for observing, describing, and forming your interpretations. The guidance offered in the previous section for undertaking the observation process asks you to recognize that as an observer, your impressions and interpretations of movement are distinct from the meaning they hold for the mover. The following discussion deepens your look at the complexities of interpretation and meaning-making in analyzing human movement.

Constructions of Meaning in Movement

You have likely encountered in pop culture and the mainstream media examples of associating certain bodily behaviors with meaning. The idea of decoding or being able to read movement as you would read a book gives the impression that something as complex as movement can be understood simply. As enticing an idea as this is, it can be dangerously misleading. Consider the following examples: Someone who slouches their shoulders is depressed; someone with broad, widened shoulders and a hardened chest is prideful; someone with a gripped hand is tense. Or, as in the example that appeared earlier in this chapter, someone with crossed arms is resistant. Making eye contact means you are trustworthy, while looking up and to the right means you are deceptive. These associations of actions with emotional states or truthfulness oversimplify the complexities of movement and hide the subtler, important questions of how a movement was done, who was doing it, and what context it was done in. In short, linking actions with specific feelings and significance is simply misleading.

Let's take the "crossed arms means resistance" interpretation. Try on the gesture as you read this. Sense into it. What does it feel like to cross your arms across your chest? Consider when you cross your arms. Do you do so when you are cold, or when you want to draw your attention inward, or when you are standing back to consider the whole picture? Perhaps you do not have pockets and would like a place to rest your arms. Now, keep your arms crossed but explore changing aspects of BESS, bulge your chest forward, or shift your weight and change your effort life. Notice how with these changes the expression also changes. On one evening, crossed arms could be a soothing and comforting act; another time it could be a distancing act. The same movement does not mean the same thing twice (Moore and Yamamoto 2012, 53). Even in moments when crossed arms do signify resistance, there are still layers to this truth. The observer may not know what the source of the resistance is or have any way of addressing it or knowing what is actually going on.

The popularity of these links between meaning and movement are unfortunate because they encourage misleading understandings of movement and lead to misinterpretations. Imagine that you are a student whose teacher has certain associations about crossed arms. And imagine that you find it comfortable and soothing to cross your arms. If the teacher never bothers to ask what crossing your arms is about for you in that moment, but becomes irritated every time you do it because he or she interprets it as a personal slight, a significant misunderstanding may brew that could lead to bigger conflict.

Constructing meaning from movement is so common that it is nearly unconscious. The practice often colors impressions of who people are and influences how relationships form. As you embark on increasingly complex ways of observing and making meaning from movement, remember that you are weaving together mover, movements, and context through your interpretative lens. As you frame your interpretations, remember that the goal is not to establish a grand truth, but to support your interpretation with details about the what and how of the movement event.

The Ladder of Abstraction

There is another inroad to considering how humans make meaning from movement, which has been articulated by Carol-Lynne Moore and Kaoru Yamamoto in *Beyond Words: Movement Observation and Analysis*. The ladder of abstraction is a concept from the field of semantics that articulates how meaning is made from language. Moore and Yamamoto propose the concept can be applied to movement as well. In this model, abstractness and concreteness are polarities.

Humans learn to make meaning from movement by moving their conceptual image schemas between abstract and concrete. Examples of concrete in movement include: delicate and buoyant movement, a gesture that uses a spoking mode of shape change to forward middle, or a rising and spreading, powerful and out of control movement. Examples of abstract in movement include: she was confident and powerful, he wanted to show me who is boss, or they were fired up and angry. The concrete is what happens in movement; the abstract is how it is interpreted (Moore and Yamamoto 2012, 49–51).

The links between the abstract and the concrete form from seeing movement in your life. For example, imagine you have an aunt who moves in a delicate, light, and whimsical manner with a large psychological kinesphere when you perceive her to be confident. From observing this you start to associate light Weight effort and large psychological kinesphere with what confidence looks like, thus you have linked the concrete "what happened in movement and how it happened" with what it signifies.

The gradations from concrete to abstract may look something like this: light, whimsical, and buoyant movements with a large psychological kinesphere translate into the way Aunt M. moves when confident, which translates into the way confident women move, which translates into the way confident people move, which translates into confidence (Moore and Yamamoto 2012, 51).

Now, say you are from a different family than the one with Aunt M. and in your household confidence looks like reserved, inward attention with a smaller psychological kinesphere; those concrete movement cues would begin to form an abstract cluster of confidence, which would look very different from the household where confidence moves like Aunt M.

Body Knowledge, Body Prejudice

The concepts of body knowledge and body prejudice suggest that your knowledge and feelings about your own body and movement frame how you experience and interpret other people's movement. As an observer you are not a neutral presence; you enter observation and meaning-making full of pre-established associations that color how a movement strikes you. And the meaning you ascribe to someone's movement could have little to do with what it means to the mover.

The concepts of body knowledge and body prejudice are developed and articulated by Carol-Lynne Moore and Kaoru Yamamoto in their book *Beyond Words: Movement Observation and Analysis*. They discuss movement observation and interpretation as a complex intertwining of the observer's present sensory and perceptive processes with their previous experiences and associations to form an impression of the movements of someone else—a person whose history may hold a very different sensibility and meaning than the observer's. Much misinterpretation arises from an observer deciphering movement through their own filter.

Again, take the example of arms folded across one's chest. You were asked to cross your arms, feel into the experience of doing so, and reflect on when you might cross your arms. Consider how your experience of crossing your arms will influence how you interpret someone else doing it. Bring to mind a time when you have seen this action and interpreted it to mean something specific. Consider what influenced your interpretation of the movement: the person and your relationship to them, the context, other aspects of their movement or body including the energetic feeling tones, and your experiences of this movement. Next, imagine that others also observed the movement. How might their interpretations differ from yours? What may have influenced their interpretations?

Each category of Body, Effort, Shape, and Space speaks to a different aspect of what is present in movement, and each category offers a unique perspective to how movement is meaningful. Consider how you experience strong Weight effort. For some, strong Weight is aggressive, intimidating, and violent. For others it is confirming, celebratory, powerful, and committed. Effort addresses a different aspect of movement than action. Layering effort information into the action gives more information and more possibilities for how a movement resonates with the interpreter. With each aspect of BESS the picture gets more complex.

The BESS frame used in Laban/Bartenieff Movement Analysis offers an inroad to addressing the nuances of movement. After using BESS to tease apart the elemental aspects of movement, you can then bring them back together to get a more complete look at what is happening in a movement and how it is contributing to its expression.

Studying L/BMA asks you to notice and claim your knowledge and prejudices associated with movement. In this process you may discover that you want to expand your associations of an aspect of movement to encompass a greater range of understanding. Reflect on your associations with different aspects of Body, Effort, Shape, and Space—for example, your associations with abound Flow effort—and get to know your values around these associations. How do your associations, your knowledge and prejudices, color and possibly limit how you experience and interpret the movement of others? How do they limit what you allow yourself to do as a mover?

Meaning-Making as the Mover

As a mover, you may not know or be tuned into what movement means to you. It may not be a common experience for you to pay attention to your own movement—to how it feels to be inside of it and what it means. There are not many contexts in which attention to one's physicality and its meaning is at the forefront. Throughout this text you have been asked to reflect on movement in your life and to expand your range of movement choices. If you are interested in pursuing this more fully, the dance therapy form known as Authentic Movement is one structure that specifically attunes the mover to how movement is meaningful to them.

What can be said about movement and meaning? As discussed in depth in this chapter, you cannot say that a movement inherently contains a specific meaning every time it is performed, yet you want to address how movement is meaningful, and how it influences perceptions and experiences.

First, recognize the meaning-making as yours. It is influenced by your lens and the perceptions you bring through preestablished associations that you may not even be conscious of.

Second, use the details provided by Laban/Bartenieff Movement Analysis to support your meaning-making: Based on what you saw in the movement, how did you come to make this meaning? Use your skills of observation and description to support how the elements that were present in the movement contributed to the impression it left you with.

Third, challenge your assumptions. When you are attached to your associations and think you know what a movement means, challenge yourself to think through other associations and consider other possibilities. Also, ask others for their perspectives. You may be surprised.

Sharing Your Insights With Others

You may have found many ways that Laban/Bartenieff Movement Analysis is useful to you. Some of these are readily suited to being shared with other people, through teaching and coaching, while others are probably more private, such as applying them to your physical presence as a teacher or improving strained interactions with a family member. The following section is specifically written to support you as you share with others how you use L/BMA in your life. Choosing to share how you use L/BMA—taking it out in the world—gives you new things to consider. In particular, where and how does movement play a role in what are you doing? And what language best conveys your message and intentions? Whether your forum is a podcast, a video, a website, a dance or performance-art piece, a presentation, or a series of workshops, sharing your movement insights means experimenting with movement and language to most effectively communicate your message.

Matters of Movement

Movement offers unique ways of knowing. As you share your insights and knowledge, consider how you engage others in movement experiences to

Eleanor Christman Cox

In order to have "good posture," cellists use their core muscles to support a straight back, which prohibits them from engaging those muscles in playing. This presents itself in various ailments, from sore arms, to tense legs, to lower-back pain, to carpal tunnel syndrome. String players, unlike other movers, are not used to being aware of their full bodies; rather, they are focused on their arms, hands, and fingers. They are not taught to be aware of breath, unless they are cuing to start a piece or a phrase. I use L/BMA to develop physicality that supports the dynamic and technical needs of playing the cello.

One of the most important Patterns of Total Body Connectivity for playing the cello is upper-lower, but it is also the least easy to use when sitting in a chair playing the cello. I teach cellists to use the power from their lower body to support the upper. That means using counterweight, pushing down into one foot or the other to add resistance to the bow on the string on the opposite side of the body, and sometimes putting weight on both feet to allow them to push the body into the cello for a burst of power, almost as though they were about to stand up out of the chair.

The technique of grounding the feet—planting them on the floor as though roots were growing out the bottoms—or imagining the feet pouring into the floor is invaluable. It gives a sense of power to the player, an attitude of "I am right here, right now," and allows mobility in the torso and arms, the range of which increases because there is no part of the upper body that is binding for stability.

In terms of Effort, the cellist is able to dynamically invest because the energy, especially in the torso, is not wasted on holding the body in a certain posture. The grounding and energy transfer from lower to upper body allow the rest of the body to make functional and expressive movements to create the sound that accurately conveys musical ideas.

support their learning. For some of the ways you might use L/BMA, this is pretty obvious—it is built into the application. For other areas, this question is a stumper: Movement is what is talked about, but not what is done. This is a fine option; you do not always need to be going to the movement. And consider that the movement experience is itself a teacher; it can help you shed light on what you are describing. Movement offers unique insights and knowledge, and as you set out to communicate about it, consider how you can offer a movement experience that supports what you are sharing. Encourage readers, viewers, listeners, and students to connect to their own sensation or get up (or down) and move, to try on in their bodies what you are discussing. Ask them to notice their experience and to see what it brings up for them.

Matters of Language and Metaphor

In *Life on Land,* Emilie Conrad writes, "Language is probably one of the greatest tissue shapers of all, primarily because it is audible breath. . . . The feet (terrain) and language (culture) probably have the greatest *external* impact on the sculpting of tissue" (Conrad 2012, 149). How you talk about movement influences how movement is understood and valued. When you talk about movement, much more is conveyed than simply words; associations, imagery, metaphorical understandings, and feeling tones create understandings and cultures around the body.

Laban/Bartenieff analysts and educators use language as an integral part of communicating. Many find that the words common in their areas of application are not the most effective for achieving the desired movement understandings and outcomes. The linguistic phrases of any movement discipline, like the movements themselves, are part of the tradition, handed down from teacher to student, echoed through facility walls, shaping the culture of the movement practices and the bodies that hear the words. Many such phrases have been successful in terms of creating the understandings for that type of training. However, linguistic phrases are rarely considered in terms of how they impact the moving body, if they actually get the results they are going for, and how they develop and limit the capabilities of the moving body. The broader subject of metaphor theory can bring important insights into the relationship between movement, body, and cognition.

George Lakoff is a linguist whose theories of cognition and metaphor offer information on the relationship between language and embodied experience. Lakoff, along with philosopher Mark Johnson, describe *metaphorical concepts* as systemic linguistic expressions and cognitive maps that demonstrate association through the words used to describe something. Simply put, we use the language of what we know—the familiar (source domain)—to understand what we don't know—the unfamiliar (target domain) (Lakoff and Johnson 2003). The known is mapped onto the unknown via image schemas, or durable and deeply embodied image-feelings based on our primary experiences of being in the world. Often, the body and movement are described through terms other than what they are; rather, they are metaphorically associated with something else in hopes of demystifying them (Culley 2015). You have been encouraged throughout this book to generate images and metaphors related to the moving body in order to create intention that supports the movement, yet these images and metaphors will leave lasting impressions on the body.

Metaphors create associations by applying language usually meant for one system to another system, and their presence is revealed through the details of language. As Lakoff and Johnson say, "[t]he essence of metaphor is understanding and experiencing one kind of thing in terms of another" (Johnson and Lakoff 2003, 5). For example, imagine the body as a machine. Movement is the result of the workings of the machine—pulleys, levers and other mechanical parts function to produce movement—that is, from simple relationships in which x action plus y action leads to z output. Consider other repercussions or associations that would be implied by this metaphor: diminished sensation and agency, or reduced expressive capacity or the capacity to be broken and fixed. With repetition, the metaphor of body as machine will deepen, and details will be filled in to establish even more associations (Culley 2015).

Continually applying machine metaphors to the moving body will shape understandings of the body and develop a palette of experience that fills in a picture of the body as machine-like. This will show up in phrases and expressions, for example, "she just keeps on ticking" or "her battery never runs out." In both cases, she is compared to something machine-like—a clock that just keeps ticking, or a toy equipped with an ever-ready battery. From these comparisons, whole conglomerates of metaphorical thought can form and take shape in phrases like "you have to shift gears" or "he is firing on all cylinders now" (Culley 2015).

The study of metaphor is important to the process of applying L/BMA to your area of interest because it highlights how language can influence understandings of the body and shape experiences of movement. It asks to you consider the metaphors you apply to movement and how they emphasize and reveal certain aspects of the body while hiding and concealing others. What understandings of the body and movement are you wanting to highlight and share in your field of interest? Is the moving body a living thing? A sentence? An ocean? An ecosystem? A factory? All of these are choices that shape movement and influence understandings of it.

Evocative and Analytical Language

As you take your Laban/Bartenieff skills into the world, using the specialized language you have cultivated is important for accuracy and precision in describing and clarifying movement. Yet, you will probably find that not everyone understands the technical terminology you're using. You will likely want to weave evocative language with your L/BMA-based descriptive language to evoke the kinesthetic experience that is movement. Therefore, it becomes crucial to cultivate the ability to describe movement in evocative and imagistic ways that still achieve the clarity and precision found in the analytic language of L/BMA.

Imagine you are a choreographer who wants to employ shape flow as a mode of shape change onstage; you might use a phrase like "adjust yourself for comfort" or "snuggle into yourself" to help the performers find this aspect of Shape. Or say you are helping a job applicant prepare for their next job interview; you want them to come across as on task, easeful, thoughtful, and relaxed, so you bring elements of the Effort category into your coaching. The goal is to achieve a fluctuation in and around direct Space, free Flow, and sustained Time vision drive; you might use the words "laser-like, relaxed, lingering" to help them manifest this constellation. These verbal translations help movement analysts communicate and coach movement to others who are not trained in the Laban/ Bartenieff perspective.

Images help translate the analytic Laban/Bartenieff language into everyday and lived experiences for people not trained in L/BMA. The choreographer seeking shape flow as a mode of shape change may suggest that the dancers imagine they are simply adjusting themselves in search of comfort. Or the interview coach suggesting a relaxed, focused, and lingering vision drive may encourage the interviewee to explore an attitude of viewing a beautiful painting hanging in a museum; their attention is channeled "out there" with prolonged thoughtfulness.

In these roles and many others that a Laban/Bartenieff movement analyst could take on, finding images that work involves:

- clarifying what is present or desired in the movement in Laban/Bartenieff terms,
- executing the movement to explore how it shows up in your life, or what creative characters and narratives arise from it, and
- crafting the images and words that help bring it to life so it is readily accessible. Ideally your image will be robust enough to contain relevant information from Body, Effort, Shape, and Space, meaning spatial and effortful information could be present.

Finding imagery that evokes what is desired in movement is a rich and creative way to bring Laban/Bartenieff skills to new audiences to help them gain insight and knowledge. Throughout this text are samples of evocative language. More fodder for creative use of the terminology is found in the actual descriptions of terms throughout the text, which provide information on *how the movement happens*. You can use these definitions to fill in the evocative with

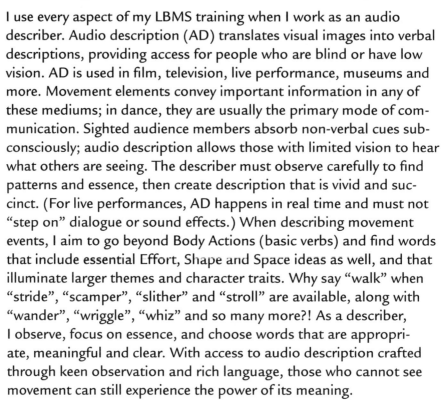

L/BMA in Your World: Audio Design

Esther Geiger

I use every aspect of my LBMS training when I work as an audio describer. Audio description (AD) translates visual images into verbal descriptions, providing access for people who are blind or have low vision. AD is used in film, television, live performance, museums and more. Movement elements convey important information in any of these mediums; in dance, they are usually the primary mode of communication. Sighted audience members absorb non-verbal cues subconsciously; audio description allows those with limited vision to hear what others are seeing. The describer must observe carefully to find patterns and essence, then create description that is vivid and succinct. (For live performances, AD happens in real time and must not "step on" dialogue or sound effects.) When describing movement events, I aim to go beyond Body Actions (basic verbs) and find words that include essential Effort, Shape and Space ideas as well, and that illuminate larger themes and character traits. Why say "walk" when "stride", "scamper", "slither" and "stroll" are available, along with "wander", "wriggle", "whiz" and so many more?! As a describer, I observe, focus on essence, and choose words that are appropriate, meaningful and clear. With access to audio description crafted through keen observation and rich language, those who cannot see movement can still experience the power of its meaning.

specific details. Such as "she channeled her focus (direct Space effort) as she indicated (directional mode of shape change) toward the broken window, as if to bridge to it," or "with uncontrolled power (free Flow effort and strong Weight effort) he swept the tchotchkes off the mantel (horizontal plane)." You can also develop personal lists of evocative terms, imagery, and examples that you can draw on.

Writing About Movement

Writing can feel disembodied; thoughts and intellect are channeled through actions of the hands to give shape to words and eventually sentences. With so little movement and so little attention paid to the body during writing, physical sensation diminishes to keep you focused on the task. This makes writing about movement ironic. Although the writer's moving body is often not part of the writing, reading writing that evokes kinesthetic sensibilities and brings forth physical sensation is delightful. Writing about movement in ways that descriptively capture the essence of what is happening and inspire a kinesthetic response is a challenging and inspiring pursuit. The Laban/Bartenieff lens is useful for developing a writing voice that both evokes the moving body and is able to communicate movement by weaving clear description with sensitizing language.

Use Movement to Check In With What Is Important

When writing about movement, it is easy to stay in your chair, attention channeled to the screen, and not execute the movements you are writing about. This means that much of what you are writing about you are imagining. Instead, leave the paper or screen, and try moving to gather information from the felt experience. Going to movement for the purposes of writing about it changes the experience. Words and imagery become more prominent as you track your experience. Moving to write about moving is a profoundly sensitizing and organizing practice in which you get to know the movement in new ways. If you are observing movement, also get up and move along with it. You will notice that you gain information that serves your understandings of the movement.

Feel the Sensations and Perceptions Present in Movement

Going to movement as part of the process of writing about it means being present with the sensations that arise and tracking the perceptions and words in order to remember them for the writing. This meditative, information-seeking practice is both creative and rigorous as you discover new sensations and details and question previously held assumptions about how movement happens and the understandings you have of it. One way of articulating sensation based on movement involves repeating a movement while describing it to yourself and asking yourself if the words truly speak to the experience. You may decide to seek other words or images to enrich the experience.

Formalities of Writing About Movement

When writing about movement, sometimes Laban/Bartenieff terms are used colloquially, as in "She is strong," and at other times they are used to specifically convey the meaning as it is known in L/BMA, as in "She uses her strong weight." These two uses of *strong* could mean very different things, one implying strength of muscle or character, the other an activation of strong Weight effort. Your reader is smart and you can trust that they can discern how you mean the words you use. Your reader's ability to understand your meaning is aided by the words you use to fill in the details. One way of being as clear as you can regarding which version of a word you are using is by adding supporting descriptive information such as "She activated her strong weighted mass to heave the rock over the wall," if you want them to get the sense of strong Weight effort.

Summary

You have likely started bringing your Laban/Bartenieff perspective and skills to movement in many areas of your life, some of which may be areas in which you share your findings with others. This chapter discussed important things to consider as you do this. The Organizing Themes, such as function-expression and inner-outer, bring a larger perspective to your work. The observation process guides you to observe evocatively and analytically in order to make meaning. Throughout this text, it has been said that movement is meaningful and that movement speaks. Yet the observation process makes it clear that the meaning-maker is at the center of how movement speaks and how its meaning is made. As you apply L/BMA and use it in your life, you are not reading minds or speaking the truth of the movement; you are organizing your perceptions of movement into your own meaning. As you share and teach your findings, weave together evocative and analytical language to inspire movement in ways both descriptively clear and suggestive of movement.

CHAPTER

9

Laban/Bartenieff Movement Analysis in Action

"Man moves in order to satisfy a need. He aims by his movement at something of value to him."

(Laban 1975, 1)

This final chapter is written entirely by other Laban/Bartenieff Movement Analysts. In their unique voices they share how they use L/BMA to augment areas of importance to them. Because they come from different fields and use L/BMA in discrete ways, the purpose of their contributions is to offer you examples and inspiration for the many ways in which you can apply L/BMA in your life and career. The L/BMA field is diverse, and each of the following contributors offers a unique perspective on the approach, bringing it to life in their own ways.

The first three contributions focus on using L/BMA in ways that support your physicality throughout the day. First, Hilary Bryan shares the approach to ergonomics used by her company, the Body at Work Ergonomics, to support the working body, including their unique approach to eye strain. Then Aida Curtis, who is finishing a master's degree in somatic psychotherapy, writes about using L/BMA in her yoga practice in ways that support the physical health of her body and help her bridge the Eastern and Western traditions to create a meaningful and more inclusive practice. This section is rounded out by Keely Song Glenn, an assistant professor of dance at Brigham Young University, who writes about her journey after knee surgery using L/BMA to return to the dance studio. Each of these contributions speaks to using L/BMA personally to support the functional and expressive abilities of the moving body.

The second set of contributions focuses on L/BMA and performance. In the first contribution, Sarah Donohue, assistant professor of dance at Utah Valley University, writes about BESS in relationship to stand-up comedy and applies what she notices to humor in dance composition. Next, Kevin Williamson, assistant professor of dance at Scripps College, writes about a choreographic process in which he worked with images and understandings of superheroes through different aspects of BESS. Finally, Amanda Huntleigh, assistant professor of music and director of chorale activities at Clarke University, writes about using elements of Shape and Space to coach different vocal styles. All three of the performance-focused contributions emphasize different aspects of performance, from recognizing patterns to exploring personal and cultural associations to coaching performers, reminding us that the options for using L/BMA in performance are vast.

The final three contributions focus on L/BMA in a therapeutic context. Again, each contributor takes a different approach to addressing how they use L/BMA. Katya Bloom writes about utilizing L/BMA as a therapist in clinical practice, citing Effort and Space as crucial to organizing her perceptions and inroads to working with clients. Next, body worker and somatic therapist Erin Law discusses the use of her body as an ashiatsu massage therapist, in which she uses her feet to give compression to and lengthen the soft tissue along the client's meridians. Finally, neuroscientist Andrea Pack discusses a case study she performed with Ralph, a stroke patient, during which she integrated neuroscience with movement through the L/BMA lens in order to rehabilitate his neural functioning. Each of these contributions highlights the L/BMA perspective as part of the therapeutic context in ways that support both the emotional and the physical.

Laban/Bartenieff Movement Studies at Work: An Integrated Approach to Ergonomics

Contributed by Hilary Bryan, MFA, PhD, CMA, RSMT. Used with permission.

In 1999 I cofounded the Body at Work Ergonomics to address the epidemic of computer injuries in the workplace from the perspective of Laban/Bartenieff Movement Studies (L/BMS). Since that time our L/BMS-based curriculum has helped thousands of office workers and other types of workers in San Francisco, New York, Kiev, Moscow, Wisconsin, and Minnesota find grounding and dynamic, internal support at work and at play. We offer individual sessions and group seminars, helping clients set up their workstations safely and navigate their space with ease. We work with private, not-for-profit, and government agencies, and in home offices of all kinds.

Our approach to ergonomics uses major themes that weave through the entire L/BMS system, such as stability-mobility, exertion-recuperation, and function-expression. We attend to both part and whole and to the moving body within the context of personal motivation and intention, as well as within the physical and emotional contexts. Our approach offers a fresh perspective and tools for repatterning that support healing and interrupt the cycle of reinjury all too common with repetitive strain injuries (RSIs), also called repetitive motion injuries (RMIs). All our ergonomics trainers are certified movement analysts (CMA or CLMA) who assume that movement injuries require movement solutions. In order to break a cycle of reinjury, we need to address the movement patterns that contribute to it.

Our ergonomics trainers employ the entirety of L/BMS so that we can draw on any part of the system as an individual session unfolds and as seminar participants raise questions. Our seminar curriculum flows from lessons on the experiential anatomy of sitting, through setting up the environment to

Hilary Bryan, PhD, MFA, CMA, is on faculty at the Moscow Institute of Therapeutic Arts; teaches modern dance, choreography, contact improvisation, and L/BMS at universities and festivals internationally; and has taught for IMS-certification programs and for the Russian Association of Dance Movement Therapy. Her dissertation research (University of California, Davis) into somatic movement practice involved extensive conversations on embodied knowing with members of Tanztheater Wuppertal Pina Bausch and Compagnie Marie Chouinard.

support three-dimensional movement in space, to an exploration of eyesight and eyestrain through exertion-recuperation rhythms. The primary goal of our foundational seminar, Unfolding the Sitting Body, is a felt experience of dynamic alignment. Participants locate the bony landmarks of heel and sitz bones and explore their relationship for dynamic lower-body grounding. They learn how stability in the lower body can support mobility in the upper body, particularly in sitting positions, because they feel it in their bodies. We provide exercises that develop awareness of fluid support through head-tail connectivity, as well as open and responsive connectivity through all six core-distal pathways. We encourage full-bodied support of breath patterning that supports both oxygenation of all the cells and vibrant shape change through the entire "body blob." I often share the image of "body blob" and "blobular-ity" as ways to access fluid organ support and encourage shape flow support in three dimensions. The word "blob" suggests that the body can feel like a single celled amoeba with its constantly growing and shrinking elastic surface and its constantly moving fluid contents. Accessing amoeba-like physicality helps me to experience my shape flow support, my blobularity. Facilitating access to this ongoing breath support is one of our main goals as movement coaches.

The interrelationships of stability-mobility and exertion-recuperation permeate our work, and our seminars provide lots of ways to experience their potency. In one of our favorite movement experiments, each seminar participant notices how much or little rotation they have available through their spines in each of several different postures (slouching, tensely leaning into their work, and sitting up "straight"). They also check in with how much breath each of these common sitting postures makes available. We then stomp our feet on the floor, roll our sitz bones on our chairs, scoot our chairs forward and back, wag our tailbones, and explore active sitting with dynamic alignment of four flexible spinal curves. Now, sitting in active and dynamic alignment, when participants check in again for both range of motion and volume of breath, they can feel how much more rotation and breath they can access because heels and sitz bones are connected, feet and sitz bones are grounded, and tail is free. This sort of felt experience builds a new body schema from the inside, by creating awareness of efficient functioning to which the body can return (including in this case upper-lower connectivity and stability-mobility). The participant can feel viscerally how the whole body is connected, how "change in one part changes the whole" (Hackney 2002, 41).

When we talk about recuperation, we clarify that we do not mean "rest" or "collapse," but rather a way to build renewal into each movement. I have coached entire conference rooms full of attorneys into swinging pretend mal-lets high into the air, sighing delicately to emphasize sustainment and light-ness at the top of each swing, and then shouting with power as they smash imaginary boulders all over the carpet. As we play, participants experience through their bodies how dynamic and spatial polarities of light and strong

Weight Effort can support one another and reanimate their movement-starved bodies. We talk about how these Efforts are diminished or nonexistent in most contemporary work environments, and we brainstorm ways to bring them back into our daily movement menu. In order to diversify our menu of nourishing movement, we pick imaginary apples along the vertical dimension as recuperation from rowing an imaginary boat along the sagittal plane. Or we row that same boat as recuperation from our other job of spinning the kids' merry-go-round at the playground, our feet planted, arms pulling from one side and heaving to the other through the horizontal dimension (the kids are spinning, but we're exhausted). We then apply these brief embodied reminders of our three-dimensional world to their office environment and together brainstorm ways to distribute their activities in space so as to design recuperation in three dimensions into their daily tasks. We talk about exertion-recuperation rhythms as integral to individual sustainability and to our ability to thrive at work as we do at play.

We developed our seminar Relief for Tired Eyes to address the eyestrain that affects 91 percent of computer users (even if they are not aware of it). Over the past fifteen years I have rearticulated basic concepts of balanced vision through the perspective of Laban's exertion-recuperation rhythms. This inter-relationship helps conceptualize an experiential anatomy of seeing in which, for example, distance vision supports close vision, peripheral vision supports detail vision, and adapting to bright light supports adapting to darkness. The result is greater ease in seeing, even with the demands of today's computer-ized office environment. Many of our clients report not having been aware of how much eyestrain they endured until discovering these simple balancing strategies to relieve it.

In addition to group seminars we do individual sessions, conducted onsite in the client's workspace. Sessions begin with observation followed by interview and discussion of the client's primary concerns. Seeing the client navigate their environment gives us a baseline for movement habits that may be contributing to their discomfort. The coding sheet we've developed to record our observa-tions includes first impressions, BESS data, and moments of recuperation. When noting first impressions we record what seems to be working well and what's not. We may include an image or question, such as, "She's fidgeting: is she nervous?" or "He's sprawled over his chair like my teenage brother on the couch." Such first impressions acknowledge the complex ways in which the relationship between function and expression inform human movement, and pose questions for us to consider as we move on to recording specific details in each different part of the system—Body, Effort, Shape, and Space. We weave first impressions and BESS observations back into our conversation with the client as the session unfolds.

We make the most detailed notes for the Body part of the system, noting body organization, parts most active, parts initiating, parts held, grounding (or what may be interrupting grounding), which kinetic chains are most available, and which are interrupted. I often find that the most revealing aspects are related to how the client recuperates. Shadowing a client's movement when he or she rubs an aching shoulder or wrist can point to discomfort they may not have noticed, factors that likely contribute to their primary concern. Subtly shifting one's sitz bones on the chair or repositioning one's feet may suggest that the body is seeking better grounding. On the other hand, a capacity for extended periods of focused attention may not allow the body to recuperate. I have seen clients go ten or more minutes before taking a deep breath or making even a tiny deviation from constantly staring forward and tapping the keys. Observations of shadow movements give us clues and something to ask the client about as the session unfolds.

After our observation, we talk. What are the client's goals for the session? What changes have they already made? What is their movement life like at work, at home, during their commute? Do they have a movement practice (gym, hiking, walking the dog, etc.)? Client responses give us a place to begin as we jump into addressing their concerns. They also give us language and imagery to use throughout the session. As often as I can, I use the same words that they used in our initial conversation. Or when their language seems to contradict an attitude or approach that I think will help them, I seek opportunities to point that out and inspire a new perspective. Paying attention to language is another way in which our work is informed by Laban's articulation of function-expression.

After this brief interview, I scan through my notes for some part of the client's primary concern that I can address easily with a movement experience or an equipment adjustment that will make an immediate difference in how the client feels. This is my "clear beginning" from which the rest of the session unfolds (many thanks to Janice Meaden). Once the client experiences even a small amount of relief, they are much more willing to collaborate in exploring the "many possibilities" together (Hackney 2002, 1). Individual sessions unfold differently with respect to each client's "Personal Uniqueness" (Hackney 2002, 51). As our hour together draws to a close, I take pen in hand and ask the client what they wish to remember, a technique I learned from Peggy Hackney and Janice Meaden. They articulate for themselves their own personal aha moments, be they images, physical sensations of internal connection, or particular adjustments to various pieces of office equipment, while I take notes, helping them expand on each memory as needed. Making the client responsible for clarifying what was memorable about the session reinforces our whole-person perspective that values each particular moving body within its overlapping contexts of intention, personal motivation, personal history, environment, and emotional life. Recording the client's own words helps the client to articulate the unique meanings they make as they perceive themselves and their world through movement.

Laban/Bartenieff Movement Analysis and Yoga: Meaning-Making in a Personal Practice

Contributed by Aida Curtis, CLMA, MA candidate in somatic psychotherapy at California Institute of Integral Studies. Used with permission.

The process of integrating Laban/Bartenieff Movement Analysis and the yoga asana tradition is a lifelong investigation. For the purposes of this text, I will share how the integration of these two traditions is currently clarifying my relationship to my moving body and supporting a renewed authenticity in my relationship to the yoga tradition, scripture, and lineage. Both of these traditions invite me to deepen my conscious experience of movement. Through this awareness, I move and experience movement differently. With this renewed aliveness in my movement, I bring integrity to how I participate in the artistic, scientific, and spiritual communities affiliated with L/BMA and yoga.

Yoga is an ancient Vedic practice. Many branches, spiritual and religious influences, and affiliated mythopoetic texts have been born from the tradition over time. There was a great deal of differentiation inside the system even before Western practitioners began to further interpret and differentiate their practice. As an instructor and practitioner of Western interpretations of the yoga practice, I feel it is important to be aware of the ways that I am actively interpreting and metabolizing this movement tradition to serve my self-connection and my connection to the philosophies that speak to the heart of the practice. L/BMA has supported the integration of movement qualities that were previously missing from my yoga practice. The integration of these movement qualities has supported a deeper connection to both self and the lineage.

At First Glance

When applying L/BMA to the yoga asana tradition, there are certain aspects of the practice that become more readily apparent. Yoga asana is a predominantly Shape-based practice. A theme of tetrahedral Shape forms predominates in the classical sequences, particularly in the virabhadrasana or "warrior" poses. Kinesthetically, I experience the tetrahedral shape-forms as kindling my alchemical fire, with my legs creating a broad, smoldering base that rises ephemerally into spatial intent. Pin and wall shape forms also predominate

---

Aida Curtis, CLMA, investigates and writes about movement and its relationship to media, culture, and society. She is currently completing her MA in somatic psychotherapy at the California Institute of Integral Studies, and continues to teach and explore L/BMA from Oakland, California.

in the classical sequences, and give me a varying sense of expansion and containment across varying spatial pulls. These shape forms, and the transitions between them, give me a sense of varying relationships to my midline, or central channel. To sense this mutation and fluidity of my central line, it is helpful for me to move slowly. As I move, I narrate: "I arrive; I unfold and expand between earth and sky; I sense my edge; I transition." Following the spatial pulls of the dimensional scale (in the octahedron), I find stability and clarity in my relationship to verticality. Spatial pulls of the planar, icosahedral scales often layer onto the dimensional scale base, creating increased complexity. These spatial pulls support my mobilization and stabilization through transitions and moments of lingering.

Sensing New Possibilities

For many years of my practice, my observations and experiences of yoga asana were largely limited to the Shape category. I would investigate these forms in an unconscious effort signature of remote state, with a tendency toward bound Flow and direct Space throughout the entire practice. Inviting broadened possibilities into my effort life has supported my shift away from limiting patterns in my movement, and has helped me to find sensual inroads back to the patterns of total body connectivity that deepen my experience of my body and my relationship with ground and space. Inviting in an effort life of Weight sensing has been key to this change. With sensuous yielding, self-touch, and minute movements of shape flow as a mode of shape change, I *feel* the quality in my tissues, and the rotations of my bones. I feel my cells organizing along spatial pulls, like lines of light to rest into and find support from. The enlivening of Weight, and my capacity to sense, supports my exploration of larger kinespheric movement. I find that with this, my Flow opens and I experience a sense of free Flow along kinetic chains. The free Flow is contained by the shape, and by the ongoingness of my energy beyond my distal edges into Space. When I have arrived and lingered in an asana, I feel the Flow, Weight, and direct Space of my limbs as they ground and reach into their given spatial pulls. Then, this moment emerges when the tensile connection of my core to distal edges coalesce, and I feel the direct Space along many spatial pulls bloom into an experience of indirect Space with my whole body. This phrasing into indirect Space gives me a different, ephemeral, felt sense of self in the world.

This delicious experience of Effort life is born from, and regenerates, a particular relationship to breath. My experience in yoga is that my relationship to breath can determine my effort life, and the conscious invocation of effort life broadens possibilities in my breath. In yoga, movement is tethered to breath, and ujjayi pranayama is often the breath pattern cued alongside asana. Ujjayi pranayama calls attention to the sensation of breath as it moves along and caresses the whisper muscles of the throat. This breath creates a sound similar to the soft whisper of the ocean or rustle of breeze in the leaves, and it also helps me to enter into my senses. Ujjayi pranayama can, but does not inherently, make certain effort factors more accessible. I feel that ujjayi pranayama may be used as an inroad and portal that supports awareness around effort life, particularly sensing. The knowledge and breadth of options around Effort, made possible through L/BMA, are what fosters this greater aspect of choice. With these sensual dynamics of Effort fluctuating and further connecting me to my energy body, I feel more tender, curious, and capable in my practice. There is an experience of strength in this openness.

Realizations

Connecting the breath pattern, effort life, Patterns of Total Body Connectivity, and spatial pulls gives me an experience of my midline, and of my consciousness, that I can bring back and relate to the philosophy and tradition of yoga as a whole. This brings yoga into my body, and gives me a "bottom-up" experience of a tradition that I was previously digesting as "top-down."

The language and description of experience made possible by Laban/Bartenieff Movement Analysis supports my self-knowledge in movement, and gives me new options to explore. These realizations, which come to life and live inside my bones, breath, and tissues, are accumulating and layering into my process of repatterning. I am repatterning habits and ways of understanding my body in movement systems. I am releasing old interpretations and assumptions about the practice of yoga asana that have held me tethered to unsupported ways of moving, a process which allows for new experiences in my body and in my consciousness. With this kinesthetic knowing and the ability to locate my experience at the intersection of the analytical and energetic aspects of L/BMA and yoga, I feel a deeper connection to my movement and to the lineages I am a part of.

Personal Journey of Rehabilitation and Hip-Hop

Contributed by Keely Song Glenn, CLMA, MFA. Used with permission.

I am a nomad, persistently seeking movement communities that can teach me kinesthetic knowledge and artistry. From ballet to capoeira, from breaking to contemporary, I find deep satisfaction in stylization cross-training.

Keely Song Glenn, MFA, is an assistant professor of dance at Brigham Young University and a dance fusionist. Her writing details how she uses the L/BMA system when acquiring new dance technique and stylization.

I am comfortable with and intrigued by the unacquainted, unknown, and unfamiliar. Training in the unfamiliar is my familiarity.

My confidence in liminality, or the space between learning and knowing, stems from my understanding and application of the L/BMA system and its systematic approach to analyzing and coaching toward greater movement efficiency and dynamics. L/BMA's physical and linguistic vocabulary offers assurance and safety within an environment and aesthetic that might feel alienating in either a physical or a social context. However, this confidence has not always felt intuitive. Rather, it has developed as I incorporate the L/BMA system in my dance training.

In the following section I discuss my training in a new dance style using aspects of L/BMA. Through observation, BESS mapping, BESS comparison, and trial and error, I move through improvement and capitalize on how I take technique classes and ultimately reveal enjoyment and encouragement along the building process. I hope that sharing my application of L/BMA serves as both catalyst and motivation for others to explore the use of L/BMA language for technique. Most important, I hope these tools serve as a support and a reference that can help others avoid feelings of self-deprecation, defeat, or discouragement throughout this lifelong journey of movement.

Empowerment in Initiation

The brace on my left leg is a reminder of the fragility and resilience of the body. Remnants of my limp remain from my ACL surgery nine months ago, but I am determined to start dancing again. "Breathe. Breathe," I remind myself. My heart pulses as I try to calm my fight-or-flight response, which has my ghost halfway out the door. I haven't even begun, and that is why I am here, on the dance floor of this dilapidated building. I am here to begin.

The air is thick and hot before class starts, and I feel perspiration already. In walks Tristan, the hip-hop instructor, with lightness and free Flow evident in his spirit and buoyant steps. His body naturally emanates the juxtaposition between free and bound Flow, heightened in its contrast with the suddenness that permeates his movement and focus. His direct focus and discipline are evident as he gestures while describing the order of the class and the work we will do. He moves mostly in the mid-reach kinesphere, but occasionally reaches the edges when demonstrating his theme for the class, which includes specifics, details, and grooves.

As the class progresses, he continues to demonstrate the combination; it appears as though he has both all the time in the world and yet no time. There is no sense of urgency, but there is a clock constantly speeding up and slowing down based on the will of the individual. I try to compose myself, to act cool, to engage the breath, but my natural bodily tendencies show through. I am neither bound nor free enough in my Flow. I am in the place where muscles can't fire and release quickly enough and everything becomes a bad smoothie recipe: The ingredients are there but not in the correct ratios.

The rapper's fast-paced lyrics versus the choreography's full-body gesturing with the rapper and the beats is a game of coordination and output. Nothing he teaches is beyond my technical ability, but the pace makes the intricacies of body in space nearly impossible to perform. I simply can't coordinate my body phrasing fast enough. I leave class in a polarized stasis of euphoria and frustration. One simple question arises as my sweat evaporates: Why can't I do the movement?

1. Observation

I consider this question on my drive home as I walk back through my experience, starting with my observation of Tristan. I'm looking for movement clues, gestures, and phrasing that might give me insight on how I can perform the choreography more successfully. Sometimes, the greatest clues for a style are not found while the music is blaring and the choreography is in motion. Sometimes, the clues for phrasing are revealed in the instructor's timing and pauses of the breath, the gestures of hands, the directionality of focus, and the rhythm and spatial attitude of the torso. Observation during these moments can be just as imperative as the fully committed physicality of the dance.

Thus, when taking a class, I note how instructors build their sequences and if they stem from their preferred bodily disposition and demeanor. If they do, I try to match aspects of their gestures and phrasing within my own demeanor. In Tristan's case, the clear, direct focus paired with succinct phrasing and pauses of speech are reflected in the choreographic timing he demonstrated. His demeanor offered clues on how to approach the movement; it is a dance swirling within the aura. As I set a goal to personify aspects of his disposition during the week, I try to keep in mind that sometimes the demeanor of a choreographer is contradictory to their movement aesthetic. When that is the case, preparing a personal BESS map takes precedence.

2. BESS Mapping

A BESS map helps me see what I already do well and where I can improve. When creating my BESS map, I consider my natural tendencies, biases, preferences, and aesthetics in the Body, Effort, Shape, and Space categories. The more detailed my map is upon entering a class, the more specific I can be in my observation, analysis, and performance integration.

Like many dancers, I have spent years emulating and copying the choreography of others and learned that it is important to differentiate between what one likes to do and what one naturally does. For example, I enjoy choreography in and around vision drive, but I naturally gravitate toward passion drive in my improvisation. Therefore, as I begin creating or editing my BESS map, I reflect upon what I like to do versus what I naturally do to design an authentic BESS map. Upon completing my map, I cross-check with outside observers to ensure that the physical manifestation reflects my inner intent. Though BESS mapping takes a substantial amount of time, its payoff in terms of technical growth makes it worth the investment.

It is important to revisit one's BESS map when training. For example, the night I first limped into Tristan's hip-hop class, my Body emphasis was cross-laterality and body-half that moved successively and simultaneously through the body. However, as I diligently returned to class, I enhanced my ability to access core-distal and upper-lower using a rapid unitary and sequential phrasing. Without an honest BESS map, traversing the landscape of my movement is difficult to document because I can't access where I have been and where I can improve. Thus, it is important to edit within each new training program.

3. BESS Comparison

With a BESS map in hand, I then compare my map with a teacher's BESS map. A BESS map is a springboard for me to streamline where I need to focus my attention and allows me to see what is missing. For example, in the Shape category, I enjoy screw-like and ball-like shapes that encompass spreading/enclosing and rising/sinking. If a class utilizes these Shape characteristics, I know I can concentrate on refining other categories, such as Body, Effort, or Space.

Next, I assess any correlations between my BESS preferences and the movement sequence I desire to learn. When my BESS partialities are in sync with a teacher's, I often find myself skating along into the momentum and sheer physicality of the movement. It becomes meditative as time and fear dissipate. However, when I attend another class, I may find fewer similarities, and my body and mind rearrange categorical identifiers.

Therefore, referring back to my question after the hip-hop class—why can't I do the movement?—I only needed to look at what our movements reveal about our partialities, habits, and tendencies. A comparison chart of my and Tristan's BESS maps indicated that our movement choices are antithetical. If he steeples, I volute; he's a square and I'm a screw; I'm in passion and he's in vision. Essentially, I have to reverse *all* the categories of BESS when taking his class.

That evening, the sheer number of changes shocked my body, but studying how I needed to reverse my preferences allowed me to train in a methodological approach that could facilitate improvement while avoiding frustration.

4. Trial and Error

It is one thing to understand why I can't do a movement phrase theoretically. It is an entirely different progression to physically embody those changes. As I returned to Tristan's class, I began a series of trial and error as I worked through each BESS category. One week, I traded my peripheral approach to the kinesphere with his mid-reach, central approach. The next week, I focused on the shape qualities of advancing/retreating versus my natural spreading/enclosing. Although I understood the need to reverse most of my preferences, I didn't know the order that would most effectively help me match the aesthetic. However, knowing that I needed to reverse most of my BESS map allowed me the patience to deconstruct the movement. Dripping sweat in sync to the beats, I began to observe the details and transitions originally invisible to my eye, and with each new detail my map was refined.

Week after week, I moved through the categories, challenging my effort configurations, a PTBC pattern, a shape quality, and spatial intentionality until I felt it crystalize or diminish in importance. As my muscle memory assisted in acquiring the movement, I began to converge both physically and theoretically the elements of BESS that most accurately represented the movement at stake. Within a few months, my vigilance in the physical and theoretical practice began to show positive results: I developed a new BESS map that converged aspects of my old tendencies with new landmarks and gave me a dynamic range of movement choices. While there is never truly a conclusion along this dance journey, my evolved BESS map infused with Tristan's hip-hop style of new jack, popping, locking, and new school is a treasure map worth keeping, and I store it away along with other BESS maps I have created.

Continuing the Journey

Before my exposure to the L/BMA system, I entered dance classes with little sense of how I would integrate new movements with previous experiences and across genres. I was merely after the physical euphoria concocted from adrenaline and excursion. It was an impetuous approach toward improvement and adaptability, like a traveler without a compass.

My training in L/BMA altered that. A sense of directionality now supports my wandering disposition across genres, creating a destination for all of my movement experiences to maneuver toward and within. Movement experiences are no longer disjointed, but are pieces that fit along the spectrum of BESS to improve my overall artistry and technique. By developing observational skills, BESS mapping, comparison, and trial and error, I have the means *and* the methods to improve how I catalog and connect my dance experiences from one genre to the next as I fine-tune my BESS maps regularly.

As my stamina and confidence continue to build, I find myself once again roaming for new maps. "Breathe. Breathe deeply," I remind myself. I walk into an unfamiliar building. Stepping into that second-floor studio where the sense of newness mingles with the thick air of sweaty capoeiristas, I am both petrified and curious. The opportunity for vulnerability and growth presented by simply entering a room gives me the adrenaline that roller-coaster addicts long for. Freshness mixes with suspense as the liminal space facilitates the freedom of the beginning and the savoring of the present. In the beginning, failure is probable, and I am liberated from the need to produce, define, or perfect.

I can't help but amusingly grin as I begin once again.

The Physicality of Humor: A Laban Perspective on Incongruent Movement Patterns

Contributed by Sarah Donohue, CLMA, MFA. Used with permission.

In the moment of humor, the senses are tickled by information and messages, both commonplace and incongruent. In fact, the juxtaposition of sense-making and altered expectations is the recipe for humor. An unexpected peek-a-boo delights a baby into laughter, the universal indicator of humor. A story is told in which the associated mental images are contradicted by an unforeseen twist at the end. With a shift in perspective, we experience humor on many perceptual levels.

This application explores the physicality of humor through a Laban/Bartenieff perspective and suggests that incongruities in movement not only contribute to humor, but are subconsciously accessed on a kinesthetic level. While acknowledging that humor is situational and relational, my research isolates the movement of the body during a humorous event and reveals that incongruent movement patterns can explain physical humor.

Since determining what is humorous is in the funny bone of the beholder, I have selected a group of individuals whose movements are generally deemed humorous: Charlie Chaplin, Buster Keaton, Rowan Atkinson, and others. I am not asking *if* their movement is humorous. Rather, I am assuming that it is and asking if they exhibit common movement patterns. Using the Laban/Bartenieff system, I have also analyzed the movement of humorous dance, such as the choreography of Monica Bill Barnes. Additionally, this inquiry prompts a search for humorous quotidian movement, such as someone walking into a spider web, which is difficult to spontaneously encounter and simultaneously analyze. Although the elements of humor-producing movement vary, I identify patterns of incongruity within the Laban/Bartenieff categories of Body, Effort, Shape, and Space.

Sarah Donohue, MFA, CLMA, is a dancer, a choreographer, and an assistant professor of dance at Utah Valley University. In her research and choreography she explores the physicality of humor and its many applications through an L/BMA perspective.

Body

Which parts of the body are moved or held and *how* they are moved or held is culturally and socially significant. In the prototypical clown, we see the legs in external rotation, knees bent and adaptable, and a narrow torso being held in line with the head. There is often superfluous action of the lower legs and feet, and walking is initiated by spoking with the knees. Picture the gait of Charlie Chaplin. This bodily posture appears paradoxically inviting (with legs turned out) and protective (with spine and torso held). The contradictory posture contributes to a pattern of incongruence.

Body-Half and Upper-Lower Patterns of Total Body Connectivity

In the movement of physical comedians and clowns, there is a tendency for locomotion to take place in a body-half pattern instead of in the natural cross-lateral gait, perhaps an intentional indication of being less physically developed. We find familiarity, and often humor, in the body-half waddling of a penguin or toddler. Perceiving someone walk in a body-half pattern is incongruent with the naturally developed human gait of cross-laterality. Additionally, an apparent separation between the upper and lower parts of the body is a trait often present in physical humor. A common theme in cartoons involves the lower body running away from peril before the upper body gets the message to flee as well. In human form, the disassociation between the upper and lower body of physical comedians indicates an incongruity on a basic level of development, as if regions of the body are being controlled by separate forces. Monty Python's sketch "Ministry of Silly Walks" demonstrates an elaborate disconnection between body parts, with the upper and lower body often moving incongruently against one another.

Shape Flow Support and Shape Qualities

The Laban/Bartenieff category of Shape reveals meaning by focusing on the growing and shrinking of the torso and how the shaping of the body connects to Space. How we move our torsos can send very clear messages to perceivers, or, conversely, incongruent messages. If a person lengthens his torso vertically while rising with his entire form to pick an apple from a tree, the experience of all parts organizing toward place high—and the apple—is both functional and congruent. Incongruence in Shape would have the apple-picking man shorten his torso like a compressed spring while the frame of his body attempts to rise to place high. This incongruence may indicate that the mover does not physically embody efficient movement phrasing, which, to those inclined to schadenfreude, is perhaps a humorous situation. From a less vindictive perspective, incongruity between shape qualities and shape flow support is prevalent in clowning and particularly humorous in dance, where the expectation is for efficient movement patterns.

Phrasing in movement corresponds well to phrasing in written language. A movement phrase, or movement sentence, is complete and congruent when there is preparation, initiation, action, and follow through. A dart player prepares by focusing on the bull's-eye, both visually and kinesthetically. To initiate throwing the dart, she carefully pulls it back toward her shoulder before suddenly and directly sending it toward the target in the main action of the phrase. To complete the phrasing, her hand follows the pathway of the dart, guiding it empathetically to the bull's-eye. In dance, a well-executed grand jeté, or leap, is an example of congruent phrasing.

Physical humor often relies on the interruption of phrasing and the viewer's preconceived expectations being altered unpredictably, as is often utilized in the choreography of Monica Bill Barnes—a pelvic gyration in the midst of a flowing modern phrase or a giant cardboard box flying onstage to hit the dancer at the height of a graceful arabesque. Incongruities in phrasing are closely related to surprise, a key element in humor (Weems 2014, 26). Our sense-making minds are stringing together visual input to create a narrative or expected outcome. When what we believed would take place shifts unpredictably, humor is the result.

Effort

Phrasing can also be interrupted in regard to Effort. Listening to your favorite song and remembering sweet memories of the past may take you into what Laban calls passion drive (free Flow, light Weight, and sustained Time). However, an unexpected knock on the door will take you into an awake state (direct Space and sudden Time). The complete shift on the effort spectrum, from indulging qualities (free, light, sustained in this case) to condensing qualities (direct and sudden) is incongruent, surprising, and can be humorous. Stand-up comedians exhibit wonderful incongruent Effort phrasing in their verbal delivery. Conversely, congruent effort phrasing is created through effort loading. The effort is a natural progression that develops out of and returns to an established effort constellation.

However, in incongruent effort phrasing, like moving from passion drive to awake state, all the Effort qualities change at once. What was sustained becomes sudden; what was missing (Space effort) suddenly appears in direct Space. We can picture the effort phrasing making a complete shift across the effort spectrum in progressions such as walking to slipping or reading a book to being startled. In choreography, being aware of how effort phrasing falls naturally into, or out of, metered music can mean the difference between predicable musicality and delightful surprise.

Space

How the human body is organized in Space is meaningful not only in humor studies but also in everyday interaction with the environment. A congruent interaction with space allows you to get to the bus stop safely and efficiently. "Natural," unaffected walking takes place in the sagittal plane (forward, with a little bit of up and down). In many clowning examples as well as Charlie Chaplin's walk, space is approached incongruently, by ambulating in the vertical plane (more side to side than forward).

Incongruence in Space is also revealed by countertension, which is what the body uses to balance when one slips or falls. From walking along in two spatial pulls of the sagittal plane, slipping requires the body to balance by moving into the third, previously absent spatial pull, the horizontal dimension (or some deflection of it). The need to move into a countertension is in opposition to the previous action or movement goal. Our expectations for regular locomotion are broken on many levels. While dance lives in the world of countertension, everyday actions meet extreme countertension when something unpredictable has happened—something incongruent.

As a choreographer and dance educator, my aim is not necessarily to create humorous dances. However, humor is an inroad to interpersonal connection, and my aim is to create dances with which a wide range of audiences can connect. Humor, like dance, has the capacity to be nonverbal and to reach beyond boundaries of culture, society, ability, and age (Weems 2014, 154). Infants laugh before they possess language—often they are laughing at motion. Humor is a primal human experience that we understand innately and kinesthetically.

The study of humor through a Laban/Bartenieff perspective offers various benefits to the arts and education. Humor in the classroom serves memory retention, allowing students to create knowledge through their individual, humorous connection to learning. Understanding the physicality of humor through a Laban/Bartenieff analysis of incongruent movement patterns allows choreographers to develop innovation in their movement, audiences to access dance on a subconscious level, and everyday people to connect with each other through the kinesthetic language of humor.

Making Dances with Laban/ Bartenieff Movement Analysis

Contributed by Kevin Williamson, MFA, CLMA. Used with permission.

As a queer artist, my goal is to celebrate excess, multiplicity, empathy, and compassion in my dance work. Working collaboratively, I disrupt binary logics by drawing from discordant sounds and imagery in live performance. For my most recent project, *Super,* which was inspired by superhero personas, I utilized the L/BMA framework extensively to both prescribe and describe movement with my collaborators while in process.

I developed a list of questions that I hoped my collaborators and I could answer through choreographic research. How do superheroes dance? Can a dance performance applaud heroes in all their glory while also subverting ideas about perfection? Can we move past binaries of valiant and cowardly in defining heroes and villains? Intrigued by archetypes and the living hero in each of us, I decided it would be a worthwhile challenge to make a dance that honored these questions in the studio.

The Process

I began the process with a group of student artists at Scripps College, where I am a faculty member. We started by discussing our various associations with superheroes: well-known and unknown archetypes, our fearless family members, courageous teachers who inspire us, and invisible heroes from our communities whose work often goes unnoticed. Memorable movements ranging from the virtuosic to the quotidian include favorite athletes, activists protesting together at the 2017 Women's March, and more personal moments with our grandparents or coaches. We also imagine renowned scientists experimenting in their laboratories, artists painting diligently in their studios, a lonely traveler searching for contentment, and those in our lives who are humbly battling illness. We describe to each other what these heroic acts look like. While chatting we notice that, regardless of context, the players from our collective memory are steadfast in their convictions as they maneuver in the world, but somehow they maintain a flexible approach to living.

For our first improvisational task, I wanted to see if the embodiment of multiple spatial pulls can demonstrate adaptability as heroic act. I invited the group to investigate Shape Qualities as they travel across the floor in the studio

Kevin Williamson is a Los Angeles-based choreographer, an assistant professor of dance at Scripps College, and a CLMA. His interdisciplinary work explores social issues through movement, media, text, and music. His essay reflects on L/BMA in the choreographic process.

and pose a question for us to consider: What happens when we advance *while* we are enclosing, or spread *while* simultaneously sinking and retreating? I'm interested in how we can embody multiple spatial pulls as a metaphor for adaptability as a heroic act. Together, we play with shaping while locomoting and soon discover that the ongoing *ingness* of shaping in one direction while being pulled in another feels chaotic and turbulent—just like life! Survival seems to demand malleability and I think this improvised score serves as an example of an aspect of heroism that is not always recognized.

As I step out to observe the dancers moving in one direction *while transitioning to another* using Shape qualities, they appear to be action stars from a superhero movie—dodging swords in an upper body retreat while slinging their imaginary shields forward, or ducking from the blow of an opponent while sliding across the floor to save their comrade. They are morphing and invincible with their abilities to shapeshift. Watching it is unpredictable and delicious. There is a special intelligence in how each dancer organizes their Body connectivity to facilitate moving in multiple directions at once. Effort is embodied deeply in one dancer's gaze—a direct look toward the sky with sudden use of time to reorient the body in a difficult transition, then an indirect gaze across the room as another dancer flow fluxes, modifying their movement choices in relationship to their peers and the environment. This episode, called "Cinematic Morph," lives in the dance as an improvised choreography.

In our second rehearsal, we decide to examine taking a stand while practicing self-preservation and inner peace. I generate phrase material that alternates distinctly among Modes of Shape Change. For example, I start with one fist flying upward into the air with strong Weight while one leg sweeps periph-erally in a calculated rond de jambe (directional Modes of Shape Change, spoking and arcing). I transition this bold movement with a carving mode to illuminate a sense of three-dimensionality and containment within my own kinesphere, fluctuating from piercing space to wrapping it around myself like a blanket. Consciously rounding into myself, I take my attention inward, with three-dimensional Shape Flow Support. Here, I give myself room to breathe and care for myself, honoring my own vulnerability before I return to face the world, which is an important theme in the work.

Imagine a dancer arriving momentarily in a Statue of Liberty pose, then slid-ing slowly into a deep and wide squat to then corkscrew her body to the floor using her hands, landing in a screw-like shape. She is twisted around herself in repose, she is protecting herself, but, quickly, she retrogrades up through the floor, unraveling as she opens the body wide to press firmly through one leg as she springs into the air, à la sissonne. After landing on two feet, she pivots, arms measuring space at the edge of her kinesphere, to then wrap around herself again in a standing coil (having phrased from a spoking leap to an arcing-carving twist). She unravels again, spreads into a giant X shape, teetering, tipping on one leg as she sends energy up and over into space as if to cartwheel, but at the last moment she pokes her gesture leg behind the standing leg and erects herself, righting herself to prevent an unnecessary fall.

These two styles of phrasing become motifs: the first, protecting oneself and then reasserting oneself in the world; the second, almost falling and catching oneself at the last moment. For me, repetition and variations on sequences that are literal (I almost fall, but I catch myself) help produce legibility for viewers within the abstract. In the movement landscape we've generated, our hero continuously rebounds and adapts to life; she falls and recovers, exerts and then recuperates by shielding herself. She does it over and over again with each new challenge, and this is why she is a hero—because she perseveres. When the piece is complete, the movement vocabulary will (hopefully) invoke a sense of risk and self-agency from one moment to the next.

We continue to build movement sequences like these, as well as partnering sections, solo dancing, and ensemble movements over the course of a few months. We add theatrical devices to the structure that provide a reflexivity—a sly wink at the audience and a strut across the stage. While paying comedic homage to films, comics, and celebrity, pop culture references and abstract phrase work combine to paint a complex portrait of contemporary heroes in action. The dance reads like a training ground for fearlessness and heroic vulnerability.

Near the tail end of our rehearsal process I ask, "What does this dance need to feel complete?" So far it had playful movement invention, fierce dancing, and quirky theatrical non sequiturs, but something was missing. I had recently shared a memory from my childhood with the cast. I had tied a blanket around my neck, pretending to be She-Ra (a fictional superhero, sister to He-Man). The students liked this image of me embodying the femme fatale as a young boy, so we gathered blankets and throws to explore our own childlike relationship to heroes in the now.

Immediately, awesome moments of Shape Flow blossomed as dancers swaddled themselves in blankets or pulled fabric taut behind them with their arms, making capes out of them, as if to fly. These subtle movements (an important contrast to the gross-motor sequences described earlier) were slow-morphing, landing in still forms. We decided to sequence together a series of these slow-moving "heroic" poses and finish with the dancers slowly tossing their capes behind them in unison. In the final image, they stand tall, repeatedly flinging their capes backward and upward, yearning for a gust of wind to help them take flight. This final image is innocent and sweet while serving as an epilogue—the characters transfixed by their imagination and the possibility of flight.

As the process concludes, the dancers and I observe videos and talk about what the dance is "doing." Together, we make decisions about the sequences we want to keep, edit, delete. Then we add a bit more choreography, and we make changes so that the dance reflects the various themes, commonalities, and differences that are important to us. The dance grows richer and more nuanced as the date of its premiere approaches. This, of course, is the most challenging and fun part—juggling what we've made, coming to understand it from various perspectives, and making choices that are deliberate in relation to our objective.

Reflection

L/BMA informs so much of my choreographic process. The BESS framework provides me with tools to consider the multiple layers of meaning-making that exist at any given moment and a framework from which to generate, observe, critique, remix, layer, and phrase it all with exactitude. As a choreographer, it is important for me to understand, with my collaborators, why we choose certain movements over others and how our use of time affects how the energy is emphasized and how the content of the piece unravels. Understanding our choices through the L/BMA lens means that we can take ownership of the material as coauthors and articulate to each other and our audiences what we have created and why.

Contemporary Vocal Music Application: Breathing Life into the Voice

Contributed by Amanda Huntleigh, DMA, CLMA. Used with permission.

In both vocal instruction and Bartenieff fundamentals, breath connectivity is a continuous underpinning; it is the life of my sound, my stability, and my mobility. Beyond breath, when singing, I attend to shape flow support and invest in upper-lower connectivity. My intention stems from the importance of feeling grounded through my core to the earth. Attending to my feet yielding in the ground is essential for preparing breath on a firm foundation. My lower body harnesses energy in a stabilizing wave into the ground, and in a mobilizing wave, via my breath, into my upper body and out into the space around me. In this way, my upper body is replaced by sound, as it is my sound that reaches out into space. Visualizing the sound moving away from my midline

---

Amanda Huntleigh, DMA, is an assistant professor of music and director of choral activities at Clarke University in Dubuque, Iowa; she previously taught public school in Illinois, Virginia, and Delaware, and collegiate choirs at the University of Washington and Smith College. With this contribution, Dr. Huntleigh outlines her use of L/BMA principles within vocal pedagogy to enhance her own artistry.

toward each side as it exits my mouth gives me a vivid sense of each foot being connected to half the sound, and allows me to remain grounded through body-half connectivity as my sound whirls through the air. Regardless of the pattern of body connectivity, focusing on that connectivity provides me the power to produce varied sounds from a place of assuredness and support.

Vocal Pedagogy Application Overview

The singing process uses the body to create sound as the torso propels air past the vocal cords, causing them to vibrate, and then moves sound through the conduit of the vocal tract, out of the body, and into the environment. The two primary variables singers can manipulate to alter the sound of their voices are: (1) breath support, created by breath speed and pressure as it moves out of the lungs and past the vocal cords, and (2) resonating space, which is the shape of the vocal tract through which the air travels. Standard technique, which reminds singers to take a better breath or to sing with more space, leaves much room for personal (mis)interpretation. Laban/Bartenieff Movement Analysis concepts allow specificity in coaching how to take and use a better breath, and how to alter the shape of the vocal tract to change the vocal tone.

Breath support is "the proper coordination of expiration and phonation to provide an unwavering sound, an ample supply of breath, and relief from any unnecessary and obstructive tensions in the throat" (Doscher 1994, 22–23). I began this application by analyzing my own breath, discovering how shape flow support, effort, and body connectivity support the inhalation of breath and the exhalation of sound. In my practice, Shape Flow support is the most important L/BMA concept facilitating breath support. Specifically, on each breath, I widen near my lower ribs. From this baseline, I then experience Time and Weight Effort, sculpting the initiation of sound via my abdominal muscles. The visibility and degree of bulging and widening are determined by the amount of air needed for a given vocal passage, and can also reinforce the shape of the desired resonating space.

This second vocal concept, resonating space, can be coached through the application of Laban's Shape and Space categories. Though subtle, the application of shape flow support in the neck and head, specifically above the clavicle up to the soft palate, can flexibly and gently sculpt the sound of the voice. These alterations, though too subtle to be visible to most observers, significantly change the shape of the vocal tract, and thus change the quality of the vocal tone. "As sound moves through the vocal tract, it encounters several places where the size of the resonating chamber changes. . . . Independent standing waves, and therefore resonant frequencies, are created each time the relative diameter of the vocal tract changes" (McCoy 2012, 35). When developing this seemingly abstract shape flow support concept, I pair the shape flow support qualities of the neck and head with shape forms and shape qualities, facilitating complementary whole-body movements. I also encourage singers to aim toward specific points in space. This pairing of outward movements with inner shaping helps people see and sense the necessary internal movements, better altering the vocal tract and the tonal quality of their sound. Speaking both from Space and Shape perspectives to address this abstract component of vocal instruction allows me to reinforce singers' resonating space descriptions using their own L/BMA-based perspectives.

Three-Dimensional Vocal Styles

To create a full-bodied, round sound for three-dimensional vocal styles like gospel music and some folk traditions, my preparatory focus is on roundness in my neck and head. To immediately accomplish this sound adjustment, I coordinate the widening and bulging in my torso, which acts as a reminder to my neck and head to express roundness. If needing an additional reminder, I can move in a ball-like shape form, including my whole body in the sound shaping. Before the phrase begins, I focus on bulging in my lower abdomen with widening through my lower ribs as my primary and secondary shape flow support qualities, respectively.

Once I begin the sounded exhale, I maintain much of the widening that I established during the inhalation by contracting my upper abdominals to help resist and slow the natural narrowing that occurs as air is expelled and the ribs work to coordinate their collapse. Bulging actively transitions toward hollowing as I use my air supply. Only once the phrase is complete does narrowing bring my lower ribs back to neutral. Throughout a musical phrase, I can pepper the vocal tone to create accents of various speeds and strengths using Time and Weight in my lower abdominals.

For a more operatic, three-dimensional sound, I must think about these concepts while also tending to the performing space around me. When I hold the image of my round shape moving out of my body and my kinesphere, my roundness can grow and whirl through the room. Roundness is not limited to the frame of my body, so the circumference of my round sound grows as it spirals into the environment like a cyclone. This creates the powerful, three-dimensional sound typical of professionally trained opera singers.

Two-Dimensional Vocal Styles

Singing using two-dimensional vocal styles requires a very different initiation than three-dimensional sounds. When creating a narrow sound, akin to that of an American twenty-first-century pop singer, my preparatory focus is relaxation. Before the phrase begins, I am still focusing on breath connectivity and grounding, as before, but the grounding has a very one-dimensional downward spatial pull. I feel narrow in terms of my shape flow support. The inhalation just before singing triggers widening from my lower ribs and down through my lower abdomen; this remains the dominant shape flow support quality throughout this two-dimensional style of singing. Depending on the tessitura, or vocal range, of the phrase, there may be lengthening as my pelvic floor descends with the preparatory breath, reinforcing the downward spatial pull. When I inhale to sing in a narrow, popular style, it is as if sound begins with breath, and then, through core-distal connectivity, it is grounded through each leg as it also ascends my vocal tract; however, as breath leaves my core to move upward, it encounters resistance from the contraction in my upper abdominals, slowing the air. To facilitate the planar quality of the sound, gestures indicating place high and forward, or whole-body movements that activate the body through the sagittal plane, are helpful for envisioning and producing the sound. Accents in this style are delivered rarely, but when they are, they tend to be with strong Weight in the lower abdominals or by slightly releasing the contraction in the upper abdominals to briefly allow more air to pass through the vocal cords.

To produce a belting quality like the kind often used in twenty-first-century musical theater, a variation on the two-dimensional style can be used. It begins like the popular sound described above, but the shape of the neck and head may feel more like an inverted triangle, emphasizing sidedness with the release of sound. This image allows the singer to maintain the narrowness necessary at the base of the vocal tract for initiating the sound and also incorporates the width necessary to achieve the style's characteristic brassiness. The two-dimensional quality of the sound is powered through body-half connectivity or upper-lower connectivity while sending the sound to right- and left-side high. The small quantity of air passing through the vocal cords de-emphasizes the sensation of breath connectivity. Additionally, the flexion needed in the upper abdominals is amplified to the degree that the upper abdominals focus on stability. Particularly for this style, each singer needs to work out their own airflow equilibrium. If one's individual balance is not achieved, the voice can crack or abruptly change registers. However, with embodied practice, this style becomes simple and rewarding.

To integrate L/BMA into vocal pedagogy, I had to listen to my body while experimenting with different vocalizations. I can now quickly identify if I am not achieving a desired sound because of an issue having to do with a Pattern of Total Body Connectivity, passivity in my abdominals, or misshaping of the vocal tract. L/BMA has allowed me to describe more specifically how each singer might achieve a desired sound, making it less of a guessing game. There is enormous potential for integrating L/BMA concepts into singing instruction for all ages and skill levels. With willingness to move and visualize these concepts, Laban/Bartenieff-based movement instruction provides a valuable supplement to solid vocal pedagogy.

Movement Psychotherapy: L/BMA in Clinical Practice

Contributed by Katya Bloom, PhD, CMA, BC-DMT. Used with permission.

When I reflect on how L/BMA has been supportive in my clinical dance/movement psychotherapy practice, I realize that it has been most useful in guiding me *before* and *after* sessions. As a general rule, I try *not* to bring it to mind *during* sessions. Of course it may pop up, and I duly note it; but then I go straight back to the more immediate experience of being present with the patient or patients and with the feelings being communicated as the session unfolds. It goes without saying that my ideas on this subject have grown out of my own practice in particular clinical settings; and I am well aware that other clinicians, perhaps working in different kinds of settings, will have found L/BMA to be useful in different ways.

Before the Session

I have found that before sessions, L/BMA (in all previous writing, Bloom has used the acronym LMA; but for purposes of uniformity, she uses L/BMA here) can provide a wonderful guide to my preparatory movement practice. I call this *tuning*. The purpose of a preparatory tuning practice is to develop my body's sensory acuity, to hone my intuition, and to cultivate my listening skills—all so that I can be receptive to both my own internal world and that of patients. The L/BMA vocabulary and framework support me in experiencing myself and my movement as seen through the various L/BMA lenses. This improvised tuning practice helps me to be more open and available, free from preconceptions when I'm with patients and whatever they may bring to a given session. I am more able to sustain what I've called *embodied attentiveness* throughout sessions, to more deeply appreciate the particular ways patients experience the world.

As I immerse myself in the practice, L/BMA can provide clarity in terms of how and where I place my attention. It can be as simple as tuning in to a single effort quality—the fluctuations in my Flow of feelings, or registering my decisions in Time. I may choose to recognize my current state and then immerse myself in a state that isn't my natural preference. Dream or near states, for example, can relax a busy mind. These particular states bring me closer to my

Katya Bloom, PhD, practiced and taught DMT for many years in London and now continues her work in Santa Barbara, California. In her book, *The Embodied Self,* she synthesized L/BMA and psychoanalytic ideas; in this piece, she describes specifically *when* and *how* she has found L/BMA to be useful in DMT.

bodily sensations, my feelings, and my intuition; they help cultivate my ability to meet and dwell in the unknown.

Using the Space harmony framework, I may choose to focus on a dimension, a plane, or the cross of axes; even the simple act of relaxing the vertical axis of my spine can enhance a sense of integration. Using the Body and Shape components, I may consciously articulate the joints of my body, and move from position to position.

I find that this kind of tuning practice, however short, supports a greater intimacy with patients. As I take in the complexity of their expression, I feel less pressured to come up with facile answers to problems. The practice helps me cultivate both a firm and a flexible presence, as well as enabling the continual development of my own body's capacity to listen and to speak.

After the Session

I find that the most fruitful time for putting on the L/BMA glasses is after a session ends and over time, when we have a chance to reflect, analyze, and hypothesize. The L/BMA frameworks help me to recognize and name key moments and emerging patterns. When something changes, I can be specific, in movement terms, about what has changed and how that change has manifested. L/BMA helps to clarify my perception of what was experienced in sessions, without reducing its complexity or imposing meaning.

Before I start to analyze things in L/BMA terms, I often take a little time immediately after someone leaves, and before making notes, to move or just be with my physical and emotional experience. By taking this time to check in with myself, I may recognize what part of someone I may have been left with, as it were, and how that may be reflected in the effort qualities or state I feel, my orientation to Space, or a specific bodily posture or gesture I have taken on. I may feel as though I need to move to give expression to feelings, or I may just sit with the residue of a session.

As I try, in making notes, to remember the sequence of how a session unfolded, L/BMA can help me to recapture the details. Over time, I have found that the Effort material—especially the states (the various combinations of two effort qualities), but also the drives (the combinations of three effort qualities)—provide an extremely useful lens for naming what I witness and experience with patients. Although, as we know, the six states of mind have no intrinsic meaning in a therapy context, individual patients' preferences for one state (or drive) over others can, in the context of their material, be very meaningful indeed. For example, a patient may present as oblivious to Time, for weeks or even months on end, perhaps arriving late and seemingly having little awareness of the movement of time within sessions. Someone like this may habitually meet the world in a remote (Space and Flow) or dream (Weight and Flow) state. Recognizing this can help to inform the therapy, even without referencing L/BMA.

Someone else may habitually present as agitated and speedy, but have little awareness of their surroundings or ease in articulating thoughts. I may, upon reflection, recognize this as a configuration within the mobile (Time and Flow) state. This recognition may inform my own decisions, words, and actions in subsequent sessions, in an effort to support the patient's growing awareness and stability.

The effort quality of Flow is, of course, of immense importance in therapy, related, as it is, to feelings. One can reflect on feelings—their absence, the resistance to expressing them, the inability to contain them, the sudden outburst of them—all in terms of how the element of Flow is manifesting and fluctuating.

Having a sense of someone's baseline state helps me to be keenly aware when something shifts, when another state emerges, even for a moment. I can also choose what feels like an appropriate moment to stimulate a change in the patient's state based on what is currently missing, and what I sense the patient is trying to move toward. Sometimes I may do this quite spontaneously, without conscious forethought. It is afterward that L/BMA can help me understand my rationale.

A memorable example of a spontaneous, intuitive intervention on my part happened during work with a young boy with autism. He had a protective habit of twirling a piece of fabric around a stick one way and then the other, ad infinitum. I'd observed his action, described it to him, and tried doing it myself—it's not easy! At some point, without thinking, I picked up a ball and placed it, with exaggerated deliberateness, beside him. He immediately grabbed it and threw it over his shoulder, while he kept on twirling. Aha, I thought, a moment of attention and meeting. I kept placing balls, and he kept throwing them, as if discarding them. After several rounds, this previously nonverbal boy plaintively cried, "Ball gone," conveying a painful feeling of loss.

In L/BMA terms, his ritualized movements had been characterized by an uncontrollable urgency and an overwhelming flow of feelings—a frenzied passion drive. The ball game seemed to provide a way of connecting to Weight, Time, and Space in a new way, drawing him outside the hypnotic vortex of his twirling. This was the beginning of building trust and communication in many forms.

Other parts of L/BMA provide helpful frameworks as well. At times, I recognize patients' patterns and changes in terms of their orientation to space and their relationship to dimensionality. When a patient seems to shy away from one of the three dimensions or planes, it will often have personal meaning for their particular narrative and worldview.

For example, some patients are less at home in the vertical dimension; they may have a hazy sense of their own vertical axis, and may be overly attentive to the outside world, including being preoccupied with the therapist. Others may have a strong vertical axis, though their relationship with the horizontal or sagittal dimension or plane may be weak. These patients may tend to assert a fierce sense of control, though they may appear or feel frozen, and their ability to connect with others may be limited.

Someone's bodily patterns of posture or gesture, reflecting the BESS components of Body and Shape, may also stand out. I may actually wonder aloud about these manifestations if the timing feels right, in addition to pondering and embodying them for myself after the session. When patients become more conscious of their bodies and their physical patterns, their verbal associations to the sensations and feelings can be enlightening.

To summarize, L/BMA can provide innumerable ideas for harnessing the therapist's fully receptive body, heart, and mind in preparation for seeing patients. L/BMA also offers many ways to help organize the data gathered during sessions for reflection afterward. The simplest L/BMA terms and categories, I find, can often have the most profound resonance. There is no question that L/BMA strongly supports the evolution of the work that goes on in therapy, enhancing the consciousness of both patients and therapists, and strengthening the relationship between them.

Surfing the Body: How the Laban/Bartenieff Material Has Shaped My Approach to Massage and Bodywork

Contributed by Erin Law, LMT, MFA, CLBMA. Used with permission.

The Laban/Bartenieff material has allowed me to understand my own moving body with clarity and wholeness and has deeply informed, shaped, and expanded my kinesthetic intelligence. The emphasis in the L/BMA teachings to "try on" the various aspects of Body, Effort, Shape, and Space by moving them in our bodies has also illuminated a wide range of possibilities outside my unique tendencies and choices as a mover, thus creating awareness of my preferences and habits. Although I had extensive dance training, the L/BMA work was what allowed me to dive in deep and to gain breadth of perspective on human movement as a whole. Now, as a bodyworker/massage therapist I am grateful for the time I spent inhabiting, observing, describing, and making meaning from the many different constellations within BESS; this has paved

---

Erin Law, LMT, MFA, CLBMA, is a bodyworker, somatic movement educator, and dance artist working in Nashville, Tennessee. She describes in this text how the L/BMA system has been integral to her understanding of her own body and to relating to her clients in her bodywork practice.

inroads for me to relate more fully to myself so I can truly empathize with my clients and their needs.

My first memorable encounter with the power of touch was in 2003, in the Integrated Movement Studies Program (IMS). We were learning how to facilitate an understanding of the Patterns of Total Body Connectivity by using our hands to indicate specific movement pathways in our partners' bodies. During this lesson on intentional touch, I was able to feel the rich inner landscape of my core as my partner's hands simply followed the movement of my breath. With no outward prompting, I could visualize and almost feel a bright, warm light channeling from her hand to my center, just from focusing on this dynamic point of contact between us. Coming from a strict ballet background, I found this hands-on work particularly compelling; it was one of the first tools that helped me seek inwardly after years of focus on the outward form. This pivotal moment, along with my growing love and appreciation for the hands-on work we learned at IMS, eventually inspired me to go to massage school so that I could develop more skills to invite others into deep awareness and appreciation of their bodies.

My massage therapy education was comprised of courses on bones, muscles, anatomy and physiology, biomechanics, business, ethics, law, Eastern theory, and more. I was appreciative of the way we took our time to learn these subjects in manageable chunks and that we did the important work of discerning their various parts so that we could learn and digest them. Without this parts-focused work, we would lack the language to talk about details. We need language to be able to understand and differentiate the uniqueness of, say, an amoeba, from that of the lymphatic system. In this particular setting, though, emphasis was not placed on considering how these parts or systems connect to the larger whole of what it means to be a human being with a physical body. As I've learned from the L/BMA work, it is important that we consider the integrated whole so we can see the inherent unity of all living things. When we fail to seek a broader perspective, we lose the ability to understand that the core essence of a *part* reflects some truth about the entirety of the *whole*. Throughout my time in school, and especially as I emerged into the bodywork field as a licensed professional, I repeatedly experienced profound gratitude for the way the L/BMA work had shaped my experience and knowledge of the body as a *whole* entity. It reminds me that when I engage with a client, one of my primary concerns is to keep the whole person in the forefront, rather than getting lost in the client's symptoms. My goal as a bodywork therapist is to co-create a space with my client where, together, we can make connections between the symptomatic "parts" and what he or she is trying to tell me about the complex and multilayered essence of the whole being.

I practice a form of bodywork called ashiatsu, an Asian modality in which the therapist uses her feet to give compression to and lengthen the soft tissue along the client's meridians. With the client lying on a traditional massage table, I work both seated on a tall stool with the wall supporting my back, and standing with one foot on the table and one moving on the client, using wooden bars securely installed in the ceiling to keep my balance and shift my weight. The phrasing of the movement commonly shifts between an alive stillness while sending channeled energy out through the heel to long strokes of the foot along a meridian. When I am engaged in mobility, it can feel a bit like surfing or skiing as my feet pass over the flowing, changing terrain of my client's body. Additionally, my particular practice is influenced by principles of traditional Chinese medicine/five elements and myofascial release (specifically the work of Ida Rolf and Tom Myers). While describing these modalities in detail is beyond the scope of this text, I mention them to highlight that like the L/BMA work, they approach the body as a whole being with many interrelated and connected parts or systems. These modalities offer a broader perspective on the body and often help unite and connect the dots of the compartmentalized model of anatomy and physiology frequently emphasized by allopathic medicine.

I work at Ha.Lé Mind and Body, a contemporary health care company in Nashville, Tennessee, that seeks to facilitate personal empowerment in the healing process by giving clients individualized tools to sustain healthy living. This philosophy supports my belief in people's autonomy and their responsibility to their relationship with their bodies. It encourages them to take an active role in their own healing processes. When we see a client for her first appointment, we spend twenty to thirty minutes discussing her health needs and desires and then design a plan to help her address what she is trying to accomplish. Ha.Lé is unique in that we offer restorative, treatment-centered movement classes in addition to bodywork, meditation, acupuncture, Ayurvedic nutrition counseling, and psychotherapy. In all contexts—classes, bodywork, counseling—we invite people to go inward on a journey to expand self-awareness and learn for themselves about their inherent wholeness. In this way, we are not simply chasing after symptoms, but offering an array of inroads to the healing process.

Spotlight on Breath, Core-Distal, and Upper-Lower Connectivity

In this writing, I discuss how the L/BMA system has shed light on and brought new information to my daily practice of giving bodywork, through an in-depth look at breath, core-distal, and upper-lower, spatial intent and space harmony, as well as effort. I also highlight how the Overarching Concepts of mobility-stability and exertion-recuperation are particularly relevant to my work and how these ideas apply to my own moving body and my relationships to clients.

Breath

The name Ha.Lé means "breath of life" in Vietnamese, thus reinforcing the importance of breath in bodywork and healing practices. When I asked the founder—my mentor and fellow ashiatsu practitioner Janice Cathey—about the role breath plays in her work, she said, "We are not just arms and legs; the client can feel when I am initiating my movements from a deeper place." This resonated with me because when I have been on the receiving end as a bodywork client, I have felt the stark difference between when a practitioner is connected to her own body and breath and when she is not. When she is connected, it feels as though she is pouring and outflowing into me, inviting me into the healing properties my own breath patterning offers. Conversely, when she is unable to access the ongoing flow of breath, I feel as though she is far away rather than present with me. Like Janice, when I initiate my movement with breath, I am reminded that I am a whole being, not just arms and legs. I find that this pattern also connects me back to myself in moments when I lose focus or presence. This, in turn, allows for a deepening of connection with the client. Within a bodywork session, the movement phrasing swings between relative stillness and reinvesting in movement. This rhythm pulses through gradations of mobility and stability, and there are endless ways these two concepts interact. For instance, in a moment of stillness where I am giving a strong Weighted and direct compression to an area, the subtle mobility of my breath patterning fuels and supports my stability. By softening and yielding my hand or foot into the point of contact I'm maintaining with my client, I am allowing the dynamic flow of my breath to create ease. The beauty of this dialogue between mobility and stability is that these two ideas are relational; they don't exist separately; rather, they feed each other. I realized that the power arises from this relationship between breath patterning, yielding, and mobility and stability when I invest in it: My whole body relaxes, and then, almost every time, my client feels this and breathes deeply.

Core-Distal

In my opinion, core-distal is one of the most important patterns for me to access for efficiency and ease in giving ashiatsu. I see three to four clients a day, and while each session is unique, I often repeat some of the same movement phrases again and again. When I get fatigued, I can feel that my big muscle groups want to take over, and when they do, I begin to feel even more tired. I also tend to move my leg and foot as though they are not connected to my pelvis and the rest of my body. When I get to the end of a stroke I can feel my ribs splaying open, tension in my lower back, and a general sense of "going beyond what I can support." When I experience these moments of discomfort, I know I need to redirect my attention. When I send my focus to the sagittal depth of my sacrum (sensing its frontness and backness) and begin to move from that place, I can feel how easily the movement flows from my center to the distal edges of my feet, as though my sacrum is a navigation hub and my foot is the ship following its guidance. When I invest in this pattern, I instantly feel a sense of freedom to move with more flow and ease. This is similar to the activities of skiing or surfing I mentioned earlier; my core is steering and responding to information that the feet are receiving from gliding over the dynamic curves of the client's body. Just as a skier shifts and responds to the contours of a snowy mountain, and a surfer becomes one with the waves by adapting and moving with the flow, ashiatsu works best when a relationship can exist in which open communication moves freely from my core through my limb to the distal edge of my foot, to the client's body, and back through my leg and into my core.

Chinese medicine associates different meridians (lines of energy that are said to flow vertically along the body from head to toe) with various organ systems. For instance, a meridian that runs along the inner thigh and the inside of the shin and foot corresponds with the spleen; another one that runs parallel along the inside of the leg corresponds with the liver. The philosophy is that we can balance the organ systems by awakening points along these meridians through acupuncture or intentional touch. I was struck by how this way of approaching the body is similar to core-distal body patterning: A superficial point at the end of the big toe connects directly to a deep core organ at the center of the body. The way I practice ashiatsu seeks to emphasize these core-distal pathways in the client's body: I often trace connections from tail to arm and back to tail, or sitz bone to heel, or sacrum to occipital ridge (base of the skull). Furthermore, I often use touch to encourage various movement pathways through the bones of my client's feet as a way to address pain or tension closer to her core. It is always proof to me that the whole body is connected when, for instance, I use my thumb to pinpoint a spot underneath a person's scapula, and she tells me "something just released in my neck."

Upper-Lower

The use of the bars installed in the ceiling affords me a unique ability to move between yield/push and reach/pull phrasing in the upper-lower pattern when I'm using my feet to give bodywork. As Colleen wrote previously in chapter 3, the lower body often provides grounding and support for upper body articulation so that we can come into ourselves in order to reach out and engage with our environment. Since ashiatsu depends on clear articulation through the feet, the upper body then holds the responsibility to offer stability, so that the lower is free to move. The crux of the practice depends on this relationship: the upper body yields and pushes (into the bars), sends the message down the arms, through the center, and out the legs so that the lower body reaches and pulls and articulates spatial pathways of the client's body. Even more complexly, there is also a boomerang effect: After this first yield/push/reach/pull pattern from upper to lower, the stable standing leg then reciprocates and ripples movement back upward into the hands. This reminds me of the image of "conversing trampolines" Colleen used in chapter 3 to describe the five diaphragms. Movement bounces between these layers of upper and lower.

Spatial Intent and Space Harmony

The concept of spatial intent gives my work clarity both in how I use my own body and in how I communicate directionality to my clients' tissue. In chapter 3, Colleen referred to this as "sending touch." My experience as a dance artist, movement educator, and contact improviser has provided me with an embodied knowledge of the dynamic relationship between spatial connections inside my body and helps me connect my body to my environment, or Space. In learning about the theory of Space harmony, wherein we encounter "balance" as a flowing dynamic experience in which we are constantly falling toward what we are missing, I got to bring awareness to the sensation of moving off of my vertical axis. This practice has come to support my bodywork practice in a significant way. Ashiatsu often has a phrasing in which I focus on a point (locating touch) with my heel with an outpouring strong directness, and then lengthen the tissue from that point with the whole sole of the foot (locating and sending touch). In order to accomplish that clear pathway of movement from initiation to completion, I must be clear about how I am shifting the weight of my body through various planes of movement. By holding onto the bars installed in the ceiling with my hands, I can truly invest in clear spatial intent with each stroke of my foot as the movement initiates in my upper body and sequences to my lower. This translates to lengthening or deepening the client's tissue in a specific direction. I am usually "falling" to the upper corner of a plane so that my foot can be moving in the diametrically opposed direction.

What follows is a more detailed description of a sequence of phrases through which I move in most sessions and in which Space harmony is of vital importance. Although I am attempting to draw a kinesthetic connection from upper to lower for the client receiving the work, I call this the "body-half sequence" because I cover an entire half of her body without disengaging from contact.

Imagine my client who is lying face down on the massage table, with her back and one half of her lower body exposed. I step onto the table and stand on one stable foot, with the other ready to engage in mobility. In order to keep a sense of calm, flowing ease, every time I make contact with my client my foot delicately and slowly enters her kinesphere, then I gradually and steadily increase the pressure. To begin the phrase, I slide my foot through my sagittal plane across her low back (in her horizontal dimension) several times, then I increase my pressure (using strong Weight) as I bind my Flow to send my heel carefully into the space between the top of her pelvis and the bottom of her ribcage, like a cat settling into the supportive corner of a couch. Keeping my heel rooted with strength and directness, my tail initiates a smooth swivel, and I change the direction my body is facing as I send the whole sole of my foot parallel along the tissue to the side of her spine and shift into a cross-lateral lunge. As I do this, I feel the power in my transition coming from two cooperating sources. The first happens as I strive to maintain a strong, free, direct spell drive throughout the phrase, and my weight pours from my back space to my front space, and energy boomerangs from my lower to my upper body and then back down to my lower body. This body patterning conspires with the second cooperating source, Space harmony, as my grip on the bars allows me to "fall" from the back of my sagittal plane, through my horizontal plane, and back into a different aspect of the sagittal plane. Here, I stabilize my distal edges in my forward high and back low corners so that my mobile foot glides easily toward my forward low. My investment in this diameter, or counterbalance, is what allows me to keep flowing through the sequence efficiently. As I reach the top of her torso, my toes drift into inward rotation so that I can hook my heel into her upper trapezius muscle for a brief moment of stability and then let my foot slide down the back of her arm.

The next phrase creates a zig-zag pathway downward and along the side of her body, much as a skier would zip down a hill. I initiate with my tail as it underlies another cross-lateral swivel. In this moment my inner thighs are pressed together so that I can fan my toes across her axillary tissue at the lateral edge of her scapula; I can feel my intense corkscrew-like nature and the connection from my center to the distal edges of my toes as the driving force. Steered again by my core, I feel the kinetic chain flow from there into the lateral edge of my foot as it gathers the tissue at the side of the client's ribcage, sending it toward her midline. I pause briefly with my heel near the side of the bottom of her thoracic spine. Then I seek to connect her upper body to her lower as I swivel again, falling into my backspace to rotate around my axis and reorient so that my toes sweep over the crest of her pelvis and my whole foot covers her gluteal muscles with outpouring free Flow. I slowly set my heel at the middle of her gluteal tissue as though I were placing a fragile china cup onto a saucer, and then I relax it into the middle of her piriformis muscle (an outward rotator of the hip), again with gradually increasing pressure. I check in to see how she is receiving this information by observing her torso for signs of a shift in shape flow support or a quickening in her breath patterning. At this point, I am again invested in the corners of the sagittal plane, my head reaching toward back high and my heel sending energy into forward low. After this brief compression, I shift the full sole of my foot to the top of my client's hamstrings, where they connect to her pelvis. Still holding the bars for support, I yield and push upward into my hands to send a message from my upper body, which leans into left side high, through my center and into my right foot, which is reaching and pulling to right side low as I steadily glide my foot all the way down the back of her leg toward her ankle with a strong, free, direct spell drive. The phrase comes to completion as the sole of my foot crests her heel and carves to adapt to the sole of her foot, swiping past her toes.

Effort and Exertion-Recuperation

I believe it is important to meet my clients where they are with compassion and respect, while also offering another perspective to facilitate healing. Here I find it useful to frame the work with the organizing theme (sometimes referred to as an overarching principle) of Exertion-Recuperation. It may seem obvious that we live in a society in which success, hard work, and pushing through until we accomplish something significant are primary values, but often people do not see how this value system actually affects their lives, and especially not how the stress of this lifestyle manifests in the truth of their bodily symptoms of pain, stress, insomnia, and tension. This constant emphasis on and allegiance to exertion has negative impacts on our health. To offer a balance, I approach what I do in our sessions as "recuperation education," in which I seek to create a safe space where people can access their dream state (Weight effort + Flow effort) to allow for full relaxation from the consistent awake state (Time effort + Space effort) of our contemporary lives. I do this by staying within the strong Weight, direct Space Effort, flow flux constellation of spell drive for most of the session. I've noticed that within my spell drive, by being in direct Space effort, I am providing certainty, comfort, and predictability; in essence, I am "holding the space," so that my client can drop out of awareness of her environment and into the deep layers of her body being. I imagine myself like the sentry in a group of meerkats, surveying the environment for trouble so that the rest can focus on living their lives free from worry.

I continue to be fascinated by the myriad ways the L/BMA material has informed and guided me in my journey as a bodyworker. I hope this peek into the world of ashiatsu and massage therapy has illuminated another way the Laban/Bartenieff framework applies to a broad range of movement activities. As I reflect on this, I realize how much I have integrated this way of embodying and interacting with movement into my worldview, and I am grateful that it affords me a unique and effective inroad to collaborating with people as they seek ultimate health.

Neuroscience: L/BMA as Movement Therapy for Stroke

Contributed by Andrea Pack, CLMA, PhD candidate in neuroscience at Emory University. Used with permission.

Neuroplasticity is a unique quality that allows connections between neurons to form or reorganize in response to experience. Consider any trained violinist; their skill requires fine-motor movement and intricate finger dexterity not required in most everyday activities. Through practice and repetition, the natural process of neuroplasticity causes the finger motor region of the brain to recruit additional neurons to help the violinist play more efficiently. This essential biological process is constantly occurring as we learn novel behaviors or information, enjoy a new experience, or compensate for a neurological disease or injury.

Around 795,000 people in the United States suffer from stroke annually (Benjamin et al. 2018). A stroke occurs when there is a disruption in the blood supply to the brain, usually caused by a blockage in or rupture of a blood vessel or artery. It results in a sudden death of brain cells due to lack of oxygen. The effects of stroke are highly dependent on its location within the brain. Common complications include loss of speech, vision, memory, touch sensations, and the ability to plan, execute, or control movement. Motor impairments are one of the more common stroke effects, because many strokes involve the middle cerebral artery, which supplies the motor areas of the brain. As many as 88 percent of individuals with acute stroke have hemiparesis, which causes weakness or inability to move on one side of the body, typically associated with the affected brain hemisphere (contralateral to the impaired body side).

When a person experiences a stroke or other neurodegenerative disease, neurons surrounding the lesion area act fast to adapt to the new environment. Surviving neurons, in combination with the generation of neurons, create new connections through mechanisms such as axonal sprouting (Carmichael et al. 2001; Dancause et al. 2005; Li et al. 2010). This leaves a window of opportunity to do various therapies—for example, physical movement with motor and sensory feedback, brain stimulation, or medication—that will aid in developing or reestablishing neural connections through neuroplasticity. Research studies have demonstrated that spared cortical (outer layer) brain areas reorganize following a stroke and correlate with spontaneous behavioral recovery (Chollet et al. 1991; Nudo et al. 1996). Additionally, repetitive rehabilitative training of the impaired limb influences neuroplasticity in spared

---

Andrea Pack, CLMA, PhD candidate in neuroscience at Emory University. In this piece, she describes the potential use of L/BMA-inspired movements as a rehabilitation method for people with motor deficits.

motor areas, promoting restoration of function or approaches for motor compensation (Levy et al. 2001; Liepert et al. 2000). Since most of our brain functions have secondary pathways, the hope is that new neural connections will allow the patient to recover some of their deficits through intact alternative pathways bypassing the lesion areas.

The purpose of this essay is to discuss the potential use of L/BMA-inspired movements as one of several rehabilitation methods for people with motor deficits caused by damage to the brain. Fundamental L/BMA categories—Body, Effort, Shape, and Space—provide a multifaceted approach to access and retrain basic neuromuscular patterns, providing possible therapeutic value in a number of neurological conditions by driving adaptive neuroplasticity through movement. The focus of this discussion will be based on my training as a motor systems neuroscientist over the past seven years, specifically researching the neural mechanisms underpinning plasticity following stroke and traumatic brain injury and sensorimotor learning, as well as my case study using L/BMA as a movement therapy with one individual with stroke, Ralph (I've obtained permission to use his first name). It is important to note that the use of L/BMA-inspired movements as a rehabilitative method is based on results from an informal research study, and further scientific experiments need to be executed to truly understand whether L/BMA movement encourages neuroplasticity, resulting in motor recovery.

Seven years prior to our meeting, Ralph suffered from a stroke on the left side of his brain after falling off a two-story ladder, leaving him with hemiparesis on the right side of his body and difficulty with speech. He was released from the hospital after five weeks and left with the inability to do everyday functions. Ralph was able to regain some of his motor functions through his initial physical therapy sessions and exercise classes, mainly by compensating with his left side.

Ralph and I worked together for 45-minute sessions twice a week for six months starting in September 2013. When we first met, he had no self-initiated mobility throughout the right side of his body. Because strokes cause deficits in balance and gait, I determined that the main theme of our sessions needed to revolve around stability and mobility. The movement exercises I created for Ralph were informed by two concepts: imagery and sensory feedback. Both are relevant to understanding and embodying L/BMA theory, as well as describing motor learning and stroke rehabilitation in neuroscience literature.

During my L/BMA certification program, imagery was regularly used as a means to understand and embody the four basic categories. Before moving through an Effort exercise, we were encouraged to imagine ourselves in two separate scenarios using spell drive (Flow, Weight, Space) and passion drive (Flow, Weight, Time) to help us discern between the use of Space and Time. Imagery is also used to understand the anatomical relationship between bones and muscles and the six body patterns. For example, imagine a figure eight starting at your heels, moving up through your inner adductors and the front

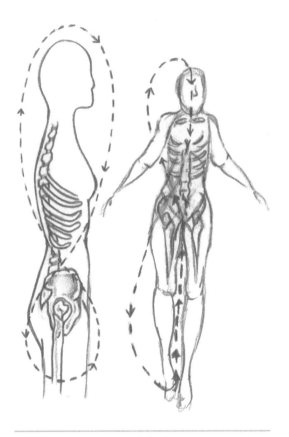

Figure 9.1 Figure-eight imagery to understand the anatomical relationship between bones and muscles.

Illustrated by Sydney P. Celio.

of the pelvis, internally crossing to the T-12 vertebra, coming up your back and over your head, moving down your chest, again internally crossing to the back of the pelvis at your lowest rib, following a line from your sitz bones and down your hamstrings to close the figure eight at your heels (see figure 9.1; Hackney 2002). The figure eight can help one access their anatomical relationship to the head-tail body pattern or how to transition from yield/push to reach/pull with the upper/lower body pattern. Most importantly, imagery is used to discover intention in one's movement, allowing one to find a connection between their Body and Space.

As in Ralph's case, many individuals with stroke are initially unable to perform movements due to the severity of the motor deficits in their affected limbs. An alternative strategy implemented in neurorehabilitation is kinesthetic motor imagery (MI), the mental execution of a specific action with one's own body (first-person perspective) without movement or muscle activation. It is important to differentiate kinesthetic MI from visual MI, another type of motor imagery in which one imagines how someone else's body performs the movement (third-person perspective; Jackson et al. 2001; Sharma, Pomeroy, and Baron 2006). Visual MI primarily activates parietal-occipital cortices (Ruby and Decety 2003; Stinear et al. 2006). Because the goal with Ralph was to regain motor functions, it was essential to use kinesthetic MI, which primarily activates regions related to sensorimotor circuitry (Ruby and Decety 2003; Stinear et al. 2006).

The neural mechanisms underpinning motor imagery are not fully understood, but various research studies using functional magnetic resonance imaging (fMRI), a technique to measure brain activity by identifying changes in blood flow, help pave the way. In healthy subjects, studies have shown many neural and muscular physiological and anatomical similarities between physical movement and kinesthetic MI. These include activation of the same cortical structures (premotor, dorsolateral prefrontal, inferior frontal, and posterior parietal; Hanakawa 2016; Sharma et al. 2006; Tong et al. 2017) and subcortical structures (basal ganglia and cerebellum; Anderson et al. 2011; Cengiz and Boran 2016) used for action planning and control, and comparable time to complete both physical and imagined movements (Decety, Jeannerod, and Prablanc 1989). In addition, repeatedly practicing the specific movement using kinesthetic MI drives functional reorganization in the motor cortices similar to what is seen in physical practice (Jackson et al. 2003) and has been shown to correlate with improvements in physical motor performance (De Vries and Mulder 2007) and increases in isometric muscle strength (the activation of a muscle without changing the muscle length or joint angle; Cornwall, Bruscato, and Barry 1991).

Most neuroscience research concerning kinesthetic MI has been done in healthy adults, while clinical studies determining the benefits of kinesthetic MI following stroke are limited due to inconsistencies between studies and inadequate instructions on the kinesthetic MI task used in the experimental design (Sharma et al. 2006). Similar to healthy subjects, the time required to complete both physical and imagined movements does not significantly differ in people with stroke. However, imagining and performing motor tasks with the affected limb is significantly slower, when compared with the unaffected limb (Decety and Boisson 1990; Sirigu et al. 1995). Nonetheless, the present literature in healthy and stroke subjects is highly encouraging of use of kinesthetic MI training to aid with motor recovery following stroke. Depending on the location of the stroke, kinesthetic MI may be more (subcortical structure damage) or less (parietal cortex damage) effective (Tomasino, Rumiati, and Umilta 2003; Tomasino, Toraldo, and Rumiati 2003). Ideally, before using kinesthetic MI with an individual with stroke, one would want to use an fMRI to verify that the location of the stroke is not obstructing cortical areas known to be involved in kinesthetic MI. Additionally, an fMRI or a questionnaire can confirm that the person has the ability to generate the imagined movement without engaging their muscles or brain regions that should not be active during kinesthetic MI (De Vries and Mulder 2007; Sharma et al. 2006).

Two critical components of kinesthetic MI are: (1) mentally embodying the Effort qualities needed to perform the movement, and (2) imagining the angular position of limb joints relative to their body (Shape) and environment (Space; Jackson et al. 2001; Sharma et al. 2006). Since the stroke left Ralph's right arm with little to no functional mobility, we relied on kinesthetic MI. The ultimate goal of the arm exercises was to get Ralph to access the upper-lower connectivity body pattern, creating a sense of grounding and stability in his lower body, while he moved his upper body by accessing his head-tail connection. Ralph pictured that he was lifting a heavy plank of wood that was sitting on both shoulders. He imagined initiating the movement from the bottom tip of his scapula using bound Flow and strong Weight to raise his shoulders to his ears. He then imagined his shoulders and arms dropping with heavy Weight in complete collapse after accomplishing the task of lifting the plank. After engaging in diligent kinesthetic MI practice every day for six weeks, Ralph started moving his right shoulder on his own with a deep, whole-body breath connectivity. Ralph's ability to eventually move his right shoulder could have been a result of the kinesthetic MI activating the neural pathways for action planning and control, priming the motor system for future implementation of physical movement.

Generally, after stroke, a person must relearn functional motor skills. The restored motor behavior can manifest itself by recruiting intact brain regions that activate the same muscles that were involved prior to the stroke, or alternative muscles via a compensatory method (Krakauer 2006; Nudo 2013). Motor skill acquisition and control require the brain to change motor patterns in response to sensory feedback, a process known as sensorimotor learning (Wolpert, Diedrichsen, and Flanagan 2011). For example, visual processing is used to see the desired (motor planning) and actual (motor execution) movement outcomes, as well as to determine how to reduce kinematic (geometry and speed of movement) performance errors (Krakauer 2006). Through sensorimotor learning, visual error feedback is integrated into the motor system. Sensory stimulation combined with motor task learning and practice has been shown to facilitate neuroplasticity within and between primary somatosensory cortex and spared motor cortices following stroke (Plautz et al. 2003; Wu et al. 2005), correlating with functional motor recovery (Bolognini, Russo, and Edwards 2016). Various neurorehabilitation therapies have explored different types of sensory input to promote motor and sensory cortical reorganization such as electromyogram-triggered neuromuscular stimulation (Sawaki et al. 2006), visual input reflecting self-produced movements (Yavuzer et al. 2008), interactive robotic therapy using multisensory integration (Fasoli et al. 2003), and proprioceptive feedback (Bolognini, Russo, and Edwards 2016; Kim et al. 2013).

When I first started working with Ralph, there seemed to be a disconnect between his movements and the sensory information he was receiving about himself and his surrounding environment. He needed exercises that empha-sized the use of sensory input. After approximately two and a half months of muscle strengthening and kinesthetic MI exercises, Ralph began to show increased muscle tone and mobility in his right arm. As a logical next step, Ralph needed to learn how to access the body-half connectivity pattern. Strengthen-ing this pattern would not only force Ralph to use sensory input, specifically eye-tracking, to initiate movement, but create a stabilization point along his midline, allowing him to fully explore the vertical plane through stability and mobility while sitting or standing. Ralph did spoke-like arm swings in a seated position, facing a mirror to provide visual feedback regarding spatial intentions of the movement. The arm swing exercise was first taught on his left side in order to sense which muscles needed to be engaged to execute the movement appropriately. To provide support for the arm swing on the right side, I gave a containing touch on his right elbow. Additionally, I used a sliding touch from the bottom tip of his right scapula to his right wrist to reinforce the movement initiating from his scapula muscles all the way through the tip of his fingers. His pinky led as his arm swung with direct Space, free Flow, and light Weight (spell drive) in a forward spatial pull through the sagittal dimen-sion to forward middle, and swinging backward in space to the starting point. I had him eye-track his fingers, particularly his pinky, to make a thoughtful connection to where he was moving in space. Initially, eye-tracking his fingers and hand on the right side was uncomfortable for Ralph; it appeared that he didn't want to look at his static hand. But as his hand became more mobile with time, Ralph would willingly follow his hand to establish spatial intention.

The engagement of the specific muscles during the arm swing can be applied to multiple functional behaviors such as grabbing a glass in a high cabinet, reaching for a seat belt, or placing a plate on a table. To encourage that the arm swing movement was not task specific and could be generalized to other motor functions (Krakauer 2006), Ralph did repetitive variations of the move-ment using different spatial pulls and level changes, sitting to standing. He first did the arm swing sitting with a different spatial intent to the left, forward, high diagonal. This allowed him to add gradated rotation, distal steering, cross-lateral body connectivity, and upper/lower body connectivity with the lower body acting as the stable ground and the torso moving with free flow toward the direction of the arm swing. Eventually, Ralph was able to execute the body-half and cross-lateral arm swings in a standing position. The arm swings used multisensory feedback—integrating vision, proprioception, and touch—combined with motor movement at varying degrees of difficulty to relearn a specific movement pattern.

With any type of neurorehabilitation, it is imperative to know the exact loca-tion of the stroke and what brain structures and connections were disrupted due to the stroke. Various brain-imaging techniques, such as computed tomography or MRI scans, can show abnormalities in the brain and blood vessels. This information can help determine which therapy will be best in driving adaptive cortical plasticity and recovery of motor functions. Ralph had considerable improvement in functional movements over the six months we worked together, reinforcing the potential use of L/BMA-inspired movements as a rehabilitation technique for people with motor deficits. In order to implement L/BMA-based movement therapy as an accredited method for motor rehabilitation, it is necessary to execute neuroscience research demonstrating whether L/BMA movements help drive constructive reorganization in the sensorimotor system supporting motor recovery and at what time point after stroke this therapy is most beneficial. The continuous advancements in neural technology will allow researchers to more accurately study how muscle activity (using electromyographic recordings) and brain activity (fMRI and electroencephalographic recordings) change throughout a L/BMA movement therapy protocol following stroke.

L/BMA-inspired movements helped Ralph explore how to use the same muscles with several different intentions. This led Ralph to gain more confidence in his movement patterns and everyday activities. To optimize emotional and physical recovery when recovering from neurological trauma, it is important to create a unified mind and body connection. Most movement-based therapies for neurodegenerative rehabilitation focus mainly on strengthening specific body parts instead of connecting the whole body and mind. L/BMA allows the recovering individual to access both mind and body with somatic, sensory, and motor feedback. Through emotional, cognitive, and motor neural connections, this system allows for someone to rediscover and strengthen developmental movement patterns and basic neurological patterns in a meaningful way. This work is supportive to the energy and time it takes to recover from a motor deficit, and, just as importantly, can help one regain physical and psychological confidence.

Summary

In the decades since Laban's pursuit of an elemental approach to the study of human movement, the seeds he sowed have continued to develop into the robust and dynamic theory it is today. The L/BMA material comes alive when it is used in people's lives. The diverse voices represented in this chapter reflect the potential of the Laban/Bartenieff lens to support inquiry and meaning-making in the many contexts in which movement matters. As each of the contributors has done, use L/BMA to shed light on and bring a more integrated and nuanced approach to your interests. Your contributions and efforts will help to increase understanding of how and why movement matters in human life.

GLOSSARY

affinity—within the L/BMA framework, two or more elements of Body, Effort, Shape, or Space that have a tendency to come together in movement—for example, lightness and rising

arc-like mode of shape change—the process of form change in which movement is directionally motivated, bridging to the environment in a sweeping pathway

base of support—the surface on which the body resides; also thought of as the points of contact between the body and the surface on which it rests

basic neurocellular patterns—movement patterns, including yield/push and reach/ grasp/pull, that describe a relationship between the body and environment and set up the locomotion into space; coined by Bonnie Bainbridge Cohen

Basic Six—elemental movement experiences that were originally outlined in Irmgard Bartenieff's *A Course in Correctives*; they support function and efficiency in full-bodied movements

beginning-emphasis phrase—a phrase in which emphasis is placed at the beginning

being with touch—a type of touch that says "I am here with you," as if to confirm your presence with another person

Body—the category of L/BMA that looks at how movement is organized in the body; it includes the patterns of total body connectivity and the Basic Six

body attitude—aspects of movement that are common and are returned to frequently by an individual; they feel like they are "of" that person; a habitual attitude of the body

body-mind centering—an approach to movement developed by Bonnie Bainbridge Cohen that integrates movement and consciousness

bony landmarks—the bony protrusions highlighted by Irmgard Bartenieff to facilitate greater awareness of the body and its movement in space, including the medial epicondyle and the anterior superior iliac spine

breath support—a concept used by Irmgard Bartenieff to illustrate the breath's ability to support and enliven full-bodied movement

carving mode of shape change—the process of form change in which movement is three-dimensionally organized in the environment so as to shape, carve, form, and mold the environment

central vertical core—the central through-line of the body that follows the pathway of the spine and spinal cord; movement organizes around it

core—the center of the body in the area of the navel

core support—an idea first developed by Irmgard Bartenieff describing a core that has a sense of dynamic internal support for movement; it is not about gripped or held core muscles, but about the ability of the center of the body to support and enliven movement

countertension—generally a spatial concept used to describe an investment in space in an opposite direction or opposite spatial pull

cross of axis—Laban's term for the point at which the three cardinal dimensions intersect

cross quadrants—the diagonal quadrants of the body related to the cross-lateral pattern of total body connectivity, such as right upper and left lower

diagonal—a line in space made up of three equal spatial pulls that change equally

diameter—a line in space connecting the opposite corners of a plane with two unequal spatial pulls

dimension—a line in space with one spatial pull, like the vertical dimension, which is comprised of up-ness and down-ness

direction—a line in space that is one end of a dimension

directional mode of shape change—form change that is directionally organized into the environment; it is often thought to be motivated by the desire to bridge or form a connection between the body and the environment

distal—the extremities of the body, including toes/feet, fingers/hands, head, and tail

distal steering—initiating and leading movement from the distal edges in order to create rotation at the proximal joints (hips and shoulders)

drive—a configuration in which three factors from the Effort category are present at the same time

dynamosphere—a term coined by Rudolf von Laban to describe the interaction between dynamic and effortful movement and the spatial environment in which it happens

Effort—the category within L/BMA that addresses the energetic dynamics manifested outwardly in movement

Effort elements—elements within the four Effort factors (see below) that are grouped into opposite ends of polarity spectrums; Weight: strong and light; Space: direct and indirect; Time: quick and sustained; Flow: bound and free

Effort factors—the four primary qualities of Effort: Weight, Space, Time, and Flow

Effort phrase—a unit or sequence of Effort in which Efforts load, unload, and amplify

Effort stroke—in the symbology of L/BMA, a line that runs from right high to left low to indicate that the symbol is in the Effort category

end-emphasis phrase—a phrase in which emphasis is placed toward the end

even-emphasis phrase—a phrase in which the emphasis is even throughout

exertion—an ongoing investment in aspects of movement that will cause shift into recuperation, a common rhythm in human movement

Flow effort—one of the four effort factors; it deals with the quality of one's energetic investment manifested in movement toward continuity; on the expansive end it is free, and on the condensing end it is bound

Full effort—when four Effort elements are present at the same time

general space—the space in which a movement event occurs

gesture—small movements of the limbs that tend to indicate or reveal meaning

grasp—an action of engulfing or wrapping around something; one of the basic neurocellular patterns

grounding—the quality of the relationship to the earth or the surface of support for the body; in L/BMA grounding is perceived as both stabilizing and mobilizing, creating a dynamic interchange between body and earth

heel rocks—a movement experience created by Irmgard Bartenieff in which the mover seeks sensation of the connection from feet to head by rocking from the heels; Bartenieff used heel rocks as a diagnostic tool to observe patterns of tension and holding throughout the body

homologous movement—a phase in motor development characterized by symmetrical movement of the upper body and hands or the lower body and feet

horizontal dimension—a line in space following the side-side spatial pulls

horizontal plane—a flat surface in space with two unequal spatial pulls of primarily side to side and some forward and backward

iliopsoas—the combination of the psoas major and iliacus muscles, which run from the lumbar spine and the iliac fossa to the lesser trochanter of the femur; it provides the major muscular through-line between the upper and lower bodies

imagery—internal processes based on images from which movement is organized

kinesphere—the sphere of movement around the body without taking a step

kinesthetic awareness—the ability to sense one's own movement

kinetic chains—relationships and pathways of movement through adjacent muscles and joints that work together to produce movement and bring a sense of continuity throughout the body

Labanotation—the system of writing about movement developed by Rudolf von Laban and colleagues that highlights the quantitative aspects of movement

locating touch—a type of touch that draws the attention of the person being touched to a specific area of her or his body, as if to say "notice this part of you"

mid-emphasis phrase—a phrase in which emphasis is placed at the middle

mobile cross—the diagonal quadrants of the body related to the cross-lateral pattern of total body connectivity; it describes the cross that is actively moving

multi-emphatic phrase—a phrase in which emphasis happens more than one time

overlapping phrase—when a new phrase begins before the prior phrase comes to its end

pathways of connection—the felt sense that parts of the body are connected to other parts through tunnels, pathways, or kinetic chains; change in one part ripples through the body's tissues to effect change in another part

Patterns of Total Body Connectivity—the perspective on movement inspired by Irmgard Bartenieff and developed by her students, including Bonnie Bainbridge Cohen and Peggy Hackney; based on developmental motor patterning in infants, they highlight how movement is organized in the body; they are applied to the adult mover to further develop the sense of connection and thoroughness throughout the moving body

personal space—the space the body takes up

phrase—a unit of movement that is in some way meaningful

phrase length—the duration of a phrase of movement

plane—flat surface containing two unequal spatial pulls

polarity spectrum—a continuum whose ends are opposites; there are gradations between the extremes

posture—the manner in which the whole body is carried

posture-gesture merger—when one's posture and gesture are congruent, as though they are linked and come together with equal importance

propulsion—the act of driving or pushing the body through space, often connected to locomotion, weight shift, and ability to drive the weight of the body to a new base of support

psychological kinesphere—the amount of space one perceives is theirs

pull—an action of actively bringing (something) into oneself; one of the basic neurocellular patterns

push—a compression pattern that is about moving away from or toward something; one of the basic neurocellular patterns

reach—an elongation into the environment; one of the basic neurocellular patterns

reach space—the amount of space around the body a movement takes up

receiving touch—a type of touch in which the toucher uses their hand as if to receive the other end of the sending touch; receiving the pathway after it has passed through the tissue

recuperation—a shift or change that brings relief from elements of movement that the mover had invested in for some time

relationship—the sense of connection and patterns of connection present throughout movement; relationships are present throughout the L/BMS lens, including in the moving body, between aspects of the L/BMA framework, and created between mover, movement, self, and environment

rotation—the ability for a joint to rotate around its axis; in L/BMS, rotation happens throughout the body, where rotary capacity is shared across multiple joints; gradated rotation is the ability for a joint to rotate gradually, over time and through a whole pathway of movement, as opposed to "flipping"

sagittal dimension—a line in space following the forward/backward spatial pulls

sagittal plane—a flat surface in space with two unequal spatial pulls of primarily forward/backward and some up and down

scales—Rudolf von Laban's specific investigations into the pattern and rhythms present in the body's use of space

sending touch—a type of touch in which the toucher uses their hands to send a message through the tissue with a sense of directionality or pathway

sequential body-part phrasing—movement that travels through the body from one part to other nonadjacent parts

Shape category—the category within L/BMA that emphasizes the form and form-ing processes of the body

shape-flow mode of shape change—the process of form change in which move-ment is organized around adjusting and accommodating to the mover's needs; it can look random or amorphous and is sometimes referred to as self-to-self, or self-referential

shape flow support—the internal support for form change that has a baseline of growing and shrinking

shape qualities—Part of the Shape category describing "toward where" in the environment the form is changing (linked to space, but not about space)

shape stroke—in L/BMA symbology, the two parallel lines that run from right high to left low and indicate that the symbol is in the Shape category

simultaneous body-part phrasing—movement in which all active parts of the body move at once

simultaneous phrasing—different phrases happening at the same time within the same body

sliding touch—a type of touch in which the toucher slides the touch along the surface of the body as if to heighten sensation about connections within the body

Space category—the category within L/BMA that looks at where and how the body moves through and engages with the space around it

Space effort—one of the four Effort factors; it deals with the quality of one's energetic investment toward their attention; on the expansive end it is indirect, and on the condensing end it is direct

space harmony—a part of the Space category comprising Rudolf von Laban's theories and practices in which he saw movement as ordered and patterned in ways that echoed existing understandings of the laws of nature; his study of Space harmony included placing the body inside platonic solids to observe and train movement in ordered ways

spatial intent—the intention to go toward and into space

spatial matrix—the symbol system used to clarify where in the kinesphere movement happens

spatial pull—the infinite and invisible guy wires of space that guide movement, like lines of inherent potential energy

spatial tension—the investment the body makes into space

spiral—a line in space with three spatial pulls that change unequally

spoke-like mode of shape change—the process of form change in which movement is directionally motivated, bridging to the environment in a linear pathway

stable cross—in the cross-lateral pattern of total body connectivity (which involves the diagonal quadrants of the body), it describes the cross that is stabilized to enhance mobility of the opposite cross

state—an Effort configuration in which two Effort factors are present at the same time

successive body-part phrasing—movement that travels through the body from one part to an adjacent part

supine—lying on the back face up

tail—usually used in relation to the head-tail pattern of total body connectivity, it references humans' vestigial tail; it includes the sacrum and coccyx

three planes of motion—the vertical, sagittal, and horizontal planes in which movement happens

Time effort—one of the four Effort factors, it deals with the quality of one's energetic investment manifested in movement toward the passing of time; on the expansive end it is sustained, and on the condensing end it is quick

vertical dimension—a line in space following the up-and-down spatial pulls

vertical plane—a flat surface in space with two unequal spatial pulls of primarily up and down and some side to side

virtuosity—highly skilled movement

Weight effort—one of the four Effort factors, it deals with the quality of one's energetic investment manifested in movement toward his or her bodily mass; on the expansive end it is light, and on the condensing end it is strong

weight sensing—an aspect of Weight effort in which one fluctuates between actively investing in their mass and giving up on it

weight shift—propulsion of the body to a new base of support

yield—a movement quality of connecting to or bonding with something or someone; one of the basic neurocellular patterns

REFERENCES

Chapters 1–8, and Chapter 9 through Erin Law

Bainbridge Cohen, Bonnie. n.d. "Basic Neurocellular Patterns." Body-Mind Centering. Accessed May 2018. www.bodymindcentering.com/course/basic-neurological-patterns-bnp.

Bartenieff, Irmgard. 1977. *Notes from a Course in Correctives*. New York: Dance Notation Bureau Press.

Bartenieff, Irmgard. 1979. "The Art of Body Movement as a Key to Perception." Unpublished manuscript.

Bartenieff, Irmgard, and Dori Lewis. 2002. *Body Movement: Coping with the Environment*. Orig. pub. 1980. New York: Routledge.

Bradley, Karen. 2009. *Rudolf Laban*. New York: Routledge.

Bryan, Hilary. 2018. "Performing the Rite[s]: Performing Bodies and Somatic Praxis in Valsay Ninjinsky, Pina Baush, Marie Choinard and Hilary Bryan." PhD diss., University of California Davis.

Conrad, Emilie. 2012. *Life on Land: The Story of Continuum, the World-Renowned Self Discovery and Movement Method*. Berkeley: North Atlantic Books.

Culley (Wahl), Colleen. 2015. "Body Language: Seeking a Living Vocabulary for the Dancing Body." Master's thesis, The College at Brockport.

Doscher, Barbara, ed. 1994. *The Functional Unity of the Singing Voice*. 2d ed. Lanham, MD: Scarecrow Press.

Fernandes, Ciane. 2015. *The Moving Researcher: Laban/Bartenieff Movement Analysis in Performing Arts Education and Creative Arts Therapies*. Philadelphia: Jessica Kingsley Publishers.

Goldman, Ellen. 1990. "The LMP Contribution to the Defense Scale and Communication." In *The Kestenberg Movement Profile: Its Past, Present Applications, and Future Directions*. Edited by Penny Lewis and Susan Loman. Keene, NH: Antioch New England Graduate School.

Groff, Ed. 1990. "Laban Movement Analysis: An Historical, Philosophical and Theoretical Perspective." PhD diss., Temple University.

Hackney, Peggy. 2000. "Phrasing Musings." DNB Theory Bulletin Board. Posted January 25, 2010. http://dnbtheorybb.blogspot.com/2010/01/phrasing-musings.html.

Hackney, Peggy. 2002. *Making Connections: Total Body Integration Through Bartenieff Fundamentals*. 2d ed. New York: Routledge.

Johnson, Mark, and George Lakoff. 2003. *Metaphors We Live By*. Chicago: University of Chicago Press.

Laban, Rudolf von. 1974. *The Language of Movement: A Guidebook to Choreutics.* Boston: Plays Inc.

Laban, Rudolf von. 1975. *The Mastery of Movement: A Guidebook to Choreutics.* Boston: Plays Inc.

Laban, Rudolf translated and annotated by Lisa Ullmann. 1975. *A Life for Dance: Reminiscences.* London: Macdonald & Evans.

Levine, Judy. 1986. "An Introduction to Theoretical Issues of Movement Phrasing." Handout. Originally introduction to PhD diss., New York University.

Maletic, Vera. 1983. "Identification of Phrasing Types in Movement and Dance." Abridged version of a paper published in the Proceedings of the Thirteenth Biennial Conference of the International Council of Kinetography Laban, 1983, pp 110–126.

McCoy, Scott. 2012. *Your Voice: An Inside View.* 2d ed. Delaware OH: Inside View Press.

Moore, Carol-Lynne. 2009. *The Harmonic Structure of Movement, Music, and Dance According to Rudolf Laban: An Examination of His Unpublished Writings and Drawings.* Lewiston, NY: Edwin Mellen Press.

Moore, Carol-Lynne. 2014. *Meaning in Motion: Introducing Laban Movement Analysis.* Denver: MoveScape Center.

Moore, Carol-Lynne, and Kaoru Yamamoto. 2012. *Beyond Words: Movement Observation and Analysis.* 2d ed. New York: Routledge.

Preston-Dunlop, Valerie. 2008. *Rudolf Laban: An Extraordinary Life.* Hampshire, UK: Dance Books.

Tobin, Susan. n.d. "Irmgard Bartenieff. " Accessed July 11, 2018. http://www.culturalequity.org/alanlomax/ce_alanlomax_profile_irmgard_bartenieff.php

Weems, Scott. 2014. *Ha! The Science of When We Laugh and Why.* New York: Basic Books.

West Side Toastmasters. n.d. "What Arm Gestures Convey." Accessed May 29, 2018. http://westsidetoastmasters.com/resources/book_of_body_language/chap4.html.

Chapter 9, Andrea Pack

Anderson, W.S., N. Weiss, H.C. Lawson, S. Ohara, L. Rowland, F.A. Lenz. 2011. "Demonstration of Motor Imagery Movement and Phantom Movement-Related Neuronal Activity in Human Thalamus." *Neuroreport* 22 (2): 88–92. doi:10.1097/WNR.0b013e328342c98a.

Benjamin, E.J., S.S Virani, C.W. Callaway, A.R. Chang, S. Cheng, S.E. Chiuve, . . . P. Muntner. 2018. "Heart Disease and Stroke Statistics—2018 Update: A Report from the American Heart Association." *Circulation* 138 (3) e67–493. doi:10.1161/CIR.0000000000000558.

Bolognini, N., C. Russo, and D.J. Edwards. 2016. "The Sensory Side of Post-Stroke Motor Rehabilitation." *Restor Neurol Neurosci* 34 (4): 571–586. doi:10.3233/RNN-150606.

Carmichael, S.T., L. Wei, C.M. Rovainen, and T.A. Woolsey. 2001. "New Patterns of Intracortical Projections After Focal Cortical Stroke." *Neurobiol Dis* 8 (5): 910–922. doi:10.1006/nbdi.2001.0425.

Cengiz, B., and H.E. Boran. 2016. "The Role of the Cerebellum in Motor Imagery." *Neurosci Lett* 617: 156–159. doi:10.1016/j.neulet.2016.01.045.

Chollet, F., V. DiPiero, R.J. Wise, D.J. Brooks, R.J. Dolan, and R.S. Frackowiak. 1991. "The Functional Anatomy of Motor Recovery After Stroke in Humans: A Study With Positron Emission Tomography." *Ann Neurol* 29 (1): 63–71. doi:10.1002/ana.410290112.

Cornwall, M.W., M.P. Bruscato, and S. Barry. 1991. "Effect of Mental Practice on Isometric Muscular Strength." *J Orthop Sports Phys Ther* 13 (5): 231–234. doi:10.2519/jospt.1991.13.5.231.

Dancause, N., S. Barbay, S.B. Frost, E.J. Plautz, D. Chen, E.V. Zoubina, . . . R.J. Nudo. 2005. "Extensive Cortical Rewiring After Brain Injury." *J Neurosci* 25 (44): 10167–10179. doi:10.1523/JNEUROSCI.3256-05.2005.

Decety, J., and D. Boisson. 1990. "Effect of Brain and Spinal Cord Injuries on Motor Imagery." *Eur Arch Psychiatry Clin Neurosci* 240 (1): 39–43.

Decety, J., M. Jeannerod, and C. Prablanc. 1989. "The Timing of Mentally Represented Actions." *Behav Brain Res* 34 (1–2): 35–42.

De Vries, S., and T. Mulder. 2007. "Motor Imagery and Stroke Rehabilitation: A Critical Discussion." *J Rehabil Med* 39 (1): 5–13. doi:10.2340/16501977-0020.

Fasoli, S.E., H.I. Krebs, J. Stein, W.R. Frontera, and N. Hogan. 2003. "Effects of Robotic Therapy on Motor Impairment and Recovery in Chronic Stroke." *Arch Phys Med Rehabil* 84 (4): 477–482. doi:10.1053/apmr.2003.50110.

Hackney, Peggy. 2002. *Making Connections: Total Body Integration Through Bartenieff Fundamentals.* 2d ed. New York: Routledge.

Hanakawa, T. 2016. "Organizing Motor Imageries." *Neurosci Res* 104: 56–63. doi:10.1016/j.neures.2015.11.003.

Jackson, P.L., M.F. Lafleur, F. Malouin, C. Richards, and J. Doyon. 2001. "Potential Role of Mental Practice Using Motor Imagery in Neurologic Rehabilitation." *Arch Phys Med Rehabil* 82 (8): 1133–1141. doi:10.1053/apmr.2001.24286.

Jackson, P.L., M.F. Lafleur, F. Malouin, C.L. Richards, and J. Doyon. 2003. "Functional Cerebral Reorganization Following Motor Sequence Learning Through Mental Practice With Motor Imagery." *Neuroimage* 20 (2): 1171–1180. doi:10.1016/S1053-8119(03)00369-0.

Kim, S.I., I.H. Song, S. Cho, I.Y. Kim, J. Ku, Y.J. Kang, and D.P. Jang. 2013. "Proprioception Rehabilitation Training System for Stroke Patients Using Virtual Reality Technology." *Conf Proc IEEE Eng Med Biol Soc* 2013: 4621–4624. doi:10.1109/EMBC.2013.6610577.

Krakauer, J.W. 2006. "Motor Learning: Its Relevance to Stroke Recovery and Neurorehabilitation." *Curr Opin Neurol* 19 (1): 84–90.

Levy, C.E., D.S. Nichols, P.M. Schmalbrock, P. Keller, and D.W. Chakeres. 2001. "Functional MRI Evidence of Cortical Reorganization in Upper-Limb Stroke Hemiplegia Treated With Constraint-Induced Movement Therapy." *Am J Phys Med Rehabil* 80 (1): 4–12.

Li, S., J.J. Overman, D. Katsman, S.V. Kozlov, C.J. Donnelly, J.L. Twiss, . . . S.T. Carmichael. 2010. "An Age-Related Sprouting Transcriptome Provides Molecular Control of Axonal Sprouting After Stroke." *Nat Neurosci* 13 (12): 1496–1504. doi:10.1038/nn.2674.

Liepert, J., H. Bauder, H.R. Wolfgang, W.H. Miltner, E. Taub, and C. Weiller. 2000. "Treatment-Induced Cortical Reorganization After Stroke in Humans." *Stroke* 31 (6): 1210–1216.

Nudo, R.J. 2013. "Recovery After Brain Injury: Mechanisms and Principles." *Front Hum Neurosci* 7: 887. doi:10.3389/fnhum.2013.00887.

Nudo, R.J., B.M. Wise, F. SiFuentes, and G.W. Milliken. 1996. "Neural Substrates for the Effects of Rehabilitative Training on Motor Recovery After Ischemic Infarct." *Science* 272 (5269): 1791–1794. doi:DOI 10.1126/science.272.5269.1791.

Plautz, E.J., S. Barbay, S.B. Frost, K.M. Friel, N. Dancause, E.V. Zoubina, . . . R.J. Nudo. 2003. "Post-Infarct Cortical Plasticity and Behavioral Recovery Using Concurrent Cortical Stimulation and Rehabilitative Training: A Feasibility Study in Primates." *Neurol Res* 25 (8): 801–810. doi:10.1179/016164103771953880.

Ruby, P., and J. Decety. 2003. "What You Believe Versus What You Think They Believe: A Neuroimaging Study of Conceptual Perspective-Taking." *Eur J Neurosci* 17 (11): 2475–2480.

Sawaki, L., C.W. Wu, A. Kaelin-Lang, and L.G. Cohen. 2006. "Effects of Somatosensory Stimulation on Use-Dependent Plasticity in Chronic Stroke." *Stroke* 37 (1): 246–247. doi:10.1161/01.STR.0000195130.16843.ac.

Sharma, N., V.M. Pomeroy, and J.C. Baron. 2006. "Motor Imagery: A Backdoor to the Motor System After Stroke?" *Stroke* 37 (7): 1941–1952. doi:10.1161/01. STR.0000226902.43357.fc.

Sirigu, A., L. Cohen, J.R. Duhamel, B. Pillon, B. Dubois, Y. Agid, and C. Pierrot-Deseilligny. 1995. "Congruent Unilateral Impairments for Real and Imagined Hand Movements." *Neuroreport* 6 (7): 997–1001.

Stinear, C.M., W.D. Byblow, M. Steyvers, O. Levin, and S.P. Swinnen. 2006. "Kinesthetic, but Not Visual, Motor Imagery Modulates Corticomotor Excitability." *Exp Brain Res* 168 (1–2): 157–164. doi:10.1007/s00221-005-0078-y.

Tomasino, B., R.I. Rumiati, and C.A. Umilta. 2003. "Selective Deficit of Motor Imagery as Tapped by a Left-Right Decision of Visually Presented Hands." *Brain Cogn* 53 (2): 376–380.

Tomasino, B., A. Toraldo, and R.I. Rumiati. 2003. "Dissociation Between the Mental Rotation of Visual Images and Motor Images in Unilateral Brain-Damaged Patients." *Brain Cogn* 51 (3): 368–371.

Tong, Y., J.T. Pendy Jr., W.A. Li, H. Du, T. Zhang, X. Geng, and Y. Ding. 2017. "Motor Imagery-Based Rehabilitation: Potential Neural Correlates and Clinical Application for Functional Recovery of Motor Deficits After Stroke." *Aging Dis* 8 (3): 364–371. doi:10.14336/AD.2016.1012.

Wolpert, D.M., J. Diedrichsen, and J.R. Flanagan. 2011. "Principles of Sensorimotor Learning." *Nat Rev Neurosci* 12 (12): 739–751. doi:10.1038/nrn3112.

Wu, C.W., P. van Gelderen, T. Hanakawa, Z. Yaseen, and L.G. Cohen. 2005. "Enduring Representational Plasticity After Somatosensory Stimulation." *Neuroimage* 27 (4): 872–884. doi:10.1016/j.neuroimage.2005.05.055.

Yavuzer, G., R. Selles, N. Sezer, S. Sutbeyaz, J.B. Bussmann, F. Koseoglu, . . . H.J. Stam. 2008. "Mirror Therapy Improves Hand Function in Subacute Stroke: A Randomized Controlled Trial." *Arch Phys Med Rehabil* 89 (3), 393–398. doi:10.1016/j.apmr.2007.08.162.

INDEX

ABOUT THE AUTHOR

Photo by Brian O'Neil.

Colleen Wahl received her Certified Laban/Bartenieff Movement Analyst (CLMA) certification in 2006 through Integrated Movement Studies (IMS). She has been a core faculty member at IMS since 2013.

Wahl has taught many graduate and undergraduate courses in Laban/Bartenieff movement analysis, including at State University of New York at Brockport, Hobart and William Smith Colleges, and most recently at Alfred University, where she is a visiting assistant professor of dance. She also served as a guest Laban faculty member for Bill Evans Dance Intensive in 2011, 2017, and 2018.

Wahl has written articles about Laban/Bartenieff movement analysis (L/BMA), including a series of fitness columns for *Epoch Times*, a section of Karen Schupp's text *Studying Dance: A Guide to Campus and Beyond,* and a chapter in *Inhabiting the Meta-Visual: Contemporary Performance Theories.* She also coauthors the monthly IMS newsletter with Janice Meaden.

Since graduating from IMS, Wahl has focused on applying the Laban/Bartenieff material in many areas. In 2007, she founded her own L/BMA-based somatic fitness business, Move Into Greatness, which has allowed her to apply Laban/Bartenieff concepts in various contexts. In addition to her fitness focus, she has applied L/BMA in sports, business, and performing arts in diverse settings, including Cornell University (with their football team and the graduate school of management) and the Rochester Institute of Technology's National Technology Institute for the Deaf.

Wahl holds a master's degree in fine arts in dance from State University of New York at Brockport, a master's degree in liberal studies from State University of New York Empire State College, and a bachelor's degree in dance and arts education from William Smith College. In addition to her certification through IMS, she is a registered somatic movement educator through the International Somatic Movement Educators and Therapists Association and a personal trainer certified by the National Academy of Sports Medicine.